The Study of Human Communication

NAN LIN **The Study of
Human Communication**

THE BOBBS-MERRILL COMPANY, INC.
Indianapolis and New York

Russel R. Windes, Queens College of the City University
of New York, Consulting Editor in Speech

Copyright© 1973 by The Bobbs-Merrill Company, Inc.
Printed in the United States of America
Library of Congress Catalog Card Number 72-77128
ISBN 0-672-61340-9 (pbk)
Third Printing

Acknowledgments

Reproduction of figures and tables from the following works was kindly permitted by the publishers and/or the authors:

C. E. Shannon and W. Weaver, *The Mathematical Theory of Communication* (Urbana, Ill.: University of Illinois Press, 1949), p. 7.

T. M. Newcomb, "An Approach to the Study of Communicative Acts," *Psychological Review* 60 (1953): 393–404 (American Psychological Association).

B. H. Westley and M. S. MacLean, Jr., "A Conceptual Model for Communication Research," *Journalism Quarterly* 34 (1957): 31-38 (Association for Education in Journalism).

E. Edwards, *Information Transmission* (London: Chapman and Hall, 1964), p. 78.

B. S. Greenberg, "Diffusion of News of the Kennedy Assassination," *Public Opinion Quarterly* 28 (1964): 225–232 (Public Opinion Quarterly).

C. E. Osgood, G. J. Suci, and P. H. Tannenbaum, *The Measurement of Meaning* (Urbana, Ill.: University of Illinois Press, 1957), P. 7.

J. R. Kirk and G. D. Talbott, "The Distortion of Information," *Etc.* 17 (1959): 5–27. (International Society for General Semantics).

T. Parsons, "On the Concept of Influence," *Public Opinion Quarterly* 27 (1963): 37–62 (Public Opinion Quarterly).

H. C. Kelman, "Processes of Opinion Change," *Public Opinion Quarterly* 25 (1961): 57–78 (Public Opinion Quarterly).

D. Katz, "The Functional Approach to the Study of Attitudes," *Public Opinion Quarterly* 24 (1960): 163–204 (Public Opinion Quarterly).

C. I. Hovland and W. Weiss, "The Influence of Source Credibility on Communication Effectiveness," *Public Opinion Quarterly* 15 (1951): 635–650 (Public Opinion Quarterly).

C. A. Kiesler, B. E. Collins, and N. Miller, *Attitude Change* (New York: John Wiley and Sons, 1969), p. 243.

J. W. Brehm, "Post-Decision Changes in the Desirability of Alternatives," *Journal of Abnormal Personality and Social Psychology* 52 (1956): 384–389 (American Psychological Association).

H. E. Pemberton, "The Curve of Culture Diffusion Rate," *American Sociological Review* 1 (1936): 547–556 (American Sociological Association).

J. S. Coleman, E. Katz, and H. Menzel, *Medical Innovation* (Indianapolis: Bobbs-Merrill, 1966), p. 98.

E. M. Rogers, "Personality Correlates of the Adoption of Technological Practices," *Rural Sociology* 22 (1957): 267–268 (Rural Sociological Association).

My research work in human communication has been supported, during the past four years, with grants and contracts from The National Science Foundation (GS-27348, GS-30820), The National Institute of Health (7R01H00654901), The Office of Civil Defense (DAH-20-71-C-0274), The Ford Foundation, and the Johns Hopkins University (two faculty grants).

Physical and moral support for my research was provided by the Johns Hopkins University Center for Research in Scientific Communication (especially Dr. William D. Garvey, the Director), and the State University of New York at Albany, Department of Sociology.

Preface

Communication has gradually evolved into a major research discipline over the last twenty years, with communication courses now being offered in such diverse academic areas as sociology, psychology, social psychology, anthropology, political science, speech, management, psychiatry, education, journalism, marketing, advertising, public health, geography, philosophy, social work, and communication. Interested students can choose from numerous readers and journal articles. However, the task becomes more and more frustrating and less and less rewarding as such choices grow in quantity. For the past six years, in order to present an integrated view of the field to my students, I have had to assemble materials that were located in literally dozens of places in the library. What is sorely needed is a volume that would systematically summarize the information currently available in this field.

My goal in this volume is to suggest a framework within which our knowledge about human communication can be integrated (Chapter 1). It is intended for students, at both undergraduate and graduate levels, who are working in a wide variety of academic disciplines and areas. Because of limitations of time, energy, and knowledge, I have not been able to cover the field with complete depth or balance. Specifically, this book will not cover the following areas: (1) the intrapersonal communication processes (for example, brain functions or the neurological structure), (2) the arts of communication (for example, training in theater and rhetoric), (3) disordered communication (for example, pathological and therapeutic communication), or (4) the structure of language (for example, linguistic elements). Most of these topics are treated in other specialty areas and my competence in them is limited. Some issues which are subsumed under these topics will be discussed, but only insofar as they are relevant to the major themes treated in this book.

What this book will attempt to do is to integrate and bring into focus what is understood about human communication in situations where the receiver(s) is a person and the message or information is transmitted to him via a unit that is distinguishable from the receiver. This unit may be either a human being or a nonhuman medium, such as radio, newspapers, or television.

The book contains some features which may be unique. One feature is a general introduction to the mathematical properties of information theory (Chapter 2). It is commonly agreed that information theory is an important tool for research into human communication. But an explanation of its techniques that would be intelligible to communication researchers whose training has been in the social sciences has up to now been lacking. To fill such a gap, I have attempted to focus on the most basic elements of information theory. But even these may prove too technical and mathematical for some readers. Therefore, I have organized the book in such a manner that the skipping of these sections, marked by asterisks, will not hinder the reader's understanding of the rest of the book.

Nonverbal communication research has become an increasingly important component in human communication. Here, for the first time, I believe, this component is systematically brought into the total context of communication research (Chapter 3).

The more traditional aspects of communication—persuasion and mass communication—are discussed as the psychological and behavioral elements of the influence of human communication (Chapters 5 and 6). Thus, the concept of influence as it is related to human communication is treated (Chapter 4) before its psychological and behavioral elements are brought into focus separately.

In discussing the structure of human communication, the source and the receiver are isolated for analytical convenience. But as soon as the source and the receiver are distinguished in this way, we are faced with the accusation that communication researchers treat communication as a one-way process rather than as a two-way interactive process. While such an accusation does not negate the need for the analytical advantage of specifying the source and the receiver for a given slice of the communication situation, such a misconception must be dispelled. Therefore, I discuss control and adaptation of communication in a separate chapter (7). Interactive concepts such as feedback and dissemination are brought out for elaboration.

Having summarized the various phases of human communication, in Chapter 8 I conclude by specifying the ways in which theories are constructed and by offering an illustrative example of how theorization can be utilized in one segment of communication. This chapter, therefore, provides conceptual tools to the student who, having familiarized himself with the major dimensions of communication research, now wishes to embark on adding to our knowledge of the field.

In preparing this volume I have benefitted greatly from the critical comments offered by Everett M. Rogers and James Roever. Important suggestions also came from Randall Harrison, Catherine Garvey, and Klaus Krippendorf. My sincere gratitude goes to Russel Windes, who, as Bobbs-Merrill editor, was responsible for supervising the final draft of the manuscript. Susan Kolodny and Meredith Prell edited and typed all the drafts. My wife, Alice, urged me on all the way. Without the advice and encouragement of all these people, I might never have completed this book.

Nan Lin
October 1971
Albany, New York

Contents

List of Tables   xi
List of Figures   xii

1. **THE EMERGING DISCIPLINE OF HUMAN COMMUNICATION: Definitions, Traditions, and a Framework   3**
   Definitions of Human Communication   3
   A Review of Research Traditions   9
   Classification of Human Communication   13
   A Conceptual Framework of Human Communication   15
   Important Characteristics of the Suggested Framework   20

2. **ENCOUNTER: The Frame of Human Communication   22**
   Definition and Measurement of Information   23
   Decomposition of the Encounter as Uncertainty Functions   32
   Summary of Measurement and Analysis of the Information System   33
   Some Applications of the Information Approach to Encounter   34
   Analysis of the Delivery System   44
   An Empirical Study of the Encounter   52
   Summary and Discussion   54

3. **EXCHANGE: The Flow of Human Communication   57**
   Definition and Studies of Meaning   58
   Generality and Specificity of Exchange   74
   Functions of Exchange   76
   Barriers to Exchange   80
   Summary and Discussion   84

4. **INFLUENCE: The Impact of Human Communication   86**
   Four Paradigms of Influence   87
   Levels of Influence   95
   Linkage Between Attitude and Behavior   98
   Concluding Remarks   101

5. **THE PSYCHOLOGICAL DIMENSION OF COMMUNICATION'S INFLUENCE: Attitude Change   102**
   The Component Approach   106
   The Social Judgment Approach   118
   The Cognitive Approach   122
   Comparisons Among the Component Approach, the Social
      Judgment Approach, and the Cognitive Approach   140

6. **THE BEHAVIORAL DIMENSION OF COMMUNICATION'S INFLUENCE: Decision and Action   145**
Indicators of Behavioral Influence   146
Effects of Mass Communication   149
Diffusion of Innovations   160
Emergent Generalizations Concerning Communication Effects
   on Behavioral Change   176

7. **CONTROL AND ADAPTATION: The Organization of Human Communication   182**
Functions of Control and Adaptation   183
Mechanisms of Control and Adaptation   185
Dynamic Contribution of Disorganization   189
Summary   190

8. **TOWARD THEORIZATION OF HUMAN COMMUNICATION RESEARCH   192**
The Concept of Theory and the Process of Scientific Investigation   192
A Critical Assessment and Reformulation of the Process of
   Communication's Influence on Behavior   201
Reconceptualization of Communication's Influence on Behavior   206
Concluding Remarks   212

References   213
Index   241

Tables

2—1. Information (I) Associated with Each Symbol in an Array of Eight Equally Likely-to-Be-Transmitted Symbols 26

2—2. Probabilities of Four Categories of Headline Events 27

2—3. Information (I) and the Weighing Factor (P) for Each of Four Categories of Headline Events 27

2—4. Digital Representation of Origins of News as Equal Probabilities 35

2—5. Digital Representation of Origins of News as Unequal Probabilities 35

2—6. Digital Representation of Single Symbols 35

2—7. Digital Representation of Combined Symbols 36

2—8. Digital Correspondence of Isomorphic Input-Output 37

2—9. Digital Representation of an Encounter with Noises 38

2—10. Results of a Series of Transmissions in an Encounter 39

2—11. Calculations of the Output Uncertainty 40

2—12. Physical Location of Respondents and Source of News of Kennedy's Assassination 49

2—13. Physical Location of Respondents Hearing from Other Persons and Information Source 49

4—1. A Paradigm of Social Sanctions 88

4—2. Summary of Distinctions Among the Three Types of Influence 89

4—3. Determinants of Attitude Formation, Arousal, and Change in Relation to Type of Function 91

4—4. A Structural Typology of Influence as the Consequence of Legitimation 93

5—1. Time 1: Attitude Toward Blacks 104

5—2. Time 0: Attitude Toward Blacks 104

5—3. Sources and Topics Selected for Credibility Study 107

5—4. Postdecision Changes in Attractiveness of Alternatives 131

5—5. Comparisons of the Cognitive Models 138

Figures

1 – 1. Shannon and Weaver's Communication Model   4

1 – 2. Balanced Configurations   5

1 – 3. Imbalanced Configurations   6

1 – 4. Newcomb's Co-orientation Model   6

1 – 5. Westley and MacLean's Mass Communication Model   7

1 – 6. Phases of Human Communication   15

2 – 1. Relationship Between Number of Symbols and Information   29

2 – 2. Relationship Between the Probability of Occurrence and Uncertainty   29

2 – 3. Probabilities in a Branching Situation   30

2 – 4. Encounter Decomposed as Uncertainty Functions   32

2 – 5. Encounter with Noises   38

2 – 6. Relationship Between Intended Information and Maximal Information Transmitted as Constrained by Channel Capacity   42

2 – 7. Pattern of Rat Dwellings in Calhoun's Experiments   46

2 – 8. Hypothesized Relationship Between Relevance of News and Effectiveness of the Mass Network   51

2 – 9. Relationship Between Stimulus Intensity and Percentage of Knowers   53

3 – 1. Symbolic Account of the Development of Sign Process   60

3 – 2. Types of Distortions   83

5 – 1. Net Change of Opinion in Direction of Communication for Sources Classified by Hovland and Weiss (1951) as "Low Credibility" or "High Credibility" Sources   108

5 – 2. Net Change of Opinion in Direction of Communication for Sources Classified by Hovland and Weiss (1951) as "Untrustworthy" or "Trustworthy"   108

5 – 3. The "Sleeper Effect"   109

5 – 4. Assimilation and Contrast Effect Graph   120

5 – 5. The Incongruent State According to the Congruity Principle   126

5 – 6. The Congruence Position Reached According to the Congruity Principle   127

6 – 1. The Study Design of the Erie County Study   151

6 – 2. Cumulative Distribution of Postage Adoption in Europe and North America, 1836 – 1880   163

6 – 3. Diffusion Rates for the Interactive and Isolated Members   168

6 – 4. The Standard Deviations of a Normal Curve as Used in the
Categorization of Adopters   172

6 – 5. The Social and Psychological System of an Individual
and His Selective Communications   177

7 – 1. Effect of Feedback   186

8 – 1. Causal Analysis of Concept Y   200

8 – 2. Effectual Analysis of Concept Y   200

8 – 3. Complete Analysis of Concept Y   200

8 – 4. The Two-Step Flow Hypothesis   204

8 – 5. A Conceptual Framework of Behavioral Change   208

THE STUDY OF
HUMAN COMMUNICATION

1

The Emerging Discipline of Human Communication:
DEFINITIONS, TRADITIONS, AND A FRAMEWORK

One of today's most widely used terms is "communication." We hear and read about "the communication gap" between the government and the people, between old and young, between black and white, between corporations and unions. We are confronted daily with the mass communication media—radio, television, newspapers, and magazines—and we worry about the effects these media will have on our children. The news media themselves remind us constantly of severe communication problems at the international level—between the United States and the Soviet Union, between Israel and the Arab countries, between the East and the West. Yet the diversified phenomena of human communication and our need to understand them have only recently become a major focus for scientific research.

The purposes of this book are simply: (1) to introduce the reader to the knowledge that has accumulated about human communication, (2) to discuss potential theoretical avenues through which our knowledge might be advanced in those areas where it is presently inadequate, and (3) to provide a single conceptual framework within which the summary of current knowledge and the discussion of crucial theoretical frontiers can be made meaningful to the reader.

In the first chapter I will attempt to introduce the reader to the emerging discipline of human communication by (1) discussing various definitions of human communication, (2) describing the major traditions in human communication research, (3) specifying several classification schemes for communication, and (4) proposing a conceptual framework that can be utilized in this book to integrate the study of human communication.

Definitions of Human Communication

What is human communication? The problem of defining "communication" is almost as old as civilization itself. Plato, Aristotle, Cicero, and other Greek and Latin philosophers all considered aspects of human communication under the heading of "rhetoric." Modern scientific approaches to defining communication, however, can be traced back only to the 1940s.

A number of the more prominent approaches to the problem of defining communication will be discussed below. Then I will suggest how communication should be defined. From here on, the terms "human communication" and "communication" will be used interchangeably.

THE DIMENSIONAL APPROACH

One of the popular ways to define communication is to attempt to specify the dimensions, components, or elements in the communication system. For example, Burke, in his discussion of motives (1945), specifies five interrelated perspectives from which communication events can be viewed: (1) the Act (what occurs), (2) the Scene (background of the act), (3) the Agent (communicator), (4) the Agency (means used), and (5) the Purpose (intent or motive). Similarly, Lasswell, a political scientist, defined communication by asking, "Who says what in what channel to whom with what effect?" (1948). Elaborating on Lasswell's definition of communication, Gerbner (1956) specified ten variables, or elements, in communication: (1) Someone (2) perceives an event (3) and reacts (4) in a situation (5) through some means (6) to make available materials (7) in some form (8) and context (9) conveying content (10) of some consequence.

Probably the best-known communication model came from Shannon and Weaver (1949), who realized the applicability of the electrical engineering model to human communication. Their model adds the "noise" component to the elements of human communication. Definitions of communication similar to Shannon and Weaver's were given by Riley and Riley (1959) and Berlo (1960).

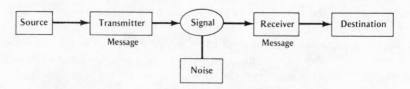

Figure 1–1. Shannon and Weaver's Communication Model

In summary, the dimensions usually singled out in the definition of communication include: (1) a source, (2) a message, (3) a channel (channels), and (4) a receiver. However, different scientists emphasize different dimensions of communication. For example, Burke (1945) stressed the intent or motive of the source in communication, while Lasswell (1948) and Gerbner (1956) focused more on the effect of communication on the receiver. Riley and Riley, two sociologists, pointed out the importance of the social milieu in communication (the social groups to which the source and the receiver belong). Although most dimensional models seem to differentiate between source and receiver, all scientists make it clear that communication can be, and most often is, a two-way activity. In one instance, there is a source and a receiver; but in the next, the receiver initiates a message and the source then becomes the receiver. Such a reciprocal relationship is the rule rather than the exception in interpersonal communication.

THE PROCESS APPROACH

In contrast to the dimensional approaches which stress the specific components of human communication, a number of definitions emphasize the process involved in communication. Heider (1946), using the cognitive model in psychology, spelled out the general principle of balanced states of (1) a person's (P) attitude toward a source (S), (2) the person's attitude toward an issue (I), and (3) the perceived assertion of the source about the issue. For example, if a person (P) has a positive or negative attitude toward legalized abortion (I), has a positive or negative attitude toward the President of the United States (S), and also thinks the President has a positive or negative attitude toward legalized abortion, then it is said that P has a cognitive configuration relative to the issue of legalized abortion and the President. The cognitive configuration is considered *balanced* if any one of the following relations exists ("+" representing a positive attitude and "−" a negative attitude):

Figure 1–2. Balanced Configurations

For example, if P has a positive attitude (+) toward legalized abortion, a positive attitude (+) toward the President, and if he thinks that the President is also in favor (+) of legalized abortion, then P should feel comfortable about the whole situation (represented by the first diagram in Figure 1–2). If P is for legalized abortion (+), but against the President (−), and if P thinks the President is against legalized abortion (−), then, again, P should feel comfortable about the situation. This is because the President's attitude toward the issue is expected by P, given P's different attitudes toward the issue and the President (represented by the second diagram in Figure 1–2).

On the other hand, the cognitive configuration is said to be imbalanced if any one of the following relations exists:

Figure 1-3. Imbalanced Configurations

For example, if P is against legalized abortion (—), is for the President (+), and if he thinks the President is for legalized abortion (+), then P is in a psychological dilemma (represented by the first diagram in Figure 1-3). This is so because given his differential attitudes toward the issue and the President, he should expect the President to agree with him and therefore to have a negative attitude toward the issue.

The determination of whether a particular configuration is balanced or imbalanced follows the simple rule of algebraic multiplication of the signs. Thus, three positive signs in a configuration indicate a balanced state $[(+) \times (+) \times (+) = +]$, as do two negative signs and a positive sign in a configuration $[(-) \times (+) \times (-) = +]$. On the other hand, three negative signs indicate an imbalanced configuration $[(-) \times (-) \times (-) = -]$, as do two positive signs and a negative sign $[(+) \times (+) \times (-) = -]$.

The model postulates that when the configuration is not balanced, the unit relations must undergo a change either through action or through cognitive reorganization in the person (P). Horowitz, Lyons, and Perlmutter (1951) elaborated on the solutions to the imbalanced states. Among the potential solutions they pointed out were: (1) the sign toward the issue is changed to agree with that of the source; (2) the reverse is done; (3) the issue is cognitively divorced from the source; and (4) the disharmony is tolerated.

Newcomb (1953) expanded Heider's basic model to include the attitude of the source toward the person. In effect, Newcomb expanded Heider's intrapersonal communication model (cognitive organization within one person) to a model of interpersonal communication—what Newcomb called a co-orientational definition of communication (Figure 1-4).

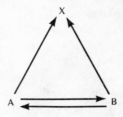

Figure 1-4. Newcomb's Co-orientation Model

Westley and MacLean (1957) eventually expanded both Heider's and Newcomb's models to suggest the situation of mass communication. In their ABCX model (Figure 1-5), communication consists of a set of abstracted events (X's) which are perceived or assimilated by an Advocate (source) who transmits this information or message to a Channel (agent or relayer) which, in turn, relays the information or message to a Behavioral Role (receiver). An example is the communication of the news of President Kennedy's assassination (Greenberg, 1964a). The event (X) was the actual assassination. The A's were the eyewitnesses of the event. The event was then relayed from the witnesses to the reporters of the mass media (C's). Such relaying was supplemented by some photos and films taken by a few witnesses at the time the event occurred.[1] Then, this event was relayed by the mass media to the public (B's). The reporters (C's) went back time and again to the eyewitnesses and partial evidence (photos and films) to verify the event, while the public (B's) kept demanding more information about the event from the mass media (C's) and the eyewitnesses (A's).

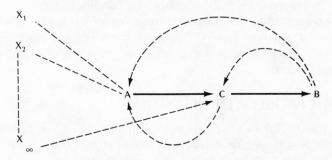

Figure 1-5. Westley and MacLean's Mass Communication Model

Several interesting processes are specified in this model. First, the model specifies the feedback which may take place between B and C, between B and A, and between C and A. Second, information can be initiated by C, bypassing A. This type of transmission often occurs in mass communication; the mass media (C's) originate dissemination without the original sources' having expressed any such intent. Third, C's are, in effect, the gatekeepers who select, edit, and relay the information or message.[2]

THE FUNCTIONAL APPROACH

Another way of defining communication is to specify the functions communication serves. Weaver (Shannon and Weaver, 1949), for example,

1. The photos and films caught only portions of the event as it happened to President Kennedy. No such direct evidence for the act of assassination itself was available.
2. This multiple-step process view is compatible with the two-step flow hypothesis, generated in empirical studies by Lazarsfeld, Berelson, and Gaudet (1948) and by Katz and Lazarsfeld (1955), to be discussed in detail in Chapter 6.

pointed out three basic functions of communication: *syntactics* (the technical function), *semantics* (the semantic function), and *pragmatics* (the use or consequence function). Many psycholinguists use such a model in discussing language features. Ackoff (1958), in suggesting three components of communication — information, instruction, and motivation — provided still another functional definition.

Many other attempts have been made to define communication. Most of them define communication in terms of alternate concepts. For example, Stevens (1950), a psychologist, defined communication as the discriminatory response of an organism to a stimulus. Stevens was, in effect, categorizing communication as one form of the general learning process. Fearing (1953), another psychologist, specified communication as involving (1) the existence of some specific tensional states related to perceived instabilities, disturbances, or needs in the psychological fields of the individuals involved, (2) the production of a structured stimulus field (communication content), consisting of signs and symbols, and (3) the achievement of a more stable organization through the cognitive restructuring of the fields induced by such content. This definition puts communication in the framework of the psychological balance (tension-reduction) theories. Anthropologist Hall (1959), for his part, suggested that communication is culture and culture is communication.

THE PROBLEM OF DEFINITION

Each of the definitions serves a specific function, of course, but one sees what difficulties result from the existence of multiple viewpoints when one seeks to establish a single definition of communication. We have discussed the dimensional approach, for example, which uses an epistemological approach to specify the elements of human communication. But since human communication is so diverse and discursive, such attempts cannot exhaust all its elements (Newman, 1960).

We have also considered attempts to define communication in terms of other words or concepts such as "balance theory," "culture," and so forth. In this way, we merely entangle ourselves in the infinite cycle of definitions and words.

Another way to define communication is by referential definition, or by linking it to the experience of the inquirer. The danger in this process of going from the general to the particular, however, is that the transfer in the inquirer's mind from the particular to the general may fail to be made or may be made incorrectly.

It seems, then, that the best way to define communication is by "implicit definition"[3] — that is, in terms of what it does, within a theoretical framework. Many scientific terms are defined in this way. Physics, for example,

---

3. For this and other kinds of definitions, see Rapoport (1953a), Popper (1959), and Kaplan (1964).

is a scientific field in which the nature of matter, force, energy, and motion is investigated. Psychology is a scientific field in which the nature of the human mind and its mental processes is explored. Political science is the study of the authoritative allocation of values in a society (Easton, 1965). Communication, used here as a scientific term, presents problems to one who would define it by verbal, epistemological, or referential methods. Thus, it should properly be defined as a *scientific field in which the nature of human symbolic exchange is studied*.[4] Whether or not we convey the meaning of communication depends on the extent to which we can describe the content of the field so that it becomes meaningful to inquirers (in terms of their personal experience). In the rest of this book, I will attempt, with the help of the various specifications of dimensions, processes, and functions to be considered, and within the scientific framework, to explore the study of human communication.

A Review of Research Traditions

A *research tradition* is defined as a *cluster of studies focusing on a similar topic in which each successive study is influenced directly by the investigations that have preceded it* (Katz, 1961; Rogers, 1962). Research traditions vary according to focal points of interest or disciplinary specialties. The study of human communication has a long and diversified history, involving a multiplicity of research traditions and incorporating contributions from disciplines as diverse as engineering and anthropology. The study of human communication is therefore considered multiple-traditional and multiple-disciplinary.

Four major research traditions have dominated the research into human communication (Berelson, 1959; Schramm, 1963). Each of these was led by one central figure, and each produced a significant and interrelated body of literature and some outstanding researchers. The four leading scholars are generally regarded as the "founding fathers" of communication research.

PERSUASIVE COMMUNICATION

One research tradition is largely attributed to the pioneering work of Carl I. Hovland, a social psychologist. In the 1940s, Hovland, together with his associates and students, mainly at Yale, conducted a series of experiments to ascertain what factors would induce change in a person's attitude. During

---

4. This definition does not apply to the act of communicating. The verb form of many other fields does not exist (psychology, physics, biology, etc.), and thus no such definitional confusion exists. Communication (along with education, management, and a few other fields) is less fortunate and therefore must constantly distinguish between the act and the discipline to avoid confusion.

the Second World War, when Hovland was associated with the intelligence branch of the army, and later, after he had returned to Yale, soldiers and college students provided the experimental subjects in his laboratory studies. These studies are acclaimed for their ingenious control and manipulation of variables. They usually focus on one or two potential change-inducing factors and control for other extraneous variables. A typical question or hypothesis tested was, "Does source credibility, such as trustworthiness, have any effect in inducing attitude change among the receivers of a persuasive message?" Source credibility was then manipulated, with a highly trustworthy source and a highly untrustworthy source presenting a persuasive message to similarly composed audiences. The findings from this series of studies, which continued into the 1950s and 1960s after Hovland's death, are presented in several volumes (Hovland, Lumsdaine, and Sheffield, 1949; Hovland, Janis, and Kelley, 1953; Hovland et al., 1957; Janis, Hovland, et al., 1959; Rosenberg et al., 1960; Sherif and Hovland, 1961). Studies in this tradition characteristically apply the classic rhetorical approach to the analysis of communication. They emphasize the psychological influences on the receiver's attitude toward a certain issue, and they utilize the laboratory setting to control and manipulate variables.

GROUP PROCESS AND COGNITIVE STRUCTURE

Another important communication research tradition originated with Kurt Lewin and his students, who investigated the small group as a social psychological force. Lewin and his students were interested in interpersonal relationships in the small group and in those characteristics associated with the small group that affect a group member's cognitive structure. A typical question would be, "Is group process more effective than nongroup process in inducing attitudinal or behavioral change?"

In one study, for example, Lewin (1943) examined the relative success of group discussion versus a lecture in changing housewives' food-selecting habits. With content controlled for, the group discussion approach (with the housewives themselves participating) proved much more effective than the lecture approach in inducing housewives to buy and cook beef hearts, sweetbreads, and kidneys.

One of his students, Leon Festinger, extended Lewin's work to the investigation of cognitive dissonance, where he focused on the discrepancy between conflicting attitudes and on how such discrepancies were resolved. A typical question was, "When a person commits himself to some behavior which he did not favor attitudinally, will he adjust his attitude [to be more favorable] toward the behavior?" Festinger and Carlsmith (1959) got college students to perform a boring and tedious task and then requested each of them to tell the next person who was supposed to perform the same task that the task was interesting and enjoyable. The students were paid either $1.00

or $20.00 for making the statement. The experimenters predicted that those who received the higher monetary reward would feel no psychological need to change their attitude toward the task, while those who received the minimal monetary reward would. The data confirmed the hypothesis; more of those who received only $1.00 stated later that the task was not so boring or tedious after all.

This tradition has its ancestry in gestalt psychology, which emphasizes the social psychological effects of groups and utilizes laboratory experiments. The representative works in this tradition include: *A Theory of Cognitive Dissonance* (Festinger, 1957), *Explorations in Cognitive Dissonance* (Brehm and Cohen, 1962), and *Conflict, Decision and Dissonance* (Festinger, 1964a).

MASS COMMUNICATION AND DIFFUSION

During the late 1930s and early 1940s, Paul Lazarsfeld was engaged in studying the impact of the mass media (such as radio and newspapers) on various public campaigns (such as advertising and elections). His investigations were subsequently expanded to include the effects of interpersonal communications. With his associates and students (such as Merton, Katz, Klapper, Menzel, and Coleman), Lazarsfeld set out to study the processes of mass and interpersonal communication as they related to elections, public taste, and innovations. Almost independently, rural sociologists (like Ryan, Gross, Wilkening, Lionberger, Beal, and Rogers) had been studying the diffusion process with respect to agricultural innovations. Both the mass communication researchers and the rural sociologists discovered the importance of interpersonal influence, even though their research methodologies (representative sample versus saturation interview) and focuses (elections and advertising versus agricultural innovations) varied. This shared discovery and the tendency of both groups to focus on the interpersonal influence caused the two traditions to converge in the early 1960s (Katz, 1961). Because almost all the contributors to this tradition are sociologists, the methodology inevitably involves a field study or a survey. The major studies and findings are presented in *The People's Choice* (Lazarsfeld, Berelson, and Gaudet, 1948), *Voting* (Berelson, Lazarsfeld, and McPhee, 1954), *Personal Influence* (Katz and Lazarsfeld, 1955), *The Effects of Mass Communication* (Klapper, 1960), *Diffusion of Innovations* (Rogers, 1962), and *Medical Innovation* (Coleman, Katz, and Menzel, 1966).

POLITICAL COMMUNICATION

The initial effort in another such tradition was made by Harold Lasswell, who was concerned with propaganda and the political system as communication processes. His colleagues and followers, all of whom are political scientists, widened the original focus to include investigation of such subjects as modernization (Lerner, Pye) and the national and international systems (Pool and Deutsch) as communication systems. This tradition is primarily concerned with the political and historical effects of societal communication. Its methodology is a mixture of content analysis surveys and theoretical and simulation analyses. Typical works include: *Propaganda, Communication, and Public Opinion* (Smith, Lasswell, and Casey, 1946), *The Passing of Traditional Society* (Lerner, 1958), *Communications and Political Development* (Pye, 1963), and *The Nerves of Government* (Deutsch, 1963).

OTHER CONTRIBUTIONS

Although the traditions described above cover the earlier focuses in studies of human communication, important contributions have also been made by scholars from other specializations and with quite different interests.

Journalistic Contribution

Journalists have had a long-standing interest in the study of the mass media. It is only during the last three decades, however, since the political polls (Gallup, etc.) joined forces with those journalists interested in the mass media as social institutions, that research has gradually become the focal point of graduate journalism programs, many of which have been renamed communication or mass communication programs. Pioneers in this field include Schramm, Deutschmann, Westley, MacLean, and McLuhan. Their intensive investigations into the effects of radio, television, and the press on the public and into the functions of mass media institutions have contributed significantly to our understanding of the function of mass media in mass society.

Mathematical and Electrical Engineering Contribution

Starting with Shannon and Weaver's communication theory, Colin Cherry, George A. Miller, and Wendell R. Garner systematically introduced the concepts and applications of the information theory to students in human communication. Because this approach requires some degree of quantitative sophistication, however, it has been minimally effective in generating communication studies.

Psycholinguistic Contribution

One important aspect of human communication is the transmission of meaning. Osgood, Jenkins, Deese, and others designed some ingenious methods to measure the "meaning" of meaning. Their investigations and methodologies have had a substantial and long-range effect on the study of human communication and have significantly influenced the nature and direction of that study during the last decade.

Scientific Communication

A pertinent issue today is the problem of communication among scientists, and between scientists, practitioners, and technologists. The last decade has seen a concerted effort to utilize the communication model to study the flow of scientific information. Contributions in this area have come from Menzel, Garvey, Griffith, Paisley, Lin, and others.

These traditions reflect the research foci of specific groups of researchers surrounding a limited number of leaders; they help shed light on the aspects of communication on which research efforts have concentrated. They do not constitute conceptual classifications of human communication research. A systematic view of the study of human communication would require a conceptually integrated framework. In the remainder of this chapter, therefore, I will review some of the attempts at classification and will then suggest a conceptual framework within which the study of human communication can be integrated and discussed in depth, throughout the rest of the book.

Classification of Human Communication

A classification is a scheme utilized analytically to distinguish classes of processes and elements for a given concept. The mass media, for example, can be classified in terms of printed media (newspapers, magazines, etc.) and electronic media (radio, television, etc.). A classification scheme helps us to identify all elements of a concept and to differentiate among the elements on the basis of a particular trait. Many attempts have been made to classify human communication; the most frequently used classifications are discussed below.

INTRAPERSONAL, INTERPERSONAL, SOCIETAL, AND MASS

One simple way to classify human communication is to focus on the level of analysis or the unit of analysis. The process of communication occurring within an individual is considered the smallest unit. Intrapersonal communication, the aspect of human communication that psychologists have investigated or discussed most often, is linked with the cognitive structure, with perception, learning, recognition, and other psychological properties. In many cases, in fact, intrapersonal communication is considered a sub-concept of the cognitive structure.

Intrapersonal communication has also drawn considerable attention from sociologists. The symbolic interactionism school of sociology, of which George Herbert Mead is a leading advocate, especially favors studying the intrapersonal aspect of human communication. As Mead saw it

(1934), intrapersonal communication is the essential bridge between an individual's behavior and his environment. Until a person can view himself objectively and respond to his own verbal and nonverbal acts as he expects others to respond, he has not learned the public attitude; in other words, he is not yet a social being.

The next level or unit of analysis is the communication which takes place between two or more individuals. Interpersonal communication represents the reciprocal interaction between two or more persons, and is called dyadic, triadic, or small-group, depending on the number of persons involved in the specific situation. Various studies have been conducted, both in the laboratory and through surveys, on the interpersonal communication process. Topics range from information flow, task performance, and group pressure, to attitudinal consonance or dissonance.

A third level, mass, or societal, communication, concerns situations involving a large number of persons. Several characteristics define the "mass," or "societal," level and distinguish it from the interpersonal level. Wright (1959) has suggested that mass communication is directed toward relatively large and heterogeneous audiences that are anonymous to the source. Societal communication may, however, take place in a group that is well defined and familiar to the communicator. Thus, the distinction between interpersonal and mass communication is somewhat arbitrary; it merely indicates two extreme points along a continuum and is based simply on the number of persons involved in the communication.

SYNTACTICAL, SEMANTICAL, AND PRAGMATICAL

Another popular approach to human communication is to classify communications in terms of the functions they serve. The syntactic-semantic-pragmatic classification has been used extensively in such areas as linguistic analysis. The syntactical aspect of communication involves the structure of the communication—the relationship among symbols; the semantical aspect of communication involves the meaning (either connotative or denotative) of the communication—the relationships between symbols and objects; and the pragmatical aspect of communication involves the influence or consequence of the communication—the relationships between symbols and their uses and effects. In this classification scheme, the focal point is the message of the communication.

SOURCE-MESSAGE-CHANNEL-RECEIVER-FEEDBACK

Communication can also be analyzed in terms of the basic components of the communication situation. These most frequently include: the source or communicator (usually denoting the originator of a specific message); the message (information and/or meaning being transmitted); the channel or channels (the medium of the transmission); the receiver (the destination of the message transmission); and the feedback (the source's assimilation, either psychological or behavioral, of the receiver's response to his message). This classification has been used in many of those persuasion studies —that is, studies concerning attitude change—which focus on the effects of the various components and their characteristics in inducing the receiver to accept the message.

A Conceptual Framework of Human Communication

The classifications mentioned above analyze human communication in terms of the unit of analysis, the functions of the message, or the components of the communication structure. Each classification serves a useful purpose. A review of the literature of human communication, however, requires a conceptual framework within which the various classifications of human communication can be integrated. I suggest one such conceptual framework here. This conceptual framework is not itself a theory; it merely maximizes the vantage points from which human communication theories have been or can be advanced. In addition, this framework incorporates the contributions from various disciplines and traditions and integrates the various classifications currently being utilized.

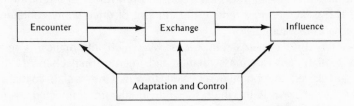

Figure 1–6. Phases of Human Communication

Human communication can be viewed as occurring in a number of phases. These phases overlap, of course, but each has its distinctive characteristics, its structure and process. These phases can be identified as (1) *encounter*, (2) *exchange*, (3) *influence*, and (4) *adaptation and control*.

ENCOUNTER

Encounter, the initial phase of human communication, *is the process by which a specific piece of information and the receiver* (or receivers) *are linked, through a particular medium.* Encounter can be analyzed in terms of: (1) the extent to which information is transmitted successfully to the receiver's cognitive boundary—the information system, and (2) the nature of the networks through which encounter becomes probable—the delivery system.

The information system examines the source's encoding process, the availability and capacity of channels utilized to transmit the information, the noise (information not intended by the source) contained in the channels, and the receiver's decoding process. Theoretical and quantitative studies of the information system have been based on a discussion of the properties of information transmission and their implications for the behavioral sciences, mainly psychology, and have been made by information scientists such as Shannon, Weaver, Cherry, Miller, Garner, Edwards, and others. Many of these efforts have direct relevance to the study of human communication.

Although there have been only limited theoretical and empirical attempts to make use of such a framework in communication research, a substantial number of communication studies can be formulated in terms of the information system, which, with its precise and powerful measures, may provide the best thrust for future assessments of the encounter phenomena in human communication. The study of news diffusion, for example, has advanced our understanding of the process by which information about major news events spreads. A study of the news diffusion of President Kennedy's assassination (Greenberg, 1964a) indicates that the probability and promptness of a person's (initial) encounter with the news is influenced by such factors as location of the person at the time the news breaks out, time and date at which the news breaks out, and relevance of the news to the person. These factors may reduce the amount of uncertainty contained in the information system.

Encounter also concerns the process by which information is relayed through spatial, network mass media, and interpersonal channels. Information is relayed to potential receivers through the social, spatial, and mass media networks with which the individuals are connected. As news diffusion studies and other experimental studies have helped us to understand, these networks can act either as relayers for or as barriers to information transmission; that is, they may facilitate or hinder one's encounter with information.

Encounter, then, is the first phase of human communication, in which the initial linkage between the piece of information and the receiver(s) is established through a certain medium. It involves the information system and the delivery system. When encounter is established, human communication can proceed to the second phase—exchange.

EXCHANGE

Exchange, defined as *the flow of shared meaning,* represents the effort on the part of the communication participants to maintain shared meaning through a set of symbols. It is because such sharing is possible that encounter can be transformed into exchange, where the meaning contained in the symbols can be transferred. Exchange is a matter not only of "talking" or "listening," but also of "understanding." In this phase, the major concern is the message, or the meaning contained in the symbols. Exchange, therefore, involves more than the information, measured by bits and network factors; it involves the meaning of the symbols, as it is shared by the participants. The study of exchange includes topics such as (1) how meaning is developed, (2) what forms and modalities exchange may take, and (3) what functions exchange serves.

Encounter does not have to be exchange; in fact, we often confuse the two phases of communication and consider exchange as a part of encounter, but encounter is the antecedent and a necessary ingredient of exchange. Exchange must contain encounter. Exchange is maintained for various reasons. Goffman (1957) describes many situations in which persons engage in exchange for no other reason than that they are bound together by time and space. Such exchange, although nonconsequential, represents a substantial proportion of human communication; it has its own formalized rituals and patterns, and offers possibilities for developing other types of human communication.

Exchange maintains its own network and structure and serves many different functions. It may integrate and solidify the participants, promote the formation of human groups of various types, effect status differentiation among the participants, or even signal the disintegration of human groups. Some of these functions require bringing into focus the third phase of human communication—influence.

INFLUENCE

Influence is defined as *the discrepancy between* (1) *a person's behavioral patterns or attitude toward an object or situation before his participation, either voluntary or involuntary, in encounter and/or exchange and* (2) *his behavioral or attitudinal patterns after such encounter and/or exchange.* Influence thus represents the impact, either psychological or behavioral, of communication.

Such impact is not always easy to measure. Some of the psychological and behavioral changes are specific and unique so that measuring them may be too costly or time-consuming. For example, because of the infrequency of such an occurrence, it is difficult to weigh the psychological influence of a president's assassination upon the population's attitude toward the issue of gun control. Also, measuring the changes is a headache, if not a downright nightmare, for the social scientist. Many of the measurements rely on constructed attitudinal scales, the reliability and validity of which may vary with the incident, the location, and the population. Other measurements rely on the respondent's ability to recall facts and opinions. Memories fade and recollections are distorted. Consequently, studies of the influence of human communication tend (1) to concentrate on laboratory experiments, where extraneous factors can be controlled and where measurement can be repeatedly tested, and (2) to focus on issues and situations which recur regularly enough so that it is the behavioral pattern that is measured rather than the behavioral incident.

Another influence problem which continuously haunts communication researchers is whether the psychological influence and the behavioral influence function in a one-to-one relationship. Does the achievement of one imply or cause the achievement of the other? Though there is some evidence that attitudinal change leads to behavioral change and vice versa, discrepancies have been observed, particularly in the area of racial prejudice. Here studies often reveal a discrepancy between a subject's attitude toward a minority group and his actual behavior. Apparently in the case of racial prejudice other factors "intervene" between attitudinal and behavioral patterns. Rokeach (1966a) has suggested that we study the interaction between the subject's attitude toward an object (a person) and his attitude toward a situation; Sherif and Cantril (1947) have proposed that we take into account the extent of a person's ego-involvement in the issue; DeFleur and Westie (1958) and Warner and DeFleur (1969) have shown that social constraint and social distance help explain the relationship between attitude and behavior.

Because human communication has so great a psychological impact, it is a major research topic in social psychology. Many theories and models are offered, under the rubrics of persuasion, social judgment, and various cognitive theories, to explain the extent of influence exerted in communication situations. The persuasion model attempts to assess the effects of various components (source, message, channel, receiver's personal and social characteristics, and so forth) on a person's acceptance of a persuasive message. The social judgment approach focuses (1) on the discrepancy between a person's position on an issue and the position advocated by a persuasive message and (2) on the relevancy of the issue to the person. According to the social judgment theorists, these are the major variables which determine the degree of attitude change. The cognitive models attempt to explain attitude change in terms of (1) the reduction of tension and (2) the restoration of consonance, or balance, in the cognitive structure of the person confronting a persuasive situation. All these approaches have their specific orientations and thus complement one another in the assessment of the psychological effects of human communication.

The behavioral impact of human communication is usually measured in connection with such recurrent and observable events as voting, the adoption of innovations by farmers, teachers, and physicians, television viewing, and the modernization process in developing countries.

One approach of special interest in the study of behavioral change is to compare the effectiveness of the mass media with that of interpersonal communication networks. One early hypothesis (Lazarsfeld, Berelson, and Gaudet, 1948) states that the flow of communication in inducing behavioral change follows a two-step process: ideas flow from the mass media to persons who are highly regarded by their peers (opinion leaders) and from them to their peers (the followers). Hypotheses advanced subsequently have modified the initial two-step hypothesis or have suggested new conceptualizations of the interplay between the mass media and the interpersonal communication in generating behavioral changes.

ADAPTATION AND CONTROL

The effectiveness over time of encounter, exchange, or influence depends to a large extent on *control, the process by which the fidelity of information flow and the efficiency of message flow and induced changes are achieved or maintained.* Thus, control can be regarded as the organizational phase of human communication. Control can be achieved by two mechanisms: (1) the feedback mechanism and (2) the dissemination mechanism. The feedback mechanism, also called the cybernetic (governing) element of human communication, focuses on negative feedback. Positive feedback informs the communication source of the extent to which the transmission has been successful; it adds little to the communication process; it merely indicates that all is well. *Negative feedback informs the source of the extent to which the transmission has failed;* in indexing the failing aspect of the communication, it provides the source with the critical information he needs to modify or improve the transmission aspects so as to make a more successful transmission, relative to his transmission intent, be it encounter, exchange, or influence.

The second law of thermodynamics tells us that any arbitrary order, once it has been formed and executed, tends toward randomness or disorder over time if the system in which the order is created and maintained interacts with its environment (an open system).[5] Since all human systems are open systems, they all face the constant threat of deterioration and disorganization. Negative feedback serves as one important means of slowing down or arresting this decay process. By supplying the consequences of the transmission, negative feedback informs the source of which aspects in the system are deteriorating.

Once feedback has received proper attention, the source must utilize another communication process to arrest the disorganization—the dissemination mechanism. The *dissemination* mechanism can be regarded as the enforced transmission in which the *transmission intent* of the source (source intent) is strong, the *delineation of the receiver system* (target sys-

---

5. A system is open if it interacts with its environment through some input and output devices.

tem delineation) is relatively complete, and the *manipulation and maintenance of transmission* (transmission manipulation) are deliberately carried out by the source. Many human communications take the form of dissemination. Political campaigns are disseminations in which the source attempts to sell himself or his ideas. (The source may be a candidate, a government agency, or a group of people.) Advertising and marketing campaigns are typical of the dissemination process; behavioral changes are induced in the consumers with regard to their particular relationships with certain products or ideas. Many activities in organizations and developing nations take the form of planned change; change is induced through dissemination via the hierarchy of the system.

The control of human communication, then, involves two interrelated mechanisms: feedback (cybernetics) and dissemination. Negative feedback provides information about those aspects in the system which have not performed effectively relative to the source's expectations. The dissemination, with the feedback, improves the probability of system success by correcting the defective aspects of the system.

Important Characteristics of the Suggested Framework

Instead of creating a completely new scheme, I have suggested a framework which integrates the major classifications already available in the literature. For example, the first three phases of the framework (encounter, exchange, and influence) closely parallel the linguistic notions of syntactics, semantics, and pragmatics. But while the linguists are primarily interested in the message aspect of the communication situation, and thus emphasize the structure, meaning, and use of the message (such as the language system), the suggested framework focuses on the human interactional aspects of the communication situation. In this framework, the message, while an important element in all human communication phases, becomes meaningful only in a context in which there are several other important components. Thus the framework goes beyond the concerns of the linguists to include the total human communication situation.

Furthermore, instead of dichotomizing mass and interpersonal communication, the framework attempts to specify their complementary as well as their unique contributions to each phase of human communication. This dichotomy is largely the result of an unnecessary but natural disciplinary bias. Interpersonal communication has long been the research focus of psychologists and social psychologists who are interested in group dynamics (Bavelas, 1950; Festinger, 1950; Cartwright and Harary, 1956), group pressure (Lewin, 1943; Asch, 1956), attitude formation and change (Heider, 1946; Newcomb, 1953), and interpersonal or group attractions, leadership, and so on. Mass communication has primarily concerned those sociologists, journalism researchers, and political scientists who are interested in the effects of the mass media in bringing about social change (Lasswell, 1948; Katz and Lazarsfeld, 1955; Westley and MacLean, 1957; Bennis et al., 1961; Rogers, 1962; Pye, 1963). Only recently has the intimate and dynamic relationship between the interpersonal and the mass channels in human communication received proper attention and treatment (Katz and Lazarsfeld, 1955; Klapper, 1960; Rogers, 1962). Separate discussions of mass media and interpersonal channels have lost their validity in the study of human communication. In the suggested framework, the interplay between mass and interpersonal channels is stressed in each of the phases of human communication.

Another popular classification, discussed earlier, treats the source, the message, the channel, and the receiver as separate entities. The separate treatment of the various elements gained impetus from the behavioral approach to the study of attitude change typified by the work of Hovland and his associates. In their attempt to isolate the attributes of the various components that affect a receiver's attitude change, they logically treated the components as separate clusters of variables. The behavioral approach has clearly demonstrated the relationship between the attributes of a component and a receiver's attitudinal change, but, because it has not threaded the factors together, the behavioral approach has failed to present a consistent theory of attitude change—a theoretical scheme integrating the attributes of the components and their effects on attitude change. While the elements' distinctiveness is important, their functional collectivity in any human communication cannot be overstressed. It is as a whole, rather than as separate elements, that they make sense of any communication situation. In the suggested framework, the components are regarded as the fundamental elements in each phase of human communication, and in the analysis of each phase, the relationships among the various components are discussed in terms of their distinctive and complementary contributions to the communication situation.

In the next six chapters, the four phases of human communication (encounter, exchange, influence, and control) will be discussed in detail. Both theoretical discussions and empirical evidence will be included.

2

Encounter:
THE FRAME OF
HUMAN COMMUNICATION

Encounter, the first phase of human communication, represents the initial linkage between a specific piece of information and a receiver (or receivers) through a certain medium. The medium can be either the original source of the information or a channel through which the information is transmitted to the receiver. A typical situation of encounter would be a person's initial awareness through a friend of President Kennedy's assassination. The information here is "Kennedy was assassinated," the medium is the friend, and the person whom the friend tells is the receiver. Thus, encounter is the crudest form of human communication; the sole criterion of a successful encounter is the fidelity of the information transmission, the extent to which the information has been accurately and speedily delivered to the potential receiver(s). The focus of this phase of human communication is, therefore, on how the information is transmitted from the source, possibly through several intermediary channels, to the receiver.

Encounter, though the crudest form of human communication, also serves as the *necessary* initial phase for the further development of human communication. Encounter establishes the link between the source, the information, and the receiver, and thus provides possibilities for the source and the receiver to develop more meaningful and sustaining communication patterns.

The fidelity of encounter depends on the working of two distinctive systems: *the information system and the delivery system. The information system concerns the symbols contained in the information.* The symbols must be somewhat familiar to and expected by the potential receiver. Some uncertainty or unfamiliarity should also be present, however; the information must have some "novel" or "new" value if the potential receiver is to consider the encounter worthwhile. Thus, analysis of the information system focuses on the measurement of uncertainty contained in the information and on finding and utilizing an optimal degree of uncertainty to induce maximal deliverable information.

The delivery system concerns the means by which the information is delivered to the potential receiver. Information can be channeled through an almost infinite variety and combination of media. An understanding of the delivery system requires an analysis of the nature of the various media (such as the social network, the mass media network, and the spatial network) and the relationship between these media and the delivery of various types of information.

In this chapter I will discuss encounter relative to the two systems. I will first introduce the notion of *information* as a quantitative and measurable concept and show how information is measured. The reader will be introduced to the mathematical properties of information measurement. Then I will try to show how measures of information can be utilized to analyze the encounter phase of human communication. The *delivery* system will be discussed in terms of the three subsystems involved (the spatial network, the social network, and the mass media network). Examples will show how the three subsystems function together in most encounters. Finally, I will summarize how analyses of the information system and the delivery system can further enhance our understanding of encounters.

Definition and Measurement of Information

Information can be defined as a set of symbols with which both the source and the receiver are familiar. *Information* differs from *message* in that information refers to the symbols contained in the transmission, whereas message indicates the semantic (meaning) of the transmission. Thus, information is the content of the encounter while message is the content of the exchange. Exchange will be discussed in the next chapter.

One convenient way of measuring information is by using an index called Uncertainty. If a finite set of symbols, all familiar to the potential receiver, composes the universe from which a certain symbol is selected for transmission in a particular situation, then the *amount of Uncertainty* is defined as the minimal number of questions (bits) the potential receiver must raise to identify every symbol being transmitted. Thus, information exists only when the potential receiver is familiar with the symbol(s) contained in it. According to this definition, the signals we presently receive from outer space cannot be considered information, since we, as potential receivers, are not familiar with the universe from which the received signals are selected.

Uncertainty is a measure of the number of bits by which the Uncertainty of the transmitted symbols can be totally reduced. Thus, the amount of Uncertainty is measured by the number of bits necessary for Uncertainty reduction, or for certainty relative to the transmitted set of symbols.

If, for example, a receiver knows that the possible symbols in a specific transmission include A, B, C, and D, and if he knows that each symbol is equally likely to be transmitted, then the most sure and economical way for him to "decode" or rightly guess the specific symbol being transmitted every time is by using the "halving method" of questioning—each question reducing the possible symbols by half. Let us assume that the symbol being transmitted is C. The first question by the receiver may be, "Is it before C?" By asking this question, he reduces the number of possible symbols to half (two). If the answer is, "Yes," the possible symbols are A and B. If the answer is, "No," the possible symbols are C and D. In our case, the answer is, "No." Then the receiver may proceed to ask another question, "Is it before D?" A positive answer will lead him to decode with total certainty. Thus, given the fact that the receiver knows the possible symbols which may occur in the transmission, and that each symbol has an equal likelihood of occurring in the transmission, a series of *binary* questions (when a question must be answered with either "Yes" or "No") will entirely reduce the Uncertainty contained in the transmission. (Actually, it might be a series of questions that could be verified by three, four, or any number of answers, but for simplicity's sake I will use the binary example throughout our discussion of information. The same principles apply to all other situations.) Thus, the simple way to measure information is to measure the amount of Uncertainty contained in the set of symbols transmitted by the sender or received by the receiver. The amount of Uncertainty, in turn, can be measured by the minimal number of questions that need be asked to decode the transmitted symbol entirely. Let us now look into this measure more rigorously.

THE MATHEMATICAL PROPERTIES OF INFORMATION MEASUREMENT*

This section develops the mathematical properties associated with the measurement of Uncertainty.

When All Possible Symbols Have Equal Likelihood of Occurrence

Suppose a reader wants to decode the headline carried by a given newspaper on a given day and suppose all the events can be categorized into the following:

   a. Politics
   b. Economics
   c. Health and pollution
   d. Education
   e. War and peace
   f. Violence
   g. Entertainment and Sports
   h. Other events

---

*This section may be skipped by readers who are not interested in the quantitative aspects of communication. Such skipping should not hinder their comprehension of the other sections of the book.

The reader can use one of two strategies. He can assume that each of the eight symbols or categories has an equal likelihood of appearing as a headline or he can assume that each of the symbols or categories has a different likelihood of appearing as a headline (for example, symbols a, b, e, and f are more likely to appear in the headline than are symbols c, d, g, and h).

Let us adopt the first strategy and assume that all symbols are equally likely to appear as a headline. The reader may ask, by using the halving method, "Is it before e?" Assuming the correct category is "b" (taxes are going up), the answer to this first question is, "Yes." This answer reduces the possible symbols to a, b, c, and d. Then, the second question may be, "Is it before c?" The answer, "Yes," reduces the possible symbols to a and b. The third question is then, "Is it before b?" and the answer is, "No." Now, it is known with total certainty that the symbol or event being transmitted is "b." In other words, with eight equally probable symbols, three binary questions will reduce the Uncertainty. So, using the symbol H for Uncertainty, we say that H = 3 in decoding the specific headline transmission.

In general, H (Uncertainty) is a function of the number of possible symbols when all symbols are equally likely to occur:

Number of Possible Symbols (n)	H (number of minimal questions)
1	0
2	1
4	2
8	3
16	4

This relationship between the number of possible symbols (n) occurring in a transmission and the Uncertainty contained in it (H) can be expressed as:

$$n = 2^H \tag{1}$$

This formula simply states that if you have a set of equally probable symbols (n) and if each question can be verified by a "yes" or "no" (binary), the number of symbols (n) equals two (binary) to the Hth power.

However, since our main interest is to find out the H for the given n, rather than the n for the given H, the formula in (1) must be transformed. The relationship in (1) can be expressed in the form of a logarithm, which is simply another way of expressing relationships involving powers of numbers of which (1) is an example. For example, given $A = B^x$, then its logarithmic equivalent is $x = \log_B A$. The latter reads, "x is the logarithm of A to the base of B." For example, $8 = 2^3$ and $3 = \log_2 8$ are equivalent statements. Most basic mathematical texts provide tables that give solutions to logarithms to the bases of 2, 10, and e (a frequently used number in mathematics, equal to 2.7182818), and it is a simple matter of finding the right answer in the appropriate table (the reader is encouraged to familiarize himself with the logarithm tables in any mathematical text).

Thus, the formula contained in (1) can be expressed as:

$$H = \log_2 n \tag{2}$$

In other words, the amount of Uncertainty (H) contained in any transmission is the logarithm of the number of possible symbols to the base of 2 (when each question is binary).

Another important concept needs to be introduced here. While *Uncertainty* (H) gives us the minimal number of questions to be asked for *any symbol* contained in the transmission, *Information* (I) tells us the number of questions that need to be asked for each *specific symbol* transmitted. For example, given the set of eight possible headline categories, we may solve for the Information (I) contained in each category:

TABLE 2-1. INFORMATION (I) ASSOCIATED WITH EACH SYMBOL IN AN ARRAY
OF EIGHT EQUALLY LIKELY-TO-BE-TRANSMITTED SYMBOLS

Symbol	I (number of questions asked)
a	3
c	3
•	•
•	•
h	3

Here we see that the information (I) contained in each of the eight symbol categories is 3. In general, *when all possible symbols have an equal probability of occurrence, then the Information (I) contained in each symbol is the same as the Uncertainty (H) contained in the transmission.* (The reader must not confuse the term "Information"—capital "I"—with the earlier general use of "information." When Information refers to the technical term, it will always bear the capital letter.)

When All Possible Symbols Do Not
Have Equal Likelihood of Occurrence

The formula in (2) gives us the measure of H when all possible symbols have equal likelihood of occurrence. In most transmissions, however, this is not the case. If the assumption of equal likelihood implies the randomness of things, then the ordering of things implies an unequal likelihood of occurrence among possible events. In fact, when symbols are randomly transmitted, a maximum effort is necessary for decoding. Thus, to reduce the amount of effort, ordering is desirable, as is an unequal likelihood of occurrence among events. In this section, I will demonstrate how to measure Information (I) and Uncertainty (H) when the assumption of equal likelihood of occurrence among symbols is removed and I will show why unequal likelihood of symbols reduces the efforts the potential receiver must make to decode.

Suppose headline events for a given newspaper can be reduced to the following categories: (A) Politics and war, (B) Economics, (C) Violence, and (D) Other events. Suppose also that over a period of 12 months, the reader finds the likelihood of occurrence of each category in the headline as follows:

TABLE 2-2. PROBABILITIES OF FOUR CATEGORIES OF HEADLINE EVENTS

Symbol	Likelihood of Occurrence
A	.500
B	.250
C	.125
D	.125

We see that B is twice as likely to occur in the headline as C or D and that A is four times as likely to appear there.

A reader wishing to decode the headline of a given day, using the same halving method to decode the transmission, would first ask, "Is it before C?" This would result in two halves with unequal probabilities. The reader could better decode this set of possible symbols by utilizing his knowledge of their unequal probabilities and assigning weights to the symbols. Using the probability of the least likely symbol as the baseline, he might arrive at the following equally weighed array of symbols:

$$A \ A \ A \ A \ B \ B \ C \ D$$

One question would then solve for A (compared with three questions with the halving method); two questions would solve for B (compared with three); and three questions would solve for either C or D. Thus, if the reader utilizes his information about the probabilities of occurrence of these symbols, he saves himself three questions.

Now we may express the Information (I) contained in each symbol and their weighing factors (P's) as follows:

TABLE 2-3. INFORMATION (I) AND THE WEIGHING FACTOR (P) FOR EACH
OF FOUR CATEGORIES OF HEADLINE EVENTS

Symbol (i)	Information (Ii)	Weighing Factor (Pi)
A	1	1/2
B	2	1/4
C	3	1/8
D	3	1/8

For equally probable symbols, the Uncertainty (H), as stated in the formula in (2), is simply the logarithm of n to the base of 2. For unequally weighed symbols, the Uncertainty (H) can be expressed as follows:

$$H = \sum_{i=1}^{n} I_i P_i \tag{3}$$

This formula states that "the Uncertainty contained in a set of weighed symbols is the sum (Σ) of the products of each symbol's Information (I) and its weighing factor (P)." Let us compute the H for the transmission problem stated in Table 2–3.

$$H = \sum_{i=1}^{n} I_i P_i = (1)\ (1/2) + (2)\ (1/4) + (3)\ (1/8) + (3)\ (1/8) = 1.75$$

If we use the unweighed (that is, treating the possible symbols as equally likely) formula (2) for the same four symbols:

$$H = \log_2 n = \log_2 4 = 2.00$$

By utilizing the weighing factors when the possible symbols have unequal probabilities of occurrence, the reader achieves a saving of .25 for the set of four symbols. This represents a saving of 12.5 percent over the H derived from the unweighed formula (H = 2.00).

In general, then, if we utilize the weighing factors when the symbols have unequal probabilities of occurrence, the amount of Uncertainty will be reduced. As the weighing factors deviate from the equal probabilities for all symbols (1/n), the Uncertainty will decrease proportionally. To state these properties formally:

1. For all weighing factors between zero and one ($0 \leqslant P_i \leqslant 1$, for all i's), the Information (I) contained in each symbol i is:

$$I_i = - \log_2 P_i \qquad (4)$$

2. The Uncertainty (H) associated with such a set of possible symbols is:

$$H = \sum_{i=1}^{n} I_i P_i = \sum_{i=1}^{n} (- \log_2 P_i)\ (P_i)$$

$$= - \sum_{i=1}^{n} P_i \log_2 P_i \qquad (5)$$

The second step substitutes I_i with $-\log_2 P_i$ from formula (4). *Formulas (4) and (5) are the general formulas for obtaining I and H.* They can be used in all cases, whether the symbols have equal or unequal probabilities. The reader should use these formulas to solve for the Information (I) contained in each symbol and for the Uncertainty (H) in the set of symbols presented in Table 2–1.

To demonstrate the generality of formula (5), let us compute the H when all n symbols in a set have equal probabilities of being transmitted. Then, the probability for each symbol to occur is 1/n. Thus, $H = - \sum\limits_{i=1}^{n} (1/n \log_2 1/n)$ by formula (5). Since there are n terms in the summation, and every term is identical, the equation becomes:

$$H = (n) - [(1/n \log_2 1/n)]$$
$$= - \log_2 1/n \quad \text{(by canceling out n and 1/n)}$$
$$= \log_2 n$$

The result, of course, is the same as in formula (2)—for the case when all possible symbols are equally likely to occur. Thus, formula (5) can be used to solve for the Uncertainty, whether the symbols have equal or unequal probabilities of occurrence.

SOME CHARACTERISTICS OF INFORMATION (I) AND UNCERTAINTY (H)*

One important characteristic of the Information (I) contained in each symbol is its relationship to the number of possible symbols in the set to be selected for transmission. An increase in the number of possible symbols (n) means an increase in the Information (I) contained in a symbol (see Figure 2–1)

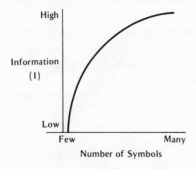

Figure 2–1. Relationship Between Number of Symbols and Information

—indicating that more and more questions must be asked to verify the use of any specific symbol. As the number of possible symbols keeps increasing, however, the increasing Information (I) contained in a symbol follows a decelerating rate. This is known as the bending effect and means simply that as the symbols increase rapidly, approaching an infinite number, the Information (I) contained in a symbol will continue to rise, but will do so

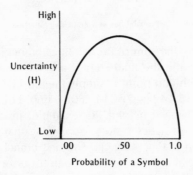

Figure 2–2. Relationship Between the Probability of Occurrence and Uncertainty

*This section may be skipped by readers who are not interested in the quantitative aspects of the subject.

slowly; in other words, after the number of possible symbols reaches, say, 30, the Information (I) contained in each symbol will increase at a very slow rate.

The Uncertainty (H) has another type of relationship with each symbol when the symbol has a different weight from 1/n. Figure 2–2 shows that given only two symbols in the set, the Uncertainty will be minimal when the weight (probability) of one symbol is zero or 1.0 and maximal when it is .50. This can be understood easily, since when one symbol's probability of occurrence is zero or one, no question would be necessary to ascertain which symbol has been transmitted, and when it is .50, then each symbol has an equal probability of being transmitted.

In summary, we may make the following observations about the Uncertainty (H):

1. H can be measured for the transmission, given the knowledge of the number of possible symbols and their weighing factors (probabilities).

2. When all P's are equal to 1/n, H is simply a function of the number of possible symbols.

3. The unit of H is additive. This can be demonstrated with a branching situation in Figure 2–3.

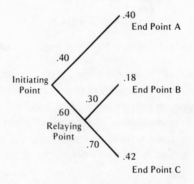

Figure 2–3. Probabilities in a Branching Situation

As can be seen here, the sum of probabilities branching from any given point is equal to 1.00 and the final sum at all end points is also equal to 1.00. Furthermore, each end point is simply the product of all probabilities leading to it. H (.40, .18, .42) = H (.40, .60) + (.60) H (.30, .70).

This characteristic can be helpful, for example, in our analysis of the interpersonal diffusion of a news story. Supposing that the news was the assassination of Martin Luther King, Jr. The first branch may indicate the probability of learning about the news through a personal source without relaying (40 percent) and with relaying (60 percent). The relayer may relay the news either to his family or friends (70 percent) or to strangers (30 percent). Then, with this simple model, we could hypothesize how many people in a community would learn the news through a personal source without relaying it, how many would relay the news to their families and friends, and how many people would relay the news to strangers. Empirically observed actual diffusion patterns can then be compared with the predicted pattern and a revision of the model made to improve future prediction of diffusion patterns of similar news events.

4. H is maximum when $P_i = 1/n$.

5. H is minimum when $P_i = 1$, or 0.

6. Relative Uncertainty (R.U.) is the ratio between the Actual Uncertainty and the Maximal Uncertainty. As stated in Formula (5), the Actual Uncertainty can be measured with $H = -\sum_{i=1}^{n} P_i \log_2 P_i$. According to observation 4, H is at the Maximum when $P_i = 1/n$ or $H = \log_2 n$. Thus,

$$R.U. = \frac{\text{Actual Uncertainty}}{\text{Maximal Uncertainty}}$$

$$= \frac{-\sum_{i=1}^{n} P_i \log_2 P_i}{\log_2 n} \tag{6}$$

7. Redundancy (R) is equal to 1.00 minus the Relative Uncertainty (R.U.).

$$R = \frac{\text{Maximal Uncertainty} - \text{Actual Uncertainty}}{\text{Maximal Uncertainty}}$$

$$= 1 - R.U. \tag{7}$$

Relative Uncertainty (R.U.) indicates the amount of saving in decoding when a certain amount of information about the probabilities of the possible symbols to appear in the transmission is known to the receiver. As a result of this saving, part of the transmission becomes redundant to the receiver. This relationship becomes more comprehensible if we return to the set of symbols presented in Table 2–3. For that set of four symbols, we find:

$$\text{Maximal Uncertainty} = \log_2 n = 2$$

$$\text{Actual Uncertainty} = \sum_{i=1}^{n} I_i P_i = 1.75$$

$$\text{Therefore, R.U.} = 7/8 = 87.5\%$$

$$\text{and } R = 1 - 87.5\% = 12.5\%$$

Thus, if we know about the probabilities of the symbols' occurrences (weighing factors in Table 2–3), we can reduce the Uncertainty in the transmission from 2.00 to 1.75 (the average number of questions that must be asked to verify each symbol transmitted). The Relative Uncertainty is now only 87.5 percent, relative to the Maximal Uncertainty (100 percent). The remaining 12.5 percent of the transmission is unnecessary because the symbol contained in the transmission has been decoded completely and is therefore redundant information.

Decomposition of the Encounter as Uncertainty Functions

The encounter can now be analyzed as a situation in which several Uncertainty functions interact. In the interest of simplicity, let us look at the source-receiver direct encounter situation where a single source transmits certain information to a single receiver. This situation can be decomposed as follows:

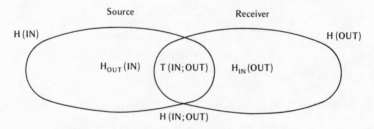

Figure 2–4. Encounter Decomposed as Uncertainty Functions

In this situation, several Uncertainty functions appear:

1. $H(IN)$: The total Uncertainty intended to be transmitted by the source, representing the *input Uncertainty*.

2. $H(OUT)$: The total Uncertainty actually received or decoded by the receiver, representing the *output Uncertainty*.

3. $T(IN;OUT)$: The Uncertainty common to the source and the receiver, representing the *transmitted Uncertainty*.

4. $H_{OUT}(IN)$: The Uncertainty that is contained in the input but is not contained in the output, representing the input Uncertainty which did not get transmitted, called *equivocation*.

5. $H_{IN}(OUT)$: The Uncertainty that is contained in the output but is not contained in the input, representing the Uncertainty not intended by the source but added during the transmission, called *ambiguity* or *noise*.

6. $H(IN;OUT)$: The *total Uncertainty* involved in the encounter, consisting of various Uncertainty functions as described previously.

We may specify some of the important relationships among the various Uncertainty functions:

1. $H(IN;OUT) = H_{OUT}(IN) + H_{IN}(OUT) + T(IN;OUT)$. The total amount of Uncertainty in the encounter is the sum of the equivocation, the noise, and the transmitted Uncertainty. Also, $H(IN;OUT) = H(IN) + H_{IN}(OUT) =$

$H(OUT) + H_{OUT}(IN) = H(IN) + H(OUT) - T(IN;OUT)$.[1] In other words, the total amount of Uncertainty in the encounter can be computed if one has knowledge of some Uncertainty functions in the encounter.

2. Similarly, $H(IN) = H_{OUT}(IN) + T(IN;OUT)$ and $H(OUT) = H_{IN}(OUT) + T(IN;OUT)$.

3. $H_{OUT}(IN) = H(IN) - T(IN;OUT)$ and $H_{IN}(OUT) = H(OUT) - T(IN;OUT)$.

Summary of Measurement and Analysis of the Information System

The encounter is defined as the initial linkage between a specific piece of information and a receiver through a certain medium. The content of the linkage is the information, which consists of some symbols known to both the source (medium) and the receiver. The information can be measured in terms of the Uncertainty contained in the transmission.

The Uncertainty represents the extent to which the information can be decoded with the knowledge of the number of alternatives and their respective probabilities of occurrence. Maximal Uncertainty exists in a transmission when no information about the probabilities of occurrence among the possible symbols is known to the receiver (the decoder) and the symbols are thus assumed to be equally probable. The Actual Uncertainty measures the actual transmission when some information about the probabilities of occurrence of the possible symbols is known. Thus, the Relative Uncertainty represents the saving of decoding effort as a result of the additional knowledge about the probabilities of occurrence among the possible symbols. As the known probabilities of these symbols' occurrence deviate from equally probable, the saving becomes greater and the Relative Uncertainty lower. The saved portion of the transmission is called Redundancy. Redundancy, therefore, is inversely related to the Relative Uncertainty; as the Relative Uncertainty decreases, the Redundancy increases.

When we focus on information, analyzing the encounter becomes a matter of investigating the Relative Uncertainty and the Redundancy contained in any transmission to the receiver (the decoder) in a given encounter.

One interesting and frequently raised question is whether the most efficient transmission has an optimal amount of Relative Uncertainty and Redundancy. It is known, in fact, that there is in many information systems a natural tendency for there to be 50 percent Relative Uncertainty and 50 percent Redundancy. One such system is language. In many languages, including English and Spanish, the common usage (transmission) will con-

---

1. $H(IN;OUT) = H_{OUT}(IN) + T(IN;OUT) + H_{IN}(OUT)$. Since $H(IN) = H_{OUT}(IN) + T(IN;OUT)$ and $H_{IN}(OUT) = H(OUT) - T(IN;OUT)$, therefore $H(IN;OUT) = H(IN) + H(OUT) - T(IN;OUT)$.

tain about 50 percent Relative Uncertainty and 50 percent Redundancy, regardless of what unit of analysis is under consideration (be it letters or words). This is so because of the distributions of the probabilities of occurrences among the units of symbols (Weaver, 1949; Rapoport, 1953b). When there is too great a deviation from this sort of split, either too much effort may be required to decode (when the Relative Uncertainty approaches the Maximal Uncertainty) or decoding may not even be justified because not enough new information is imparted (when the Redundancy approaches one and the Relative Uncertainty approaches zero). In a study of the Spanish language, from the very ancient to the modern version, the distribution of the Relative Uncertainty and Redundancy oscillated around the 50 percentile point (Greenberg, Osgood, and Saporta, 1954).

Schramm (1955) applied the same type of analysis to the various news sources used by major newspapers in the United States and Europe (among others, the *New York Times,* and *Chicago Tribune,* the *Washington Post,* the *Times* of London, and *Le Figaro* of Paris) and found that in terms of the probabilities of the possible sources being used, the distribution of the Relative Uncertainty and Redundancy varied from 41 percent to 57 percent in all cases. The remarkably consistent results indicate that if the transmission of information in an encounter such as news dissemination and diffusion is to be successful, the information must have an optimal structure (in terms of the information contained). Empirical evidence almost guarantees exciting applications of information analysis to many human encounters on both the interpersonal and mass communication levels.

Some Applications of the Information Approach to Encounter

I will now present some specific cases where the information analysis can be applied to the study of encounter. Here I must rely primarily on hypothetical or experimental studies, most of them carried out by psychologists, since direct applications of the information theory to the study of human communication are lacking. However, I hope that by demonstrating the feasibility of such measures, I will generate an understanding of the potential applications of the information theory to the study of human communication both among communication students and researchers.

ENCODING OF THE SOURCE

Let us assume that a source has to transmit information (in binary digits) regarding the origin of a news event: U (United States), E (Europe), A (Asia), or M (Middle East). Is there an optimal strategy for transmitting such information? More specifically, if the knowledge about the probabilities (or frequencies) of occurrences of these four locations in the transmission is known, can an optimal strategy be developed to code these symbols? From the uncertainty measure, we know that the Maximal Uncertainty would be 2 ($H = \log_2 4 = 2$); thus, at least two digits have to be allocated to decode the transmission (Table 2-4).

TABLE 2-4. DIGITAL REPRESENTATION OF ORIGINS OF NEWS AS EQUAL PROBABILITIES

News Origin	Digital Code (when $P_i = 1/n$)
U	00
E	01
A	10
M	11

It, however, the probabilities of news occurrences from the four locations differ, for example $P_U = .50$, $P_E = .25$, $P_A = P_M = .125$, then our coding scheme could be changed as shown in Table 2-5.

TABLE 2-5. DIGITAL REPRESENTATION OF ORIGINS OF NEWS AS UNEQUAL PROBABILITIES

News Origin	Digital Code
U	1
E	01
A	001
M	0001

If the probabilities of news occurrences from the four locations are not known or utilized, transmission of the information UUEUEAUM will take 16 digits (0000010001100011); if such knowledge is utilized, however, it will take only 15 digits (110110100110001). As the transmission comes to involve more news events, the saving also increases. Thus, the strategy is to code the more frequently used locations or symbols with a smaller number of digits.

So far, all the examples have contained even numbers of symbols to be transmitted. When odd numbers of symbols are to be coded, a modified strategy must be used. If, for example, there are three items—P (political), M (military), E (economic)—to be coded and if every item has an equal probability of occurrence, then $H = \log_2 3 = 1.58$. The minimal coding scheme would be represented in Table 2-6.

TABLE 2-6. DIGITAL REPRESENTATION OF SINGLE SYMBOLS

Symbol	Digital Code
P	1
M	01
E	00

The H for this scheme is 1.67, representing a loss of .09 as compared with the expected H. This is because an extra digit has to be utilized in coding M and E. To minimize the loss which results because odd numbers require additional digital codes, the grouping method may be used. Instead of assigning a specific digit code for each symbol, we can try to group two symbols and assign a digital code for each pair (Table 2-7).

TABLE 2-7. DIGITAL REPRESENTATION OF COMBINED SYMBOLS

Paired Symbols	Digital Code
PP	111
PM	110
PE	101
MP	100
MM	011
ME	010
EP	001
EM	0001
EE	0000

With this method, the 2H becomes 3.22 and the H is 1.61. This is an improvement over the previous single-symbol coding because the loss is now only .03. The grouping can be developed further into three-symbol coding, four-symbol coding, and so forth. As the groupings become larger, the loss continues to be minimized. The marginal improvement also becomes smaller and smaller, however. This method shows that optimal strategies can be devised, and several principles can be stated:

1. The more frequently used symbol should be assigned the shorter code.

2. When odd numbers of symbols are to be coded, the grouping method should be used; the symbols should be grouped and digital codes should be assigned to the grouped symbols. As the grouping size increases, the loss of effort will be reduced. However, as the grouping increases, the marginal reduction of the loss will rapidly decrease.

DECODING OF THE RECEIVER

In a perfect (noiseless) encounter, we say the transmission is complete when T(IN;OUT) approaches maximal, that is, when $H_{OUT}(IN)$ and $H_{IN}(OUT)$ both approach zero and H(IN) approaches H(OUT). Let us demonstrate this situation with the following example:

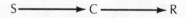

$$S \longrightarrow C \longrightarrow R$$

Here, S represents the source which transmits input into the encounter situation, C represents the channel, and R represents the receiver which "outputs" the information. When there is no noise, the information in input and output should be isomorphic (in a one-to-one correspondence). If the input consists of two signals (0 and 1) and eight transmissions take place, then the input-output correspondence is as shown in Table 2-8.

TABLE 2–8. DIGITAL CORRESPONDENCE OF ISOMORPHIC INPUT-OUTPUT

Input	Output
0	0
0	0
0	0
0	0
1	1
1	1
1	1
1	1

We may calculate the information functions in this encounter:

Input	Output	P(IN;OUT)	$-P \log_2 P$
0	0	1/2	.50
1	1	1/2	.50

Therefore: $H(IN;OUT) = -\Sigma P \log_2 P = 1.00$ bit/signal
$\quad\quad\quad H(IN) \quad\quad = -P(IN) \log_2 P(IN) = 1$ bit/signal
$\quad\quad\quad H(OUT) \quad = -P(OUT) \log_2 P(OUT) = 1$ bit/signal
$\quad\quad\quad H_{IN}(OUT) = H(IN;OUT) - H(IN) = 0$
$\quad\quad\quad H_{OUT}(IN) = H(IN;OUT) - H(OUT) = 0$
$\quad\quad\quad T(IN;OUT) = H(IN;OUT) - H_{IN}(OUT) = 1$ bit/signal

Thus, no information is lost and the transmission is perfect (T = 1 bit/signal). However, in most human encounters, noise exists. The noise can be introduced by the source—when his unintentional verbal and nonverbal gestures vary, when the selected coding scheme is imprecise or can be confused with other schemes known to the receiver, and so on. Noise can also be introduced by the receiver, who may misinterpret the information because of past experiences and decoding schemes. The channel is another source of noise, as both the structure and the function of the channel may induce noise.

Noise can also be categorized according to whether it is systematic or random. Systematic noise occurs when the noise itself forms information, although such information may be irrelevant or may contradict the information intended for transmission.[2] Random noise, on the other hand, may be caused by incidental codes that somehow get through in the transmission.

When noise occurs in the transmission, T(IN;OUT) is less than maximum. How far it deviates from maximum depends (1) on the encoding of the source—how effectively the source or the channel transforms the information into proper and economic codes, (2) on the extent of noise that exists, and (3) on how effectively the receiver decodes the information transmitted. Once we know about the information encoded, the noise, and the outcome

2. It is possible that systematic noise may affect the pattern of the transmitted signals without affecting the amount of uncertainty contained in the transmission. For example, with the input (0, 0, 1, 1) and the output (1, 1, 0, 0), the amount of transmitted uncertainty remains the same, but the pattern is a reversed one. In other words, information measures are insensitive to directions.

of the transmission, we are equipped, with the information theory, to analyze the fidelity of the information transmission, or, in other words, the degree of success of the encounter.

Using the same example as before, we may have the encounter as shown in Figure 2–5. Here, the N's are noises—N_1 and N_2. Both are assumed to

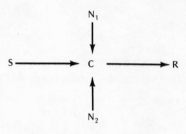

Figure 2–5. Encounter with Noises

be systematic noise. Let us assume that the transmissions occur in this particular encounter as shown in Table 2–9.

TABLE 2–9. DIGITAL REPRESENTATION OF AN ENCOUNTER WITH NOISES

Input	N_1	N_2	Output
0	0	0	0
0	0	1	0
0	1	0	1*
0	1	1	0
1	0	0	1
1	0	1	0*
1	1	0	1
1	1	1	1

*Error

In six of the eight transmissions we find a correspondence between input and output. The other two are erred—one possibly due to N_1 and the other to N_2. As a result of the transmissions, we can now compute the various information functions by using the formulas in (5) and on pages 32-33.

Input	Output	P(IN;OUT)	− P logP
0	0	3/8	.531
0	1	1/8	.375
1	0	1/8	.375
1	1	3/8	.531

Therefore:

$$H(\text{IN};\text{OUT}) = - \Sigma P(\text{IN};\text{OUT}) \log_2 P(\text{IN};\text{OUT})$$
$$= 1.81 \text{ bits/signal}$$
$$H(\text{IN}) = - \Sigma P(\text{IN}) \log_2 P(\text{IN})$$
$$= - (4/8) \log_2 (4/8) = 1 \text{ bit/signal}$$
$$H(\text{OUT}) = - \Sigma P(\text{OUT}) \log_2 P(\text{IN}) = 1 \text{ bit/signal}$$
$$H_{IN}(\text{OUT}) = H(\text{IN};\text{OUT}) - H(\text{IN}) = 1.81 - 1 = .81 \text{ bit/signal}$$

$H_{OUT}(IN)$ $= H(IN;OUT) - H(OUT) = 1.81 - 1 = .81$ bit/signal
$T(IN;OUT) = H(IN) + H(OUT) - H(IN;OUT) = .19$ bit/signal

Therefore, by knowing the input and output signals, we can calculate the total information contained in the encounter (1.81) and the information transmitted (.19), which shows the reduction of the amount of uncertainty as a result of the existence of noise in the channel. The reader may feel that T decreases rather rapidly from 1 bit/signal, in the noiseless transmissions, to .19 bit/signal, when noise erred two of the eight transmissions (in fact, when noise causes only one transmission error, the T is reduced from 1 bit/signal to .45 bit/signal), but the reduction is so rapid because all these information functions are logarithmic in nature. Therefore, if four errors occurred in the eight transmissions, T would become 0—indicating no correspondence between the input information and the output information.

The reader who is familiar with correlational analysis and the analysis of variance should notice a strong analogy between the information theory and these other statistical methods. T, in fact, has been interpreted as the main effect in the analysis of variance (Garner, 1962) and it is a measure of the amount of correlation (rather than the degree of correlation) in the correlational analysis. While the correlational and variance analyses assume at least some variables to be metric (interval or ratio data; for example, in the analysis of variance, the dependent or criterion variable is always assumed to be metric), information analysis can be used for nonmetric (nominal or ordinal) data such as the binary codes.

The same analytic procedure applies to the more complicated situation in which the information transmitted involves a series, rather than a pair, of signals. For example, a source is transmitting nine signals and transmits each signal 20 times during the encounter by showing on a board a sequence of nine positions. The positions run from left to right and each has a signal light. At each transmission, one signal light of one specific position is flashed on for one-fourth of a second in time. The input order of the signals

TABLE 2-10. RESULTS OF A SERIES OF TRANSMISSIONS IN AN ENCOUNTER

		Input Signal									Total
		1	2	3	4	5	6	7	8	9	
	1	20			1						21
	2		19	1							20
	3			18							18
	4				17						17
Output	5		1		1	20	1				23
Signal	6			1			19				20
	7				1			19	2		22
	8							1	17		18
	9								1	20	21
Total		20	20	20	20	20	20	20	20	20	180

SOURCE: Adapted from Edwards, 1964.

is random and the receiver, sitting 20 feet in front of the board, is asked to record the specific position at each transmission on a record sheet. One such encounter may result as presented in Table 2–10. This table was constructed after 180 transmissions in which each signal was transmitted 20 times in a random sequence. From this table, we can compute the H(IN) in terms of the total presented in the last row. However, since each signal was transmitted 20 times, all the input signals are equally probable, and we may use the formula in (2):

$$H(IN) = \log_2 9 = 3.17 \text{ bits/signal}$$

The output Uncertainty H(OUT) can be computed with the totals in the last column. As shown in Table 2–11, the probability of each signal's occurrence in the output derives from the ratio between the frequency of each signal received and the overall total (180).

TABLE 2–11. CALCULATIONS OF THE OUTPUT UNCERTAINTY

Output Signal	Frequency	P(OUT)	$-P(OUT) \log_2(OUT)$
1	21	.12	.37
2	20	.11	.35
3	18	.10	.33
4	17	.09	.31
5	23	.13	.38
6	20	.11	.35
7	22	.12	.37
8	18	.10	.33
9	21	.12	.37
Total	180	1.00	3.16

$$H(OUT) = -P(OUT) \log_2 P(OUT) = 3.16 \text{ bits/signal}$$

The total Uncertainty H(IN;OUT) can be computed from the ratio between each cell's frequency and the overall total:

$$H(IN;OUT) = -P(IN;OUT) \log_2 P(IN;OUT)$$
$$= 3.52 \text{ bits/signal}$$

Now, we may compute for the information that was transmitted (correctly):

$$T(IN;OUT) = H(IN) + H(OUT) - H(IN;OUT)$$
$$= 3.17 + 3.16 - 3.52 = 2.81$$

We can also compute for the equivocation (the input information which was not received by the receiver) and the noise (the information received but not intentionally transmitted by the source):

$$H_{OUT}(IN) = H(IN) - T(IN;OUT)$$
$$= 3.17 - 2.81 = 0.36$$
$$H_{IN}(OUT) = H(OUT) - T(IN;OUT)$$
$$= 3.16 - 2.81 = 0.35$$

As these findings show, a large amount of the information is successfully transmitted; that is, T is relatively high and $H_{IN}(OUT)$ and $H_{OUT}(IN)$ are relatively low. But precisely how successful is the transmission, in terms of the input signals and the output signals? The following indices estimate the extent of the success or failure of such an encounter.

In terms of the transmission source, a Relative Encoding Success can be constructed from the ratio between T(IN;OUT) and H(IN):

$$\text{R.E.S.} = \frac{\text{Actual Transmission}}{\text{Input}} = \frac{T(\text{IN};\text{OUT})}{H(\text{IN})}$$

$$= \frac{2.81}{3.17} = 88\%$$

Thus, we know that 88 percent of the input information has been successfully transmitted, while the other 12 percent is lost (as the relative equivocation which can also be computed from the ratio between the equivocation $H_{OUT}(\text{IN})$ and $H(\text{IN})$; the reader is advised to verify the result).

From the receiver's point of view, a Relative Decoding Success can be constructed from the ratio between T(IN;OUT) and H(OUT):

$$\text{R.D.S.} = \frac{\text{Actual Transmission}}{\text{Output}} = \frac{T(\text{IN};\text{OUT})}{H(\text{OUT})}$$

$$= \frac{2.81}{3.16} = 88\%$$

Again, approximately 88 percent of the output information was the genuine information intended by the source for transmission and only about 12 percent of the output information was due either to noise occurring in the transmission channel (the flashing light, the visibility in the laboratory) or to decoding error.

CHANNEL CAPACITY

A channel is defined here as the source which originates the transmission, as the medium through which the transmission is relayed to the receiver, or as the receiver of the transmission. From our discussion of Figure 2–4, it should be clear that the T(IN;OUT) cannot exceed either H(IN) or H(OUT); in other words, the transmitted information is limited by the total transmission capacity of the source and the receiver. An extension of this observation is that *when the source and the receiver have different transmission capacities, the information transmitted (T) cannot exceed the minimum capacity of the two*. When the information to be transmitted is less than the minimal channel capacity of both the source and the receiver, the information has a certain probability of being transmitted in its entirety, depending on the extent of the encoding equivocation, $H_{OUT}(\text{IN})$, and the decoding noise, $H_{IN}(\text{OUT})$, and the relationship of the information with each of these as an inverse one. When the information to be transmitted is greater than the minimal channel capacity of either the source or the receiver, then the channel (source or receiver) capacity is the upper bound (the maximum) of the information which may be transmitted. The function of channel capacity can be demonstrated in the following diagram (Figure 2–6).

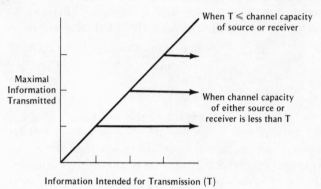

Figure 2–6. Relationship Between Intended Information and Maximal Information
Transmitted as Constrained by Channel Capacity
Adapted from Garner (1964), p. 64

When T (information intended for transmission) is less than the channel capacity of both the source and the receiver, the relationship between the maximal information transmitted and the information to be transmitted is a linear function. When the channel capacity of either the source or the receiver is less than the information to be transmitted, the maximal information that can be transmitted is reduced to the capacity of the lesser of the two channels. Psychologists have observed in experiments that the channel capacity of a human being (as a receiver, in discriminatory response) is quite stable and low, having a value of about 2.3 bits (Garner, 1962, p. 97). Thus, in encounters, the information transmitted should not exceed 2.3 bits; otherwise, some portion of the information is destined to become equivocation and thus to be lost in the transmission.

The English language can be used as an interesting example of the transmission limitation imposed by the channel capacity. If every letter in English had an equal chance of occurring in a passage, the amount of uncertainty contained in English would be $H = \log_2 26 = 4.7$ bits. This amount of information uncertainty exceeds the human capacity to decode. Investigations of the frequencies with which English letters appear in printed texts, however, show that some letters (E, T, A, O, N, R, I, and S, for example) occur much more frequently than others (the least likely letters to appear include J, Q, Z, V, X, and W). Thus, the amount of information (Relative Uncertainty) contained in printed English is reduced to 4.129 bits/letter (Edwards, 1964, pp. 44–45) when such differential probabilities are taken into account.

Furthermore, we have found sequential dependencies in the use of letters in verbal and printed English. That is to say, the likelihood that u will follow q approaches 100 percent and the likelihood that t will follow s is much greater than that z will follow s. This characteristic follows the "stochastic process," a system which produces a sequence of discrete symbols according to certain probabilities. When the probability of a letter's occurrence is dependent upon the immediately preceding letter, then the stochastic process is called a Markov Chain. Various methods have been devised to measure the interletter dependence of English letters (Shannon, 1951; Newman and Gerstman, 1952). However, an actual frequency count becomes extremely difficult beyond a string of three letters. It is estimated that the redundancy is in the neighborhood of 50–60 percent. In other words, the Actual Uncertainty of specific English letters being used is about 40–50 percent of the Maximal Uncertainty. Since the Maximal Uncertainty is 4.7, the Relative Uncertainty is between 1.0 and 2.3. This is remarkable because the Relative Uncertainty approaches, but is less than, 2.3 bits/signal, found in laboratory experiments to be the human channel capacity in decoding. A similar analysis has been conducted on word frequencies (Zipf, 1945). It may be hypothesized that if we analyze the word strings in verbal and written English, the Relative Uncertainty of English words will also approach but be less than human channel capacity.

These examples demonstrate that indeed the basic set of symbols used by English-speaking people approaches but does not exceed the human decoding capacity. It seems, in fact, that if a set of symbols is one that will be used regularly by humans in transmitting information, there is a natural tendency for that set of symbols to have a Relative Uncertainty less than but approaching that of the human decoding capacity.

Yet another remarkable fact about the way human beings design symbols for information transmissions is that the more frequently used sets of symbols also approach a balanced distribution between the amount of Uncertainty and Redundancy. The Spanish language has survived many centuries with its Uncertainty and Redundancy always approaching a 50–50 percent distribution. This is also true for English, with its Redundancy of 50–60 percent. And it is true for the selection of news sources by the mass media (Schramm, 1955). The natural tendency of Uncertainty and Redundancy in information transmission to balance each other reminds one that both order and unpredictability have an important role in the development of human civilization. Rigid order tends to cause breakdown and decay (the second law of thermodynamics demonstrates the decaying process of all organizations), while total randomness is chaos. Thus, survival requires a balance between order and randomness, and humans, as part of this surviving world, show such a balance in many of their activities. Thus, communication, the generalized mechanism in human transactions and exchange, must also, given the decoding capacity of human beings, maintain the delicate balance between Uncertainty and Redundancy.

The phenomenon of balance between Uncertainty and Redundancy can be explained on a much more individual level in terms of the efficacy of the encounter. In an encounter we are trying to transmit a maximum of information with a minimum of effort. When the information contains a great amount of Uncertainty, much effort (continuous attention, comprehension, and retention) is required for decoding. But when the information contains little Uncertainty (and thus a great deal of Redundancy), it may not be worth the effort of decoding the whole transmission just to obtain that little "new" information.

Analysis of the Delivery System

In analyzing the information system, we studied the content of the encounter, information. In this section we will examine the other important component of the encounter, the delivery system.

At least three types of networks constitute the delivery system. One type of network involves the individual's social contacts, his kinships, friendships, professional ties, and other social events and constraints. These relationships establish and maintain a network of limited membership—called the social network—around him. Another type of network is the result of physical and spatial contiguity. Living in a neighborhood, being exposed to transportation facilities and barriers, all cause the formation of a spatial network. Still a third type of network links persons with the mass media. The printed media initiated a chain of impact upon human activities (McLuhan, 1964) and the electronic media continue to expand the individual's encounter with information far beyond his immediate social and spatial reach.

While encounters do occur by chance, they are much more likely to occur within given social, spatial, and mass media networks. Also, chance encounters do not facilitate planned investigations, while social, spatial, and mass networks provide stable information transmission patterns for empirical studies. In what follows, I will discuss each of these three types of networks and will then consider the simultaneous effects of the three networks on the encounter.

THE SPATIAL NETWORK

It has long been observed in experimental as well as in empirical investigations that *the frequency of interaction among people is inversely related to the physical distance between them.* For example, Festinger and others (1950) found that the shorter the physical distance, the greater the possibility of friendship among married students in two housing projects at a university. Caplow and Forman (1950) found the same sort of relationship in their investigation of a housing project in another university. Galluhorn (1952) found that the arrangement of desks, file cabinets, chairs, and so forth affected the flow of communication in an office.

Further data about the relationship between distance and the likelihood of communication comes from geographers who call the phenomenon the neighborhood effect. Hägerstrand (1952, 1965) observed a relationship between physical distance and the frequency of telephone calls as well as between distance and within-the-community migration in Sweden.

In constructing various (computer) models to predict the pattern of local migrations, for example, Hägerstrand utilized the concept of the neighborhood effect. The neighborhood effect states that the probability of a person's local residential movement is inversely related to the physical distance between where he resides now and where he intends to reside. In other words, people are much more likely to move to a nearby location than to a location farther away when they migrate locally. Hägerstrand constructed a transparent probability "grid" which assigned high probabilities to near-the-center cells and low probabilities to distant cells. Placing the transparent "grid" over the actual location of a potential mover, he drew a random number to determine the cell to which the potential mover was expected to move. With this method, he was able to predict well the local migration patterns in several Swedish communities. Other models by Hägerstrand improved on this basic model by taking physical barriers such as rivers and mountains into account. Hägerstrand also suggested that the neighborhood effect exists for physical distance and telephone calls; we are more likely to call people who live close to us than those who live far away. Similar effects have been observed in other parts of the world.

Too little spatial distance between people, however, may have disruptive effects on human associations. Anthropologists (Hall, 1966) have long observed the various effects of overcrowding on behavior. In a series of experiments with rats, Calhoun (1950a, 1950b, 1962) found that overcrowding disrupted important social functions such as courting, sex, nest building, and caring for the young and that overaggression and disorganization followed. In a typical experimental situation, Calhoun constructed a four-unit room for the wild rats. The four units, in a row, were connected by gates. All the rats were allowed to explore all four units. As the number of rats increased to about 24 per unit, the crowding caused an interesting social pattern to develop. Each of two dominant male rats established his territory in units I and IV (see Figure 2–7). Each maintained a group of eight to ten females. Social orders were maintained in these two units. The two central units (II and III) developed into what Calhoun called "sinks," where chaos reigned among the rats. The crowded rats attacked one another, killed the young, disrupted nesting, and so on.

Social problems may result not only from actual spatial relations but from the perception of space as well. And this is true among animals as well as among humans. Many urban problems are associated less with an actual shortage of space than with architectural design defects which create the impression of crowdedness (Hall, 1966).

These observations demonstrate that while closer physical space can promote interpersonal communication, it can also generate problems if such closeness is perceived to exist continuously. Thus, selectivity of association and regulated frequency of actual contacts constitute the additional activities within the spatial network.

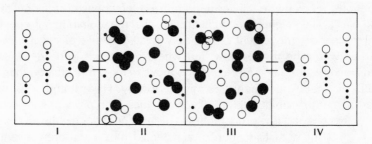

Figure 2-7. Pattern of Rat Dwellings in Calhoun's Experiments

The effect of spatial distance on human communication should not come as a surprise, for the shorter the distance, the less the effort required to engage in communication activities. As a group becomes stabilized and as people within the group have the opportunity to meet and interact with one another, another type of network begins to evolve. This is the network created by social contacts and interactions.

THE SOCIAL NETWORK

Social contacts do not occur in a vacuum. In fact, there are specific patterns of social contacts. One pattern indicates that social contacts are more likely to occur among persons of similar social status than among those whose socioeconomic characteristics differ substantially. Lazarsfeld and Merton (1954) have pointed out that the frequency and effectiveness of social interactions tend to be associated with the homophily-heterophily characteristics of the participants. The homophilous participants, those with similar socioeconomic status, tend to engage more often in contacts and their contacts are more effective (Rogers and Bhowmik, 1970). Laboratory experiments support such a hypothesis.

Thaibaut (1950) found in an experiment that the flow of communication was related to the status of his subjects. Low-status subjects initiated communication with high-status subjects much more frequently than high-status subjects did with low-status subjects. In another experiment, Kelley (1951) found that those who were of low status and who were blocked from attaining high status tended to communicate upward with those who enjoyed high status. He interpreted this finding to mean that for low-status subjects, upward communication was a substitute for real status improvement. Larsen and Hill (1958), in an empirical study, found essentially the same relationship among children. King (1961), in a review of four studies, concluded that there was a consistent tendency, regardless of what factors conferred status, for individuals to choose friends from among those of the same or higher status. Barnlund and Harland (1963), in an empirical study of sorority houses, found that prestige, more than physical distance, influenced interpersonal contacts. Allen and Cohen (1969), in their investigations of research and development laboratories, found that communication flows upward (from the non-Ph.D. personnel to the Ph.D.'s and among the Ph.D.'s rather than from the Ph.D.'s downward to the non-Ph.D.'s or among the non-Ph.D.'s themselves).

Another pattern of social contacts suggests that informal contacts tend to be more effective than formal contacts. For example, in a series of systematic investigations of scientific communication, Garvey, Lin, and Nelson (Lin et al., 1970; Garvey et al., 1970a, 1970b) have found that the informal network among scientists constitutes the most effective and expedient means of information exchange, feedback, and work modification for social, physical, and engineering scientists.

In fact, informal social contacts are so pervasive and effective, recent studies by Milgram (1967) and by Travers and Milgram (1969) have shown that a chain letter, initiated in Nebraska, could reach the target receiver in Boston through an average of four intermediary acquaintances (persons who are on a first-name basis with the preceding person).

The evidence is thus overwhelming that social networks can be based on a variety of criteria. They can be based on friendship, kinship, professional ties, or other social choices. Once such a social network has formed, the chances for an encounter among members becomes much greater than the chances for an encounter between a member and a nonmember.

THE MASS NETWORK

A third network which provides opportunities for encounters is that linking people and the mass media such as radio, television, and newspapers. As mass media become more accessible with the availability of inexpensive receivers (like transistor radios, portable TV's, and low subscription rates to the printed media) and as the transmission of world events becomes faster, the mass network plays an increasingly important role in disseminating information. In this type of encounter, the mass media are the medium in the transmission. They have been labeled the relayers, gatekeepers, and so forth, and they are efficient channels for rapidly transmitting information. Mass media may not provide the only impetus for *attitudinal* or *behavioral change*, but they are important transmitters of *information*. The mass media's ability to communicate facts, as Klapper (1957–1958) pointed out, cannot be underestimated. More recently, Wade and Schramm (1969), in summarizing national survey data, indicated that the mass media have become increasingly useful in transmitting information about science, health, and public affairs. They suggested that television is more effective in transmitting facts and findings, while the printed media such as newspapers and magazines are more effective in explicating concepts and deepening understanding. Definite empirical evidence for such a distinction is still lacking, but the mass network has clearly played an integral part in the transmission of information in the modern world and it is safe to conclude that as the facilities become more and more accessible (De-Fleur, 1966; Rogers, in press), the mass network's dominance in the future will increase even further.

Having specified the importance of the mass network, I must nevertheless point out that the mass network seldom, if ever, operates alone in delivering information. During the 1930s and 1940s, it was widely believed that the mass media were overwhelmingly effective in transmitting information about news events and public activities. Such a hypodermic model was quickly modified, however, by numerous findings indicating that the mass media were of only partial importance in information diffusion and even less effective in generating change (Katz and Lazarsfeld, 1955; Klapper, 1957–1958). Here I will consider only the interactive nature of the various networks in the transmission of information; the factors in attitude and behavior change I will discuss in a later chapter.

INFORMATION TRANSMISSION IN SPATIAL, SOCIAL, AND MASS NETWORKS: SOME EMPIRICAL INVESTIGATIONS

Diffusion of news events provides the most direct evidence of the complementary interaction among the spatial, social, and mass networks in the transmission of information. Several studies have dealt intensively with news diffusion and supply clues as to how information flows through the three networks.

Miller (1945) conducted a survey of the diffusion of the news of President Roosevelt's death among students on a university campus. Within half an hour after the announcement of the President's death on Thursday, April 12, 90 percent of the students sampled had learned the news. The news initially flowed through the mass media (mainly radio) and was then relayed among the students. The social network (interpersonal transmission) accounted for 85 percent of the sampled students' initial awareness of Roosevelt's death. However, the average radio informant relayed the information to seven persons, while the average word-of-mouth informant told only one person.

Larsen and Hill (1954) conducted a study in a university faculty community and in a working-class interracial community of the diffusion of the news of Senator Robert A. Taft's death. They, too, reported rapid diffusion. About 90 percent of the sampled respondents heard the news within 11–14 hours. The flow again started with the mass media and was then relayed among people. In contrast to the Miller finding, however, Larsen and Hill found that radio was the most effective source in transmitting the news. Radio was followed by personal sources, newspapers, and television.

Deutschmann and Danielson (1960) conducted a series of studies in three locales (Lansing, Michigan; Madison, Wisconsin; and Palo Alto, California) of the diffusion of three news stories—President Eisenhower's light stroke; the orbiting of Explorer I; and the announcement of Alaskan statehood. They found that for 77–98 percent of their respondents, the mass networks were the initial source of the news events and that TV was the most effective source in transmitting the news, followed by radio and newspapers. The social network was the least effective information source.

TABLE 2-12. PHYSICAL LOCATION OF RESPONDENTS AND SOURCE
OF NEWS OF KENNEDY'S ASSASSINATION

Location	First Source			
	Radio	Television	Personal	(N)
Home	22%	44%	34%	147
Work	22	3	75	136
Out	49	9	42	78

SOURCE: Adapted from Greenberg, 1964a.

In a study of the spread of the news of President Kennedy's assassination, Greenberg (1964a) found that about 90 percent of his respondents (a sample of a northern Californian community with a population of about 200,000) heard the news within 60 minutes after it was broadcast over radio and television. Fifty-three percent of the respondents heard the news through the social network (interpersonal sources), while 26 percent of them heard it through radio and 21 percent through television. Greenberg also showed the relationship between the physical location of the respondents and the social and mass networks. For example, among respondents who were home, 22 percent heard the news on radio, 44 percent heard it announced on television, and 34 percent were informed by another person. Among respondents who were working at the time they heard of the shooting, 22 percent heard the news on the radio, only 3 percent heard it announced on television, while 75 percent were told by other people. Among respondents who were "out," 49 percent heard the news on the radio, 9 percent heard it on television, and 42 percent were told by other persons.

TABLE 2-13. PHYSICAL LOCATION OF RESPONDENTS HEARING FROM OTHER PERSONS
AND INFORMATION SOURCE

Location	Information Source				
	Spouse	Other Relative	Friend or Neighbor	Co-worker	Stranger
Home	12%	35%	49%	3%	1%
Work	3	2	2	77	16
Out	3	6	27	0	64

SOURCE: Adapted from Greenberg, 1964a.

For those informed by personal sources, the physical location also affected whom the respondent heard the news from. The neighborhood effect was verified by the fact that the "home" respondents tended to be told by friends, neighbors, and relatives, the "working" respondents by co-workers, and the "out" respondents by strangers.

More recent studies—on the diffusion of President Johnson's TV announcement that he would not enter the race for another term (Allen and Colfax, 1968) and of Pope Paul's announcement regarding the Catholic Church's position on birth control (Adams and Muller, 1968)—have also proved the effectiveness of the mass network in delivering news stories fast.

The seemingly inconsistent findings concerning the differential effects of the social, spatial, and mass networks in transmitting news are subject to theoretical discussion. It seems clear that the following influence the effectiveness of the various networks:

1. The increasing effect of the mass media. DeFleur (1966) pointed out that the circulation of daily newspapers in the United States grew from .21 per household in 1850, to .94 in 1900, to 1.23 in 1950, and that it recently declined to 1.05 per household in 1967. Similarly, movie attendance in the United States increased from 1.56 weekly attendance per household in 1922 to 2.33 in 1942, and declined to .77 weekly attendance per household in 1965. These declines in the use of newspapers and in movie attendance are more than balanced by the fantastic growth of radio and television ownership during the last two decades. The number of radio sets per household, for example, jumped from .016 in 1922, to 1.45 in 1940, to 2.25 in 1950, 3.00 in 1960, and reached 4.55 in 1967. In 1953, there were 20 million black and white TV sets in the United States and 47 percent of the households owned sets. In 1967, there were 58 million black and white TV sets and almost every household (98 percent) in the United States owned at least one set. Since the early 1960s, color television sets have increased in popularity; the latest statistic shows that about 43 percent of U.S. TV households owned color sets in the winter of 1970 (26,200,000 sets).

Such phenomenal growth in the availability of the mass media has also occurred in other parts of the world. The transistor radio has virtually revolutionized the process of news transmission in most developing nations. With the potential worldwide satellite hookup near realization, there is no forseeable limit to the capability of the mass network in transmitting information. Mass media, through their extensive availability and coverage, also generate "incidental learning" (Schramm et al., 1961, p. 75). DeFleur and DeFleur (1967) found that TV serves as an important source in transmitting knowledge about and role descriptions of various occupations to children.

2. The time of day and the day of the week when the news breaks. It seems that the mass network is more effective in transmitting information when the news is announced during working hours and on a workday,

while the social network becomes more effective during the evening hours and over weekends. However, more research is needed to substantiate this difference.

3. Extensive interaction of the spatial network with the social and mass network. The physical location of the potential receivers determines to a large extent whether relaying will take place and how such social diffusion will proceed (who will be the receivers of such relay—fellow workers in the office or factory, relatives, neighbors, or strangers). Such spatial distribution of potential receivers benefits those locations with access to and use of the mass media. As the news breaks, persons at these locations tend to be the early knowers or receivers of such information—again following the neighborhood effect proposition.

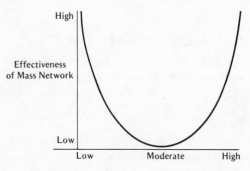

Figure 2-8. Hypothesized Relationship Between Relevance of News
and Effectiveness of the Mass Network

4. An interesting hypothesis has been advanced concerning the effectiveness of the mass media relative to that of the social network. Greenberg (1964b) suggested that the effectiveness of the mass network in diffusing news is related curvilinearly to the extent of the relevance or importance of the news to the potential receivers. When the news is either very important or unimportant to the potential receivers, the mass network is more effective than the social network in transmitting it. When the news is of moderate importance or relevance to the potential receivers, the social network is more effective than the mass network. This hypothesis is based on the following: when the news is most relevant, the potential receivers, due to the selective exposure principle, will give immediate attention to the information transmitted through the mass network; when the news is of least importance, receivers will have a minimal interest in relaying the information through the social network; when the news is of moderate importance or relevance, there is a great likelihood of potential receivers missing the transmission through the mass network and there is also a great likelihood that those who receive such information through the mass net-

work will use it as a casual conversation piece. Again, there is no real empirical test of the hypothesis yet available so that confirmation awaits further research.

An Empirical Study of the Encounter

Due to the vast complexity of the information system and the delivery system involved in an encounter, data on the encounter, which take into account both the information and the delivery systems, are lacking. One field experiment, which encompasses the two aspects of the encounter, however, is available. The study reported by DeFleur and Larsen in 1958 is discussed in this section.

THE MATHEMATICAL MODEL*

Using the basic learning theory approach, DeFleur and Larsen constructed a function which indicates that the response intensity (R) is a logarithmic function of the stimulus intensity (S). Then, ΔS denotes the increase of S. The ΔS is a function of S; in other words, $\frac{\Delta S}{S} = C$ where C is a constant. If ΔR denotes the increase in R, then the positive relationship between S and R can be expressed in the differential equation:

$$\Delta R = a \, \frac{\Delta S}{S} \text{ where a is a constant coefficient.} \qquad (8)$$

This equation simply states that the increase in the intensity of the response is a function of the increase of the stimulus intensity relative to the existing intensity of the stimulus. Integration of both sides of the equation results in:

$$R = a \log S + b \text{ where b is another constant.} \qquad (9)$$

To solve the equation, DeFleur and Larsen assumed that the existing (or original) S equals s(S = s) and the existing (or original) R equals O(R = O). Thus, the above equation (9) can be expressed in the following:

$$O = a \log s + b$$
$$\therefore b = - a \log s$$

Substituting the value of b into equation (9):

$$R = a \log S - a \log s$$
$$= a \, (\log S - \log s)$$
$$= a \log \frac{S}{s}$$

---

*This section may be skipped by readers who are not interested in the quantitative aspects of communication.

Since s is the unit measure of S, this equation becomes simply:

$$R = a \log S$$

Translating this equation, they postulated that if the response intensity in a given community i is P_i, then the intensity of stimulus S_i (amount of information transmitted to the community i) should be a good predictor.

$$\therefore P_i = a \log S_i + d \text{ where d is a constant to be empirically determined.} \quad (10)$$

THE FIELD EXPERIMENT

In their experiment, they controlled S_i by air-dropping leaflets regarding a specific civil defense issue over a number of communities. The number of leaflets dropped was varied according to the community population density to achieve the following ratios: 1/4 of the population, 1/2, 1, 2/1, 4/1, 8/1, 16/1, and 32 leaflets to 1 person ratios. The populations of the communities selected for study ranged from 1,000 to over 300,000.

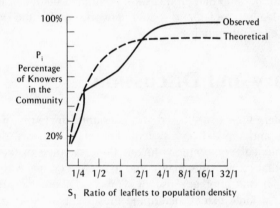

Figure 2–9. Relationship Between Stimulus Intensity and Percentage of Knowers
Adapted from DeFleur and Larsen, 1958

Three days after the leaflet-dropping, interviews were conducted in the communities to investigate the spread, among the residents, of the information contained in the leaflets. The percentage of "knowers" in each community was plotted and compared with the prediction of equation (10). The d term was found to approximate 20.

THE FINDINGS

The empirical results fitted reasonably well with the predicted ones. In other words, the extent of information flow can be predicted reasonably well from the extent of information transmission. It was also found that the flow of information increased absolutely, but at a decreasing rate, as the community size increased; that is, small towns seemed to have a higher intensity of social interaction, or "gossip," as DeFleur and Larsen call it.

In studying the social interaction patterns more closely, they found that children tended to be early knowers, largely, no doubt, because of their curiosity about the transmission method—air-dropping leaflets—and that they served as important interpersonal transmitters. As a result, members of large households tended to be early knowers (receivers of children's dissemination effect).

DISCUSSION

If we compare DeFleur and Larsen's equation with the information measures discussed earlier in the chapter, we cannot fail to see the close relationship between them. In fact, equation (10) is an information measure as formula (4), and the resulting graph is exactly the same function as presented in Figure 2–1. Interestingly, DeFleur and Larsen did not specify that they were applying the information measure in their study.

Their use of the information measure, combined with their investigation of the mass (leaflet), social, and spatial networks, makes the study a major landmark in encounter analysis.

Summary and Discussion

In this chapter, I have discussed the encounter in terms of its content (information) and the delivery system. Information theory demonstrates important potential contributions to our understanding of the encounter. It shows us that participants may come to the encounter with differential familiarity with one another's use of symbols. Different degrees of such familiarity, to a large extent, determine the extent of effort necessary for encoding and decoding. When such familiarity is low, then a participant must assume that many symbols are equally likely to be transmitted by the other participant and must use maximal effort to encode and decode. On the other hand, when the participants are fairly familiar with one another's use of symbols, they can assign differential probabilities of occurrence to the symbols and thus reduce the effort needed for encoding and decoding.

Information theory also tells us that the amount of information transmitted in an encounter cannot exceed the encoding and decoding abilities of the participants. Furthermore, information is transmittable only up to the minimal capacity for encoding or decoding among the participants. In other words, when two participants have different degrees of encoding and/or decoding capacity, the amount of information that can be transmitted from one to the other is limited by the lower capacity of the two. This fact has important implications for those who plan strategies for encounters as well as for those who themselves are participants in an encounter. Unless there is an awareness of the participants' encoding and decoding capabilities, either redundancy must be utilized extensively or certain portions of the information may be lost during the transmission.

A third feature of information theory is its application to multistage diffusion processes, as interpersonal transmissions are often characterized. Information theory can be utilized to specify the various branching probabilities. Quantitative models of the diffusion process can be constructed for empirical testing.

Still another contribution of information theory to the study of the encounter comes from its taking into account the element of noise. Human encounters do not occur in a vacuum; many kinds of "noise" can distort the transmission. Information theory allows for measurements of most noises, especially the random variety.

Finally, information theory provides insight into the delicate balance between Uncertainty and Redundancy. It implies that encounters must be a balance between novelty and acquaintance. Where the balance lies presents an interesting research question. Research findings from other areas, such as languages and news sources, suggest that the balance lies somewhere near the midpoint—50 percent Uncertainty and 50 percent Redundancy. A research strategy may focus on the learning of the various symbols being transmitted. Varying the weights of the symbols should provide data as to whether the most effective learning occurs when the Relative Uncertainty approaches 50 percent of the Maximal Uncertainty.

While information theory can be utilized to analyze the content of encounters, various networks add to our understanding of the delivery system of the encounter. Studies on the physical network show that the closer the distance between two persons, the more likely people are to engage in interactions. Such physical distance barriers, however, can be overcome by means of the social network. Studies have shown that people of identical or similar social status tend to interact more often and more effectively than those of dissimilar social status. The spatial and social barriers are further overcome by the availability of the mass network. The growth of mass media has substantially facilitated human encounters.

We have an uneven knowledge of the various aspects of the encounter. The theoretical and mathematical literature is abundant in the area of the information system, while empirical applications are almost entirely limited to the structure of language and the psychological component of the receiver in the encounter. We have a great deal of experimental and field evidence as to how the various networks in the delivery system function. In fact, we also have the tools (theoretical and mathematical) to study the networks. These tools include the various graph and sociometric techniques and the information measure, such as the use of the stochastic model or the Markov Chain, to study the flow of information in mass media chains and interpersonal chains. But somehow the empirical investigations and the theoretical models have not been utilized simultaneously.

One such simultaneous application of information measure and network analysis would be the tracing of the information flow in mass and interpersonal networks. When we trace the diffusion of information originating at a national news agency to a specific locale, for example, we may use the Markov Chain technique to trace the flow of the information through various channels, from the national level to the regional, local, and individual levels. For an event, we may calculate the probability that it will be covered by the various television networks, radio networks, and press agencies. Once the networks and agencies transmit the information, we may then calculate the probability of its being relayed by local stations and newspapers.

Finally, we may trace the flow of information in social and spatial networks. This type of analysis combines the information measures (in terms of the amount of Uncertainty and Redundancy involved), the theoretical model (such as the one proposed by Westley and MacLean [1957], in which the role of relaying as well as feedback is considered), and the tracing of the flow on the interpersonal level—all of which have been investigated so far with only very crude methods. We should utilize the more sophisticated sociometric techniques to measure the extent of contact (diffusion), the intensity of contact (speed), the effect of the contact (awareness of the events), and the accuracy of the knowledge. Admittedly, such a study would require an enormous amount of effort and time. However, the study conducted by DeFleur and Larsen has demonstrated both the feasibility of such an approach and the fruitfulness of its theoretical and practical implications.

3

Exchange:

THE FLOW OF
HUMAN COMMUNICATION

Encounter has been defined as the *initial phase of human communication in which the receiver or receivers decode some information transmitted by either the source or some intermediary media.* An encounter occurs whenever the symbols (all or some of them) in the transmission are successfully decoded by the receiver. Decoding involves recognition of the symbols only; whether the symbols have any meaning to the receiver, whether the receiver responds to the symbols, and, if so, how he responds are all beyond the encounter analysis. When the receiver not only decodes the information transmitted but also "understands" and reacts in some manner to the message, source, or media, then communication moves into its second phase—exchange.

Exchange, then, may be defined as the *flow of shared meaning;* that is, the communication participants exert some effort to respond to each other's transmissions and to maintain and increment some shared meaning. The *content of exchange* is *message,* just as the *content of encounter* is *information.* The *unit of message* is *meaning,* as *that of information* is the *symbol.* Exchange, which goes beyond the recognition of symbols, represents some effort on the part of the receiver to grasp the source's intention in transmitting the message and measures the effect the message may have on the receiver's psychological and behavioral patterns.

Exchange occurs on many levels of human communication. Two persons may engage in extensive exchange; groups of people may exchange, either through delegations of representatives or through mass participation by the members of the groups. On a still larger scale, societies engage in discourse and exchange. While we focus in the following discussion on interpersonal exchange, similar principles can be applied to larger scales of exchange.

In this chapter on exchange I will first discuss how "meaning" has been defined and measured. Does meaning exist in words, in gestures, or in people? How are meanings transferred from one person to another? And how do we measure, in a quantitative manner, the meaning transferred in both verbal and nonverbal behavior? Attempts by social scientists to tackle these problems will be presented.

Then I will relate the modes of exchange to culture and human perception. Do different cultures operate with different rules of exchange? If so, do the differences in expressing meaning also induce different structures of exchange?

Another section will deal with the various functions that exchange serves in our lives. Some exchanges are primarily for intrinsic benefits such as information relay and verification (as, for example, many interactions at cocktail parties), whereas other exchanges offer extrinsic benefits such as identification with a group, gaining recognition, or affecting influence.

In the next section I will describe some barriers to exchange. And, finally, I will summarize our knowledge of human exchange and suggest directions for future investigations.

Definition and Studies of Meaning

As Osgood (1952) pointed out, there are at least as many definitions of meaning as there are disciplines, since even within a given discipline, more than one definition of meaning is likely to be offered. The linguists, for example, have a long-standing interest in the semantic structure of language. A *language* is defined as a *set (finite or infinite) of sentences, each of finite length, all constructed from a finite alphabet of symbols* (Chomsky, 1956). In each language, there is a device which produces all the strings that are sentences and this device is called the grammar of that particular language (Chomsky, 1956). Analysis of a language includes two important aspects: the sound structure of the language and its grammatical structure. The sound structure analysis focuses on the verbal expressions of various combinations of the alphabet of symbols; the grammatical structure analysis emphasizes the logical linkage between the different parts of sentences. Usually the basic unit of the sound structure is the phoneme, while the basic unit of the grammatical structure is the morpheme (Greenberg, 1954). Many linguists (Bloch and Trager, 1942; Joos, 1950; and Harris, 1951) attempt to incorporate the study of meaning under the grammatical structure. For example, meaning is defined as the morpheme's function or position in the code system as a whole (Bloch and Trager, 1942). In general, the definition of meaning discussed by linguists concerns the relationships among the symbols or signs used in a given language. It is part of the formal and logical structure of a language (Osgood, Suci, and Tannenbaum, 1957). Other linguists tend to dismiss the discussion of meaning in their logical and formal analyses of linguistic structure (Bloomfield, 1933; Chomsky, 1956).

The intercode relationship definition of meaning used by the linguists does not bear on the study of exchange in human communication, since it does not indicate how users of the language receive and respond to morphemes or sentences. In exchange, we are interested in human responses to codes, as these responses at least indicate what the codes "mean" to people. In other words, for human exchange, *meaning must exist in people.* So let us turn to the psychologists (in particular, the psycholinguists) in our search for a possible useful definition of meaning.

The psycholinguists are interested in the meaning of meaning defined as the relationships between objects (significates), and signs (artificial symbols), and between signs and assigns (artificial symbols assigned to describe relationships among signs). For example, Ogden and Richards (1923) took a mentalistic view of meaning by defining it as something which is not the significate if it gives rise to the "idea" or "thought" or "expectation" of that significate. They clearly grasped that signs are never identical with significates. However, the mental process by which the association between a sign and a significate is made received no treatment. Some other psychologists interpreted meaning as simply another form of conditioning, theorizing that if a sign generates the same reactions in an organism that a significate would, then the sign contains the meaning of the significate in the organism. Although a sign never generates the identical reactions in the organism that the significate would, behavioral psychologists such as Watson point out that some transfer occurs in the organism between the sign and the significate. The definition was further modified by Morris (1946), who stated that if a sign produces a disposition in the organism to make any of the responses previously elicited by the significate, then that sign produces the meaning of the significate in the organism.

A further revision of this transferring process was proposed by Osgood and his associates (Osgood, Suci, and Tannenbaum, 1957). Calling it a representational model of meaning, they conceived of the transferring process as a two-phase development. They argued that "whenever some stimulus other than the significate is contiguous with the significate, it will acquire an increment of association with some portion of the total behavior elicited by the significate as a representational mediation process [p. 6]." As shown in Figure 3−1, the sign $\boxed{S}$ elicits part (r_m) of the response (R_T) to the significate itself ($\dot{S}$). This partial response (r_m) mediates another stimulus (s_m) which generates some response pattern (R_x). Thus, through this mediating and representing process, the organism is able to transfer some of the stimulus-response pattern for the significate and to provide another response pattern that would not have occurred if there were no such association between the significate-sign.

Not only are relationships between signs and significates established as more and more signs are generated in this process, but relationships among the signs also emerge. This second phase of the development constitutes the meaning for assigns. Such meaning again results from the representing and mediating process, but this time the relationship is between an assign and a sign rather than between a sign and a significate. Most of the symbols used in a language are assigns which by themselves in no way resemble the significates whose meaning they have come to share. Few of us have seen the panda—the little bearlike animal. Some of us have seen pictures of it and many of us are familiar with the word "panda." Panda, the word, elicits in us some of the responses we would give the animal panda; the word evokes an image of a small animal found in some parts of Asia, which loves to eat young bamboo shoots.

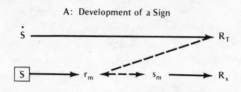

A: Development of a Sign

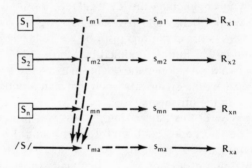

B: Development of an Assign

Legend:

$\dot{S}$ = Significate
S = Sign
r_m = Mediated Response
s_m = Mediated Stimulus
$/S/$ = Assign

Figure 3–1. Symbolic Account of the Development of Sign Process
Adapted from Osgood. Suci, and Tannenbaum (1957), p. 7

These psychological attempts to define meaning clearly point to one important fact about meaning—namely, it exists in people. A sign or an assign has no universal meaning unless or until, either by natural association or arbitrary decision, some people agree to react to the sign or assign with similar transferring processes and stimulus-response patterns.

Exchange is the process by which such meanings, as shared in significates, signs, and assigns, arise and are transferred from a source to a receiver. The receiver must not only recognize the symbols being transmitted; he must also perceive the symbols as meaning the same thing the source intends them to mean. In turn, the receiver's response may indicate to the source that shared meaning has been received by the receiver.

To measure meaning—the shared stimulus-response patterns attached to signs, assigns, and significates—is a difficult task. Unlike the measurement of information as objective functions outside people, the measurement of meaning must incorporate the subjective evaluation of the symbols by the participants in communication. Measuring is further complicated by the multitude of ways in which shared meaning can be exchanged. The spoken and the written expressions of language are but two of the ways. The motions we make with our hands and various parts of our bodies, our facial and eye expressions, our manipulation of sound and control over our voices all contribute to the measurement problem. In the following, I will describe some attempts to measure the meaning contained in both verbal and nonverbal modes. In so doing, I will demonstrate some approaches to the study of meaning and I will also show how limited our knowledge of the meaning contained in exchange messages is.

MEASUREMENT OF VERBAL MEANING

The psychologists' measurements of verbal meanings usually follow one of three psychological models: the classical conditioning model, the free word-association model, and the mediated word-association approach.

The Classical Conditioning Approach

While explicit statements about "meaning" have appeared only in the last two decades or so, interest in the meaning of meaning is reflected in much early psychological work. For example, the classical conditioning approach initially focused on the simple pairing of an unconditioned stimulus (a stimulus which draws a certain response before the experiment takes place) and a conditioned stimulus (a stimulus which does not draw the response before the experiment takes place) over time to result in the conditioned stimulus' "acquiring" the response after the experiment. The classical experiment, conducted by the Russian physiologist Pavlov (1927), paired the sight of food (the unconditioned stimulus) and the sound of a tuning fork (the conditioned stimulus) in evoking salivation in a dog's mouth. Initially, the sound did not produce salivation. But as the sound was made either immediately before or during the appearance of the food, the dog began to produce salivation when the tone sounded. Over a series of such trials, the dog would produce a large quantity of saliva (the response) at the sound of the tuning fork (the conditioned stimulus) without the sight of the food (the unconditioned stimulus).

This approach was later employed by other Russian psychologists to pair words or sentences (Razran, 1939). A word or a sentence was first used as a stimulus to evoke a certain response. When the word or sentence had become an unconditioned stimulus for the response, a second word or sentence was used as the conditioned stimulus. Various experiments have shown that indeed a response could be conditioned to a word or sentence and then be generalized to other words or sentences, irrespective of any physical similarities among the eliciting words or sentences. Razran called such an approach "semantic generalization." These conditioning experiments demonstrated that a word or a sentence can acquire some portion of the meaning of another word or sentence to evoke the same response.

Bingham (1943) later showed that the response could be either some words or physiological phenomena. In one experiment, he asked 50 subjects to rate each of 72 words in terms of their meaningfulness, significance, and importance. He then developed an index of the pattern of these ratings (the MSI index) and correlated the index with a physiological measure of changes in the resistance of the skin to the passage of a low-voltage electrical current—the Galvanic skin response (GSR). A high positive relationship was found between the GSR and the MSI index, suggesting that the physiological measure and the verbal measure share similar meaning.

Other experiments by Russian psychologists have demonstrated that semantic generalizations can be achieved at various levels; meaning can be generalized from a physical object to a word and also from one word to another (Brazier, 1960).

This conditioning approach was then adopted by American psychologists. DiVesta and Stover (1962), for example, reported a study in which they used fifth-grade children as subjects and demonstrated generalization of evaluative meaning over a three-step process: (1) nonsense syllables were conditioned when they were paired with words with evaluative meaning; (2) nonsense figures were conditioned when they were paired with the nonsense syllables that had acquired meaning; and (3) these figures acquired similar semantic generalization.

In sum, the conditioning experiments have clearly demonstrated that meaning can be acquired through the pairing of the unconditioned and the conditioned stimulus. The conditioned stimulus can be a nonsense syllable, a word, a sentence, or other symbols (such as figures). In other words, meaning is defined as a semantic generalization of the conditioning process.

The Free Word-Association Approach

While the classical conditioning model specifically tests preselected unconditioned and conditioned stimuli as well as the response, another model (the free word-association) focuses on preselected stimuli but leaves the responses entirely open for the receivers to elicit. Jung (1918) presented words to normal and abnormal subjects who were instructed to respond with the first word that came to mind. Any unusual extension of reaction time or deviant word response was considered to be indicative of a "complex," defined as a constellation of ideas with associated affect. One of the consequences of the word-association approach has been the utilization of this approach in the study of verbal meaning. Based on the assumption that words which tend to be elicited by an eliciting word must share some portion of the meaning of the eliciting word, numerous associative indices have been constructed as measures of word-relatedness (Marshall and Cofer, 1963).

The free word-association approach, in essence, offers a selected set of stimuli to the subjects who respond in an open-ended manner; theoretically, they can select responding words from a large set of words. Consequently, the results must be interpreted with care. Jenkins (1963), for example, suggested that research in free word-association has not dealt adequately with the problem of how to reinforce a certain responding word from the subjects for the selected eliciting words. That is, we do not know whether or how the subjects can be reinforced so that the words they select to respond will be of a limited and predictable set. Nor has this approach dealt adequately with the characteristics of the task confronting the subjects or with the subjects' past history of reinforcement as it affects their responding patterns. In other words, we need control over the valuations of the experimental task given the subjects for the word-association activities and over the variations of the subjects' individual differences.

The conditioning approach usually focuses on one unconditioned stimulus, one conditioned stimulus, and one or a few responses. It attempts to uncover the process of meaning-acquiring by reinforcing the relationship between the conditioned stimulus and the response via the unconditioned stimulus. Thus, it narrowly focuses on the selected conditioned stimulus and the response. On the other hand, the free word-association approach selects a number of eliciting stimuli (words) and leaves it to the subjects to define the meaning of these stimuli with responses (words) of their choice.

Somewhere between the restrictive conditioning approach and the open-ended free word-association approach is the mediated word-association approach, which suggests that for any eliciting stimuli (words), the human subjects define them in a limited number of "meaning" dimensions. This approach was systematically developed and investigated by Osgood and his associates (1957), and has generated numerous studies in both verbal and nonverbal meanings. I will now discuss this approach in more detail.

The Mediated Word-Association Approach

The rationale behind Osgood and his associates' attempt to measure meaning as contained in language was their assumption that there is a semantic space in the human brain which has a limited number of dimensions or factors. When an incoming message is received, the human brain evaluates the meaning contained therein in terms of the various dimensions in the semantic space. The result of such assessment is the meaning of the message for the individual. If such a semantic space does exist in our brains, and if we have more or less identical dimensions across individuals so that symbols can be assessed similarly by different individuals, then the measurement of meaning consists in deciding the various dimensions of the semantic space. Osgood and his associates believed that the dimensions of the semantic space could be studied through people's verbal responses to various significates, signs, and assigns.

Osgood and others believed that the measurement of the semantic space should contain three ingredients. First, a large number of potential verbal responses had to be identified. This task involved finding the segments in a language that were generally used to assess meanings of ideas and things. Second, these potential verbal responses had to be presented to the subjects who would then be asked to mark their preferences from among these responses relative to some eliciting ideas or things. For example, when asked to "describe" the concept "mother," the subjects should be able to choose from a long list of possible responses as many responses as they feel applicable. On the other hand, a prepared list of potential responses might reduce the variability of subjects' "encoding fluency" and thereby eliminate different levels of verbal ability among the subjects. However, if a list of potential responses were to be provided, it would have to include all the applicable responses for the majority of subjects, for the majority of ideas and things, and for all the important dimensions or factors which exist in the semantic space. Thus, the third ingredient in the measurement had to be that the potential responses would include most, if not all, of the assigns which adequately represent the major ways in which people attach meanings to ideas and things.

To ensure the inclusion of these ingredients, Osgood and others used the following procedures in their study of the meaning contained in language:

1. Selection of polarized adjectives. They felt that the verbal responses which represent the semantic dimensions are mostly contained in polarized adjectives such as good-bad, fast-slow, hot-cold. Their strategy was to collect as many such verbal opposites as are commonly used by people speaking a common language. Thus, in many different surveys, respondents were asked to write down adjectives that came to mind when they were confronted with 50 selected nouns. This procedure was repeated several times and the number of polar adjectives used ranged from 50 to 76 (the latter number indicating the limitation of the computer program used to analyze the data at the time of the study).

2. Sample of people. Because of the investigators' academic affiliation, the samples used were mostly college undergraduates, although other types of respondents were used in some later studies. The final construction of the polarized adjectives and the semantic dimensions was based on samples of college and high school students.

3. Sample of concepts (nouns). A sample of concepts (nouns) was used in each investigation. The selection of the concepts was based simply on the criterion that nouns with as diverse meanings as possible should

be included. Usually, in an investigation, 20 concepts were used.

4. Measurement. The respondents were asked to rate each of the concepts with the polarized adjectives. For example, for the concept "mother," the subject was to determine for the good-bad scale:

good _____: _____: _____: _____: _____: _____: _____: bad

Each scale contained seven categories, and the rating indicated both the direction and the magnitude. This type of *scale*, consisting of *polarized adjectives and seven rating categories*, has come to be called a *semantic differential*. For example, the good-bad semantic differential consists of the seven categories which may be labeled "very good," "quite good," "good," "so-so," "bad," "quite bad," and "very bad." Thus, each respondent was to rate each concept with all the semantic differentials.

5. Cluster of semantic ratings. If the majority of people in a given culture share meanings for a given concept, Osgood and others figured, then they should rate the concept with certain semantic differentials consistently. For example, if "mother" is associated with "very good" on the good-bad semantic differential and with "very pleasant" on the pleasant-unpleasant semantic differential, then consistency between these two semantic differentials must be found for the concept "mother" for most people. Thus, the task becomes to find what semantic differentials tend to be used as a "cluster" for many concepts. Osgood and others (1957) used a statistical procedure called the factor analysis to find the clusters of semantic differentials. These analyses resulted in *three major dimensions of the semantic space* and several minor ones, as measured by the semantic differentials. The three major dimensions were: (1) *evaluation:* including such semantic differentials as good-bad, pleasant-unpleasant, and positive-negative; (2) *potency:* strong-weak, heavy-light, and hard-soft; and (3) *activity:* fast-slow, active-passive, and excitable-calm.

In other words, American respondents tend to use "good-bad," "pleasant-unpleasant," and "positive-negative" semantic differentials in a consistent manner for most concepts. For the concept "mother," for example, if a person tends to rate it toward "very good," he also tends to rate it toward "very pleasant" and "very positive." Another person might rate "mother" toward "very bad," but he would also rate it toward "very unpleasant" and "very negative." Similar consistencies were found to exist among strong-weak, heavy-light, and hard-soft semantic differentials and among fast-slow, active-passive, and excitable-calm semantic differentials.

Osgood and his associates thus concluded that there are three major dimensions in the semantic space, along with several minor ones. These dimensions constitute the basis upon which the significates, signs, and assigns assume meaning for people.

One interesting aspect of the semantic differentials is that they apparently generate similar dimensions in different languages. The same procedure was applied in studies of many other linguistic cultures and the results showed that three major dimensions occurred among the Japanese, Korean, Greek, Navajo, Zuñi, and Hopi peoples, relative to their languages (Osgood, 1963).

Another interesting aspect of the measurement is that various semantic ratings were used for the various concepts. Different persons evaluate different concepts with different patterns of semantic differential ratings. The dimensions are not uniformly applied by different people to the same set of concepts. As in the example I gave earlier, "mother" can be rated either toward the positive extreme by one person or toward the negative extreme by another. Osgood (1963) concludes that the semantic factor structure has generalizability across people, but not across concepts.

Numerous studies have utilized the semantic differentials to measure meaning in various contexts. For example, Berlo, Lemert, and Mertz (1970) have used the scales to measure the dimensions of source credibility. They found three major dimensions: trustworthiness, expertise, and dynamism.

Questions have also been raised, however, about the semantic differentials in measuring meaning. The major questions focus on the following:

1. How completely do the three major dimensions represent the total semantic space? It was clear that in most cases the evaluation dimension was the dominant factor, accounting for about one-third of the scale variability (the total variance in the factor analysis), while the potency factor accounted for only 7-8 percent of the variance and the activity factor for only 6 percent. Thus, a total of less than 50 percent of the scale variance was accounted for. In other words, if the semantic differentials selected for study represent the total semantic space, then less than half the total space was accounted for by the three dimensions. What is the other half of the semantic space? Apparently, according to Osgood and his associates, part of that space consists of many small dimensions such as stability, novelty, receptivity, aggressiveness, and so on. These dimensions are "small" only in the sense that each contains few semantic differentials. However, they may occupy a place in the semantic space just as "meaningful" as the major dimensions of evaluation, potency, and activity. They suggest that further testing should deliberately incorporate semantic scales for these possible dimensions. However, each one of them would probably account for less than 1 percent of the semantic space. Another portion of the semantic space may be due to individual differences. As has been found, people do rate different concepts differently, indicating that there are probably individual factors that are utilized in assessing meaning contained in adjectives. This is also plausible methodologically, since the factor analysis does show that a certain portion of the variance is common to all subject-ratings, while the other portion is unique to each subject. Certainly, further research is needed on the number of common dimensions among the semantic differentials.

2. Do adjectives—particularly the polarized adjectives—exhaust the

meaning contained in language? This is difficult to answer, since no one has yet devised a better method to measure the meaning contained in language. Thus, although there is some question as to how thoroughly the polarized adjectives cover the meaning in language, there is as yet no comparative basis according to which the question can be answered. One suspicion is that probably most, if not all, adjectives are by nature "evaluative." Thus, what has been measured with the semantic differentials may simply be the evaluative dimension of the semantic space. How, then, do we measure other dimensions of the semantic space? Again, ingenious devices may be used to answer this question in future research.

3. Do the semantic differentials also measure meaning as contained in strings of linguistic structure such as morphemes, phrases, and sentences? What the semantic differentials have measured so far are single concepts. Empirical evidence as to whether the scales work with strings of concepts, and with strings of other linguistic syntactics, is lacking. Again, only further research can tell.

In short, the verbal aspect of meaning has been measured under one of the following assumptions: (1) the meaning of anything (stimulus) can be defined in terms of the response to it; (2) meaning can be understood in terms of simple associative (direct) connections between stimulus and response; and (3) meaning can best be conceptualized as a hypothetical construct or as an intervening variable (Creelman, 1966). No doubt, significant advances have been made in measuring the meaning contained in some aspects of language in the last two decades, but more work must be done and better methods devised before a definitive statement can emerge about the various aspects of meaning which occur in the verbal exchange among human beings.

MEASUREMENT OF NONVERBAL MEANING

While verbal communication may play a major role in many social situations, nonverbal exchange is also pervasive and often complementary to the verbal. Because nonverbal exchange involves any part of the human body and any combination of the parts, the measurement of nonverbal meaning constitutes an even more difficult task than the measurement of verbal meaning. Systematic efforts have been made in several areas, however, and though these are far from conclusive, they do show great promise.

The measurement of nonverbal meaning takes a number of steps. The first involves *identification of nonverbal modalities*. For each modality, an exhaustive list of variations (or forms) has to be constructed. Furthermore, an exhaustive list of all human nonverbal modalities must be attempted. These two tasks form the basis for constructing the basic nonverbal codes used by humans. While the verbal codes are limited and readily available for analysis, the nonverbal codes, as contained in the modalities, are far from clear or finite.

A second step involves *analyzing the relationships between each such code* (and combination of codes) *and the meaning attached to it* by the people of a given linguistic culture. Although an exhaustive list of nonverbal codes is conceptually desirable in the analysis of the attached meanings, this second task need not, in fact, wait until all the codes are identified. As soon as the most salient codes have been identified, the meanings attached to them should be studied. This strategy has generally been followed by the nonverbal communication researchers.

Our knowledge of the nonverbal modalities has greatly increased during the past 15 years due to a small dedicated group of researchers (most of them psychiatrists, anthropologists, psycholinguists, and psychotherapists), and our knowledge about the nonverbal meanings has begun to accumulate (Duncan, 1969; Mehrabian, 1969; Ekman and Friesen, 1969b). However, segmentation of concepts and theories is still pervasive and our discussion will necessarily be less systematic than that on the verbal meanings.

Identification and Codification of Nonverbal Modalities

A list of nonverbal communication modalities, according to Duncan (1969), would include: (1) body motion or kinesic behavior: gestures and other body movements, including facial expression, eye movement, and posture; (2) paralanguage: voice qualities, speech nonfluencies, laughing, yawning, and grunting; (3) proxemics: human use and perception of the physical space; (4) olfaction; (5) skin sensitivity to touch and temperature; and (6) use of artifacts, such as dress and cosmetics. Three of these modalities have drawn more research attention than the others and an important pioneering researcher has been associated with each of these three areas —George Trager with paralanguage, Ray Birdwhistell with kinesics, and Edward T. Hall with proxemics.

According to Trager (1958), paralanguage has two principal components: (1) vocalizations and (2) voice qualities. Vocalizations are variegated noises which do not have the structure of language. They include (1) vocal characterizers, such as laughing, crying, and belching; (2) the vocal qualities of intensity, pitch height, and extent; and (3) vocal segregates, such as "un-un" for negation, "un-huh" for affirmation, and "uh" for hesitation in English (p. 6). Voice qualities are "modifications of all the language and other noises, and include pitch range, resonance, articulation control, and vocal lip control" (p. 4). Trager (1960, 1961) found that his classification system applied adequately to Taos, an American Indian language, and speculated on the generalizability of the system across linguistic boundaries. Recent contributions to paralanguage classifications have come from, among others, Crystal and Quirk (1964), who, drawing data from educated English adults in spontaneous interaction, employed a pitch-contour approach to analyzing intonation, as opposed to the phonemic-level approach usually employed by American scholars.

Birdwhistell (1952, 1970) has attempted to classify body motions. Hoping to develop a transcription system that would index every possible movement, Birdwhistell constructed microkinesic recording, which consists mainly of a set of pictographs for the various body parts and a set of symbols for movement and position modifiers. He also attempted to construct a syntactic structure for body motions, analogous to the phoneme, morpheme, and syntactic units in spoken language (Birdwhistell, 1970). This macrokinesic system employs common typewriter symbols.

Grant (1969) has attempted to categorize facial expressions. Based mainly on observations made in interviews between individual psychiatric patients and doctors, in group meetings of patients and doctors, in free-acting groups of patients, in groups of normal adults, and in normal, free-playing groups of nursery school children, he summarized a total of 118 distinguishable expressions, which were categorized according to the part of the face involved (for example, direction of gaze, eyebrows and forehead, mouth, lips, and tongue, as well as the full face).

In the area of proxemics, Hall (1963) devised a notation system that provides scales for eight different dimensions: postural-sex identifiers, sociofugal-sociopetal orientation, kinesthetic factors, touch code, retinal combinations, thermal code, olfaction code, and voice loudness scale. More recently, Hall (1966) has felt that four spatial distance categories are sufficient; these are: (1) the intimate distance, which includes a close phase and a far phase ranging from physical contact to 6−18 inches; (2) the personal distance, which also includes a close phase (1½−2½ feet) and a far phase (2½−4 feet); (3) the social distance, whose close phase ranges from 4 to 7 feet and its far phase from 7 to 12 feet; and (4) the public distance (the close phase being 12−25 feet and the far phase 25 feet or more). He also attempted to construct a typology of these four distances and eight phases as they are related to various other nonverbal modalities such as kinesthesia, thermal receptors, olfaction, vision, and oral aural (pp.107-122).

While all these attempts are directed at specific areas of nonverbal modalities, several authors have tried systematically to examine all modalities of nonverbal behavior. For example, Ekman and Friesen (1969b) have categorized nonverbal behavior into five categories: *emblems, illustrators, regulators, affect displays,* and *adaptors.* Emblems are "those nonverbal acts which have a direct verbal translation, a dictionary definition, usually consisting of a word or two, or perhaps a phrase" (Ekman and Friesen, 1969b, p. 63). For example, among some groups, a raised clenched fist inevitably implies, "Right on!" Emblematic status is determined by the shared decoded meaning and the conscious intentional usage across some group of individuals, and emblems occur most frequently where verbal exchange is prevented by noise, external circumstance, or distance, by agreement (for instance, the sequential touchings and contacts of hands and arms among U.S. black soldiers in Vietnam), or by organic impairment.

Illustrators are movements which are directly tied to speech, serving to illustrate what is being said verbally. Efron (1941) and Ekman and Friesen (1969b) identified six types of illustrators: (1) batons (which time out, accent, or emphasize a particular word or phrase); (2) ideographs (which sketch a path or direction of thought); (3) dictic movements (which point to a present object); (4) spatial movements (which depict a spatial relationship); (5) kinetographs (which depict a body action); and (6) pictographs (which draw a picture of their referent). Efron (1941) pointed out that batons and ideographs have no meaning or connotation independent of the spoken word, while other illustrators have meaning regardless of the words. He also found that different ethnic groups use illustrators differently. For example, Jewish immigrants used more batons and ideographs while Italian immigrants used more kinetographs and pictographs. However, such differences tended to disappear among the offspring of the assimilated first generation.

The face is considered as the primary site of affect displays (Tomkins, 1962, 1963). Some of the common affect displays found in most cultures are: happiness, surprise, fear, sadness, anger, disgust, and interest. Usually, at any given instance, the face displays a multiple number of affects simultaneously rather than a single affect.

Regulators, like illustrators, are related to the conversation. Ekman and Friesen (1969b) pointed out that while illustrators are linked with the moment-to-moment fluctuations in speech, regulators are instead related to the conversational flow, the pacing of the exchange. The common regulators include the head nod, eye contacts, slight movement forward, small postural shifts, and eyebrow raises.[1]

Adaptors are movements which were "first learned as part of adaptive efforts to satisfy self or bodily needs, or to perform bodily actions, or to manage emotions, or to develop or maintain prototypic interpersonal contacts, or to learn instrumental activities" (Ekman and Friesen, 1969b, p. 84). When these movements are made by adults, only a fragment of the original adaptive behavior is seen. For example, although chapped lips or a dryness of the mouth may induce the wiping of the lips with the tongue or hand, the movement may appear in adult life independent of the chapped lips or dryness in the mouth. Other examples of adaptors are clicking or slapping the tongue against the roof of the mouth (originally associated with cleaning away debris from the mouth and lips after a satisfying meal) and wiping around the corner of the eye with the hands (for removing tears).

Ekman and Friesen (1969b) provided a detailed analysis of the usage, coding, and origins of these nonverbal behavioral categories.

While such pioneering efforts have been made to identify the major nonverbal modalities, much of the work needs empirical verification to

---

1. Ekman and Friesen (1969b) reserve the label "regulators" for those behaviors which do not fit into any of the other categories.

ascertain their *salient occurrences* as well as their *significances* as codes for nonverbal meanings.

More ambitious attempts have been made to determine the relationships among verbal and nonverbal modalities. For example, selected segments of a filmed and taped interview involving a research anthropologist (Bateson), a middle-class American housewife, and her young son were used to identify vocal behaviors with phonetic, phonemic, and paralinguistic symbols, and body motions with Birdwhistell's microkinegraphic and macrokinegraphic systems (Birdwhistell, 1970). Scheflen (1966), viewing communication as a cultural system consisting of successive levels of patterning that support, amend, modify, define, and make possible human relationships, suggested a structural approach to specify the units, rules, and organizations of the communication activity. This position was given support by Condon and Ogston (1967a, 1967b), who found that a high degree of "self-synchrony" existed among body motions and the phonetic articulations of normal speakers and that such synchrony exists among people in interaction sequences.

Furthermore, studies have been conducted to assess the relative contributions of the verbal and nonverbal modalities in conveying meanings among communicators. Levitt (1964) filmed communicators as they attempted to communicate six emotions facially and vocally, using neutral verbal materials. He found that the decoding of facial and vocal stimuli in combination was only as accurate as the decoding of facial stimuli alone, and both conditions were more accurate than the decoding of vocal stimuli alone. Thus, for the two-channel facial-vocal communication of emotions, the facial channel contributes more to the transmission of the message than the vocal channel. Subsequently, Mehrabian and Ferris (1967) paired three degrees of liking (liking, neutral, and disliking) in facial expression with three degrees of liking communicated vocally in the transmission of a neutral word ("maybe"). They found that both facial and vocal communication were effective in conveying the differential liking, with the facial component receiving approximately 3/2 the weight received by the vocal component.

What happens if the verbal and nonverbal modalities carry "inconsistent" (positive versus negative) messages? In an experiment, Mehrabian and Wiener (1967) found that judgments of "inconsistent" messages contained in words and tones were primarily based on the tonal component.

Research attention to the codification of nonverbal modalities has accelerated during the last 15 years, and also systematic classifications of all such behaviors and the structural relationships among them have begun. The latter task is most complex and exhausting, as the permutations of such behaviors and the combinations of them approach infinity. However, during the past 15 years, considerable headway has been made on the construction of lists of the most salient nonverbal codes, that is, those which constitute the basis on which the meanings of nonverbal exchanges can be systematically studied.

Meanings of Nonverbal Codes

That meaning does exist in and is conveyed by nonverbal modalities has been well documented. For example, Sainesbury (1955) found significantly more movement occurring during stressful periods of interviews. Dittmann (1962) found that different body areas were active for different moods. Dittmann, Parloff, and Boomer (1965) found that on the basis of body cues, both therapists and dancers could differentiate degrees of pleasantness of effect. The therapists tended to concentrate on facial cues, while the dancers were receptive to the rest of the body as well.

Duncan (1965) found that the peak and the poor interviews between a therapist and a client in psychotherapy sessions could be differentially detected when their paralinguistic behaviors were analyzed separately.

Hesitation phenomena, such as types of pauses (filled and unfilled), and stutters and repetitions, have drawn considerable research attention. Panek and Martin (1959) found that filled pauses and repetitions, were both related to emotional arousal. Livant (1963) found that the time required for the solution to addition problems was significantly greater when the subject filled his pauses than when his pauses were silent. Duncan's study (1965) showed that high proportions of filled pauses were characteristic of the speech of both client and therapist in interviews perceived as poor by the therapist. Such a relationship between emotional disturbance and speech disturbance has also been reported by Boomer (1963), Boomer and Dittmann (1964), and others.

Visual interaction (looking into the eyes of another) has also been intensively studied (Exline, 1963; Lambert and Lambert, 1964; Exline, Gray, and Schuette, 1965; Exline and Winters, 1965; Argyle and Dean, 1965; Exline, Thibaut, Brannon, and Gumpert, 1966; Efran and Broughton, 1966; Kendon, 1967; Argyle, Lalljee, and Cook, 1968). The data conclusively show the following patterns:

1. More use of the "line of regard" (looking at the other person) when a person is listening than when he is speaking.

2. More visual interaction when the interactants are farther apart physically.

3. More use of the line of regard and more of the feeling of being "observed" by females than males.

4. More use of the line of regard when the other person is more friendly (expressed in nodding and smiling).

5. More use of the line of regard when a person is ending his utterance and less use of the line of regard when a person is initiating an utterance.

6. Some functions of the line of regard: (a) cognitive (to look away at difficult encoding points); (b) monitoring (to indicate conclusion of thought

units and to check interactant's attentiveness and reaction); (c) regulatory (to control the interactant's responses); and (d) expressive (to signal degrees of involvement) (Kendon, 1967).

As to proxemics, Hall's basic thesis concerning the various groupings of physical distances has been subjected to several empirical examinations. Watson and Graves (1966) found that the association between distance and other communication modalities varied for an American group as compared with an Arab group. The Arabs were more intensely interactive. Willis (1966) found that distance between interactants was a function of their sex, age, and race. Altman and Haythorn (1967) found a general increase of territorial behavior (defending a fixed spatial territory from intruders) in isolated groups over time. Hutt and Vaizey (1966) found that as group intensity (crowding) increased, children showed a deterioration in behavior (aggressive/destructive, social, and withdrawal to the edges of the room).

Tactile communication (touching) also has received some research attention (Frank, 1957). Jourard (1966) found that females were much more accessible to touch than males and that tactile communication occurred more frequently between opposite-sexed friends than between other pairs.

Another fascinating area of research focuses on the clues to deception that are provided by the nonverbal behavior of a sender. Ekman and Friesen (1969a) suggested that because of sending capacity, external feedback, and internal feedback, the behavior of the head/face was much more salient to both the sender and the receiver than the behavior of the hands or legs/feet and thus received more conscious attention from the sender. They hypothesized that clues of deception would be more detectable if the hands or legs/feet, rather than the head/face, were observed. However, only a few case studies seemed partially to support this hypothesis. Further studies are needed to verify such effects differentially for different persons (that is, good deceivers and bad deceivers).

In a series of experiments, Mehrabian (1968, 1969) has attempted to measure and review the relative contributions of various nonverbal modalities to the conveying of meaning. He found that distance, eye contact, body orientation, arms-akimbo position, and trunk relaxation were consistently indicators of a communicator's feelings toward the potential receiver of the message. These variables, along with the degree of arm openness of female communicators and the degree of asymmetry in the arrangement of arms and legs, tended to indicate the status relationships between the communicator and the receiver.

In summary, our knowledge of the meanings contained in nonverbal behavior is accumulating rapidly. In some areas, such as visual interaction and hesitation phenomena, systematic conclusions have emerged, while in others, the research effort has only begun. The problem is compounded, however, because the literature is scattered among many different academic disciplines. Several forthcoming volumes summarizing the current state of the art (Mehrabian; Harrison; Knapp) should substantially integrate the nonverbal literature.

In order to integrate our knowledge of the role of verbal and nonverbal modalities in conveying meanings, it is important to determine the extent to which the dimensions of verbal meaning, as suggested by Osgood and his associates, apply to the dimensions of nonverbal meaning. Should our means of assessing nonverbal codes be similar to our means of assessing verbal codes as measured with polarized adjectives? Is there a nonverbal semantic space that is more or less independent of the verbal semantic space? Some recent studies (William and Sundene, 1965; Osgood, 1966; Mehrabian, 1970) suggest that a semantic space, measured with polarized adjectives, may also apply to nonverbal modalities. The major dimensions also seem to include (1) evaluation, (2) potency, and (3) activity, as in the case of the verbal modality. Intensive research along this direction in the future should prove fruitful.

Generality and Specificity of Exchange

Exchange, as we stated, takes two major modes—one involving the use of language in its verbal and written forms, called the verbal mode of exchange, and the other involving the nonverbal modes of exchange.

The influence of language on human perception and behavior is well documented in the so-called linguistic relativity theory. Boas (1938), an anthropologist, was the first to suggest that there was some relationship between language and culture. He observed, for example, that whereas in English there is only one word for snow, in Eskimo there are many words, each describing a different state or condition of snow. He attributed the linguistic differences to the differential geographical locations of the two cultures. The speculation was formalized by Whorf (1956), who extensively studied the Hopi Indians in North America. He hypothesized that language plays an important part in molding the perceptual and cultural world of the speaking people. While not negating the other direction of the relationship —that culture and the physical environment also influence language—the discovery that language actually molds human perception and thought gave impetus to the study of human exchange as it is to some extent governed by the specific code system a people use—the verbal and non-verbal modes. Osgood (1963), in his recent studies of meaning in other cultures, has found that while the major dimensions of meaning as measured by the semantic differential scales have generality across languages (namely, people of different languages tend to assess concepts with similar clusters of semantic differential scales), there is no generality in terms of how people of different languages actually assess various concepts with the semantic differentials. This seems to lend some support to the hypothesis that *language affects human perceptions,* even the perceptions and assessments of similar concepts.

Another example of how language structures human exchange can be demonstrated by the different responsive modes exhibited by Orientals and Occidentals. In Chinese, when a person responds to a statement made by another person, his affirmative "yes" or negative "no" indicates whether he *agrees with the person who made the statement,* rather than whether he *agrees with the statement itself.* In English, only the latter mode is used. Thus, when a Chinese agrees with the statement, "It did not rain this morning," he says, "Yes, it didn't," whereas an American says, "No, it didn't." This interesting differentiation, demonstrating how one language structures around personal agreement while another structures around statement agreement, provides further evidence of the diversified modes of verbal exchange in different languages.

The nonverbal mode of exchange is just as extensive as the verbal one. Anthropologist Hall made extensive studies and observations in the United States, Europe, the Middle East, and the Far East of how the spatial factor affects culture. In *The Silent Language* (1959), he discussed various distances as they serve to identify the situation in which exchange is defined. In his recent book, *The Hidden Dimension* (1966), he observed that the intimate distance ranges from actual physical contact between the participants, as in love-making, wrestling, comforting, and protecting, to about 6–18 inches. At this distance, because of the distortion of the other participant's physical features and because of the low voice involved, much exchange results from slight movements of the body, body temperature (warmth), olfaction (various odors of the body), and the feeling of the breath. The personal distance ranges from 1–2 feet to about 4 feet. At this distance, the features of the upper part of the other participants become visible, the bodies are not in direct contact, the voices are still low, and body movements are slightly exaggerated in the exchange. Body heat and odor are not that perceptible. At the social distance, which measures from 4 to 12 feet, impersonal exchange, such as business or meeting people for the first time, takes place. At this distance, personal odors, heat, slight movements, and so forth, are not generally transmitted and participants may engage and disengage in exchange with relative ease. The public distance, defined at 12 or more feet apart, signifies a formal exchange, usually involving more than two parties. While the above four distances, measured for Americans, are similar in other cultures, the defining measures may vary. Little (1968), for example, when he requested people of different nationalities to position dolls relative to one another for a variety of social situations, found that, on the average, Greeks, Americans, Italians, Swedes, and Scots, in that order, assigned increasing distances to the space between the dolls.

In each culture, then, there is a set of defined distances, each of which identifies the proper stance for a particular situation and a particular participant. An erroneous use of the distance either leads to the bewilderment and embarrassment of the participants (Garfinkel, 1964) or induces immediate disengagement from the exchange and discourages future exchange (Felipe and Sommer, 1966). Erroneous use may also be a signal of discontent with the situation or the participant. For example, when a baseball coach objects to an umpire's decision, he may burst from the dugout and engage in an exchange with the umpire at the "intimate" distance, with eyes directly confronting those of the umpire. This exchange, totally inappropriate for the defined situation and the defined roles of the coach and the umpire, clearly signifies the dissatisfaction one party has with the other. Such exchange, of course, cannot be allowed to persist. Should the coach continue the exchange, the umpire would have to resort to the "thumb out" technique to disengage the exchange formally so that the rules of distance could be maintained. Similarly, when a man finds that an intimate female friend is keeping him at arm's length, he will soon wonder if the close relationship is deteriorating or being terminated.

Facial and bodily movements also constitute important modes of exchange. Some recent experiments (Izard, 1968; Ekman, Sorenson, and Friesen, 1969) have shown that facial expressions alone transmit messages of happiness, anger, fear, surprise, sadness, disgust, and interest. While cross-cultural similarities were found linking these basic messages and facial expressions, gestural (facial and bodily), as well as spatial and linguistic, relativity does exist. The Chinese will nod their heads when they agree with a person who makes a negative statement, regardless, while Americans will nod only if they agree positively with the proposition contained in the statement. A certain gesture with fingers may mean "A-OK" in North America, but the same gesture is considered indecent in South America and should never be made in front of ladies there.

Thus, just as some linguists argue for a linguistic relativity, so is there strong evidence for a *spatial relativity* and a *gestural relativity* (body motions and facial expressions) as well. These various modes serve both as the *codes* and the *media* to convey messages for exchange to take place or not to take place.

Functions of Exchange

Exchange serves many functions. We may classify exchanges under two major headings: those undertaken for their own sake, and those undertaken for the sake of some external benefit (Blau, 1964). In the first category, exchange brings benefits to the participants without imposing on one or more of them for actions or attitudes external to the exchange itself. The second category includes those exchanges which are only means to an end which must be attained through situations and actions beyond the exchange itself. We will look at each of these two categories.

EXCHANGE FOR INTRINSIC BENEFITS

1. Information relay and verification: Information, as indicated in the last chapter, flows in the social, spatial, and mass media networks. Exchange facilitates the flow not only of information regarding major news events but of facts and figures which may be of trivial importance to people other than the participants. Exchange also facilitates the verification of information by receivers. Studies of news diffusion show that once a person has heard about a news event, he is likely to seek confirmation, either through the mass media or from another person, depending on his accessibility to the mass media and other persons (Deutschmann and Danielson, 1960). For information not available through the mass media, confirmation is sought entirely through the social network. The information that Mr. and Mrs. Jones had a quarrel last night may not determine how a woman receiving the news will react, but the lady may consider confirmation of such information of such value to her "status" in the social circle that she will give it top priority among her activities, probably spending the afternoon on the phone.

2. Interaction ritual: There are exchanges in which the situation itself brings the participants together. Sociologist Goffman (1959, 1961, 1963, 1967, 1969) extensively discusses the "dramatic" nature of face-to-face interaction, which has its own rituals and rules, yet has no binding effect on the participants once they disengage from such interaction. The participants' sole reason for engaging in such interaction is to preserve the situation. Each participant maintains a certain front in staging the interaction and tries to acknowledge the fronts of the other participants. Furthermore, the messages sent by each participant must be constructed so that they will be maximally useful to other participants as sources for constructing their messages. This is necessary if exchange is to be maintained. Likewise, each participant should expect the other participants to elicit messages which can, in turn, be maximally used by him to construct new messages. As Goffman points out, it is these two tendencies, "that of the speaker to scale down his expressions and that of the listeners to scale up their interests, each in the light of the other's capacities and demands, [that] form the bridge that people build to one another, allowing them to meet for a moment of talk in a communion of reciprocally sustained involvement. It is this spark, not the more obvious kinds of love, that lights up the world" (1957).

This art of impression management constitutes almost a theatrical performance and can be most successfully staged only if the performers and the audience all act according to one another's expectations and according to certain rules—for example, that the front stage and the backstage, onto which the audience is not allowed to intrude, are separated and that everyone demonstrates his enthusiastic front in certain ways; for example, the actors perform as if they were actually characters in a play staged for the audience and the audience applauds to show its appreciation that the actors are indeed successful in the characters they have chosen to portray. The rituals involved in interactions thus have definite and almost rigid rules: there is loyalty, as shown by all the participants to the interaction; there is discipline in that the actors follow the prescribed character roles and avoid interaction messages and gestures that might disrupt the interaction; and there is circumspection with respect to the staging of the action so that the participants will already have prepared themselves to the best of their abilities before entering the interaction and so that they will enter in anticipation of a successful interaction (1959, pp. 208–237). Although Goffman tends to consider such interaction as a closed system, interactions are very seldom closed or separated from the outside environment. Thus, while the interaction is being staged, stimuli from the environment may alter or even disrupt the interaction. Participants may be attracted by other interactive groups and drift out of the particular interaction in which they are engaged —a phenomenon frequently encountered at cocktail parties. A person who chronically makes himself or others uneasy in conversation and perpetually kills interactions is a faulty interactant (Goffman, 1957). Most people are aware of the risk of disrupting a particular interaction. Each, however, must weigh the effect of staying in the interaction against the alternative. If a participant finds other participants totally inadequate in their performance, if the interaction is badly staged, or if the messages generated do not provide stimuli that will generate further messages of interest to most, if not all, the participants, he may well be willing to be a faulty interactant in that particular interaction situation and try to make up for it later by taking part in another interaction more to his liking and more in keeping with his ability to contribute and perform.

3. Friendship: A more permanent form of exchange than the ritualized interaction is friendship, which provides the expectation of future interaction for the same participants at the end of each exchange. Friendship is based on the mutual liking of the participants, and usually involves a small number of participants. It is built upon status symmetry among the participants (Wright, 1970), serves no extrinsic purposes, and results from free choice. This does not imply, however, that people of different social, political, or economic status cannot be friends. They can, but only where they find symmetric relationship and equal basis. Thus, the rich and the poor may befriend one another on the basis of their bridge playing, fishing, or other common interests. Homans (1950) suggested, for example, that there is an interdependence between liking (sentiment) and interaction. Liking includes

both similar and complementary characteristics. As Wright (1970) points out, having similar interests provides a common meeting ground, while having complementary skills and knowledge insures that the interactions that occur will be minimally competitive, as competition creates status differentiation and status differentiation in turn disrupts the basis for friendship. In friendship, confiding those secrets which are usually kept backstage of the ritualized interaction becomes the distinctive characteristic of the interaction. Indeed, in the ritualized interaction, the form of delivery or the performance of the role is just as important, if not more so, than the content of the message. In friendship, however, the form of delivery is no longer vital; it is the message that really counts. As Wright said, "One of the functions of friendship is to provide a context within which misjudgments in social skill are not fatal and where attention can be concentrated more fully upon the content of what is to be communicated than upon the art of communication [p. 633]."

4. Play: Exchange also takes the form of pure pleasure that can be generated by the interaction. Stephenson (1967) has proposed a play theory for mass communication: people often use the mass media for no other purpose than to be entertained. The same principle can be applied to many occasions where people interact. Because of the daily ritualized interactions required by many situation-defined occasions, people seek opportunities where they can relax, entertain, and be entertained.

EXCHANGE FOR EXTRINSIC BENEFITS

5. Group identification: Exchange may take place among people who belong to the same group, whether it be formally structured, like the Rotary Club, or informally organized, like a neighborhood group. Exchange also takes place between members of different groups. Exchange thus serves either an integrative or a differential function for the participants.

Guetzkow and Simon (1955) found that the extent of interaction affects or depends upon the organizing ability of the participants. Leavitt (1951) found that interaction itself constitutes the most important function for group and member activities. As mentioned in the first chapter, Newcomb's co-orientation theory is a statement about the relationship between participants' attitudes toward a certain subject and their attitudes toward each other. Shaw and others (1957) have found that interaction provides a means whereby members in a group can reach decisions. This is an example of how exchange serves to integrate group members.

Exchange also serves to differentiate members in and between groups. Schatz and Strauss (1955) discussed the relationship between interaction and the differentiation of social classes. Mulder (1960) also showed that interaction brings power to a member in a group, which in turn increases the member's satisfaction with the group. Thus, exchange provides the opportunity to differentiate. Differentiation usually brings inequality relative to class or status, which, in turn, generates satisfaction for the members who have thus acquired higher status or greater power.

6. Recognition: Exchange also promotes recognition of one's work or effort. This phenomenon is most pervasive in the scientific community (Merton, 1957). Scientists are engaged in various forms and extents of exchange through which scientific information is transmitted and the scientist's efforts recognized. Although the formal mechanisms such as publications, awards, and rewards are also important means of achieving recognition, the effect of the "invisible college" (Price, 1963) is well documented (Crane, 1969; in press). The "invisible college" facilitates the scientist's becoming aware of new information, receiving feedback for his own work much before the publication of the work (on the average, about one to two years before) and thereby getting important and early recognition for his contributions.

7. Influence: Obviously one of the critical roles which exchange plays is to enable the participants to affect one another's attitudes, beliefs, behavior, and so forth. This brings us to the third phase of human communication, to be discussed in the next three chapters.

In sum, exchange serves many functions. It may constitute the mechanism for relaying and verifying information. It may be a simple ritualized interaction among people who are bound by the situation and who have no other obligation to each other or to any further interaction. A more permanent function of exchange occurs in friendship, in which the participants are bound to regular interactions—more by the messages exchanged than by the form of the exchange, which is so important in the ritualized interaction. Exchange may also serve a play function for the participants. Exchange involving more than two participants and a bond defined by common interest or purpose usually integrates and differentiates group members. Exchange also provides avenues for recognition. When such integration, differentiation, and recognition are carried to a relatively constant psychological and behavioral level, influence is exerted by one member on another.

Barriers to Exchange

Since modes and functions of exchange vary, many factors may disturb exchange. These factors may be due either to situations over which the participants have little, if any, control or to deliberate efforts on the part of some participants to break up an exchange for which they no longer feel any need.

1. Exchange, like any other phase of human communication, requires a delicate balance between organization and disorganization. Or, in information theory terminology, it requires a delicate balance between uncer-

tainty and redundancy. As Colby (1958) pointed out, there are two aspects each of organization and disorganization. For organization, the active aspect is the effort to create a form in which activities (in our case, exchange) may take place; the passive aspect is the repose or maintenance of the form created. Thus, the active organization means creativity, or freedom, while the passive organization indicates culture, or determinism. For disorganization, the active aspect is represented by a striving for a better or different organization, while the passive aspect of disorganization is the innate need for novelty. While active disorganization replaces the existing organization with a different or new organization, passive disorganization involves the disruption of the existing organization accompanied by no such move toward a better or different organization. Translating these theoretical discussions into the situation of exchange, we see that the participants are required to form the exchange—there is active organization. Once exchange takes place and if the participants strive to maintain it, then the mode of organization is passive. When some of the participants feel a need to change the structure or substance of the exchange but to maintain the exchange, we observe active disorganization. Finally, there is the situation in which some participants simply want to get out of the exchange and have no desire to create or form a new exchange to replace the existing one. This represents passive disorganization. Either active or passive disorganization are barriers to the existing exchange. For active disorganization to develop, some participants must feel discomfort about the existing structure or substance of exchange. Passive disorganization, of course, terminates the existing exchange.

While disorganization may bring discomfort to the participants or an end to the exchange, an organized exchange is not necessarily the most desirable one. A totally organized exchange (the passive organization) is a static form of exchange. In other words, no new information (uncertainty) or form is involved in such exchange. A static exchange eventually leads to a breakdown of exchange. Only the active organization represents the creation or formation of a particular exchange; once an exchange is formed, then there is always the danger that it will approach a static state. Thus, what is most desirable is a balance between organization and disorganization. An exchange must be formed and conducted in a certain systematic and structured fashion, but it must also be continuously prepared to change and disengage to avoid the static form. Any overwhelmingly organized or disorganized exchange constitutes a barrier to exchange.

2. One serious barrier to exchange may lie in the meaning of the messages being exchanged. The linguists have reminded us time and again of the difference between connotative and denotative meanings. The denotative meaning can be regarded as the dictionary meaning—a strict interpretation of the message according to well-defined meanings contained in the codes and the universal (within the receiver's linguistic universe)

interpretation of the codes strung in the message. The connotative meaning, on the other hand, conveys the mood or feeling and the implications and associations contained in the message. Thus, it represents a much deeper level of exchange; it requires a substantial amount of agreement between the source and the receiver in their beliefs, attitudes, and general outlook on life. A "V" sign, for example, may have one meaning to a student participating in a peace march and quite another to a soldier just returning from a battlefield.

Furthermore, many messages have both a surface and a latent meaning (Schramm, 1963). When we say, "How are you doing?" we indicate pleasure at seeing somebody and we intend to initiate some form of exchange rather than to ascertain the specific details of how the person is really doing.

Another barrier can result from the discrepant meanings contained in the verbal and nonverbal messages. Ekman and Friesen (1969a) noted that nonverbal messages may carry leakage or deception clues in interaction situations. In contrast to Goffman's interest (1959) in interactions where there was moderate to low saliency about deception and collaboration to maintain the deception, they emphasized situations where the deception was highly salient (for at least one participant), where there was antagonism (such that one participant wishes to maintain and another wishes to uncover the deception), and where there tended to be role asymmetry (such that one participant is primarily deceiver, the other primarily detector). In some case studies of mental patients, they found that body movements provided observers with more clues to deception than did the movements of the head and face. Such discrepancies create barriers against continuous exchange among normal people as well.

3. The messages may be distorted by the receiver for a variety of reasons. He may be unfamiliar with the codes used by the source in the message, he may attach different meanings to the codes in the message, there may be noise in the channel or situation in which the exchange takes place, or he may deliberately interpret the message in a way not intended by the sender. Distortions take many different forms. As Kirk and Talbott (1959) pointed out, there are at least three major types of distortions.

There is the systematic, or stretch, distortion, a distortion of the form or shape of the message. Many rumors have this characteristic and gossip contains much of the stretch distortion. Then, there is the fog distortion, a distortion in which a portion of the message is lost. Only a certain amount of the message sent out by the source is received cognitively and semantically; the rest is simply lost. Finally, there is the mirage distortion, the distortion by which meaning other than that intended by the source is added to the message. The combined effect of these distortions is shown in Figure 3–2.

All these distortions are related to the basic problem of the receiver's cognition. Because of the limitation and structure of his cognition, a person has to be selective in his attention, perception, retention, and interpretation. The incoming message must, first of all, be of limited quantity. Its meaning will inevitably be interpreted in such a way as to be compatible with some portion of the receiver's existing cognitive system. Also, distortions occur not as a result of the person's selective attention, perception, retention, or interpretation, but simply as a consequence of defective channels. But, the effect is the same—the meaning of the message is received in a distorted form by the receiver.

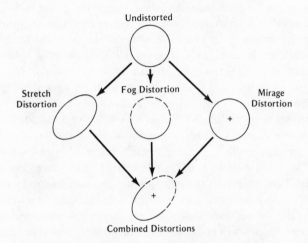

Figure 3–2. Types of Distortions
Adapted from Kirk and Talbott (1959)

Distortions can be corrected by the source if they are detected. Kirk and Talbott (1959) suggest means of providing such corrections. The systematic, or stretch, distortion can be corrected by transformation, by transforming the form or shape of the message back to its intended form or shape. The fog distortion requires an improved decoding method on the part of the receiver and more redundancy in the message by the source. In other words, the receiver must make more and better inferences from the message and the source must increase the length of the message so that redundancy can be added to that portion of the message which was missed. The mirage distortion also can be corrected by the source's increasing the redundancy in the message and by more frequent attempts on the part of the receiver to make inductions from the message.

Distortion, therefore, signals an excessive amount of uncertainty in the message, as received by the receiver in the exchange. Reduction of uncertainty can be achieved by the increase of redundancy. However, we are dealing here not merely with the uncertainty or redundancy of the information but rather with the uncertainty or redundancy of the meaning contained in the message. Thus, reduced uncertainty and increased redundancy must be imposed both on the codes used (information) and on the meanings attached to the codes by the source and the receiver.

4. Exchange failures also result from the cultural, geographical, linguistic, racial, and psychological differences in makeup among the participants in the exchange. Not only are there differences in the more obvious forms of linguistic system and spatial distance, but the effects of these forms and distance on the participants' perceptions and on their interpretation of messages also vary. Jokes in one culture may be meaningless or insulting in another; slang, colloquialisms, and local twists of idiom and accent all create problems for exchange. A distance regarded as social in one culture may be considered intimate in another, while a certain smile merely containing social meaning in one culture becomes erotic in another. Within a given culture, barriers exist among participants from different social, educational, sexual, economic, and racial backgrounds. The forms, the content, the gestures, and the sustaining effort all vary when participants from different segments meet. The breakdown of exchange among participants from the same culture is often as severe as the breakdown among participants from different cultures. These intracultural breakdowns often result from a relaxation of effort. When participants are all from the same culture, they tend to assume that the meanings carried in messages are uniform for everybody. Their selection of language and gestures becomes less rigorous and the effort to interpret the messages is also reduced. The outcome is not only a breakdown of exchange, and resultant misunderstanding, but that people part with misconceptions about one another and about the exchange itself. Such failures generate further difficulties for future exchanges.

Summary and Discussion

Human communication begins with the occurrence of an encounter, defined as the phase in which a receiver decodes some information transmitted either through the originator of the information or some intermediary media. When such flow of information leads to a flow of shared meaning between the source and the receiver, then human communication moves to its second phase—exchange. While the content of encounter is information, the content of exchange is message. While the unit of information is the symbol, the unit of message is meaning.

Meaning is shared by people. By associating one stimulus with a second stimulus in generating a certain response, the second stimulus may eventually acquire some portion of the meaning contained in the initial stimulus and thus be able to elicit the same response even when the initial stimulus is absent.

Most forms of human behavior can be made meaningful if the source and the receiver both share the association between such behavior and certain responses. Behavior can be categorized into the verbal and the nonverbal modes. While verbal and nonverbal types of behavior approach infinity in permutation and combination, it is generally believed that a limited number of salient meanings can account for most forms of behavior in exchange. Research has shown that among the salient dimensions of meaning, evaluation, potency, and activity seem to account for a significant portion of the "semantic space."

Not only is the number of salient dimensions of meaning limited, but there is evidence that the acquisition of meaning for behaviors is affected by the cultural, social, and individual characteristics of the exchange participants. While certain basic meanings universally appear in certain verbal and nonverbal behaviors such as happiness and anger, I have suggested that spatial relativity (perception of space affects human perception in exchange) and gestural relativity (use of gesture affects human perception in exchange) must exist in addition to the well-known linguistic relativity (language affects human perception). Therefore, we should expect cultural, social, and individual factors to serve both as barriers and as vehicles in human exchange.

Exchange serves different functions, some of which are intrinsic such as information relay, interaction ritual, and friendship. Other exchanges bring extrinsic benefits such as group identification, recognition, and influence.

Although exchange is well researched, there is still much that we do not know about it. We do not know enough about the ways in which we combine various verbal and nonverbal modalities in transmitting or concealing meaning in exchange. We do not know what modalities are or should be used to make it easier for exchange to serve different functions. Furthermore, we know little about how different modalities are or should be used to increase or decrease barriers to exchange. Finally, we are only beginning to speculate about the conditions under which various exchange rules (such as rationality, reciprocity, altruism, status consistency, or competition) are utilized (Meeker, 1971). Future research along these lines should greatly enhance our understanding of the second phase of human communication—exchange.

4

Influence:

THE IMPACT OF
HUMAN COMMUNICATION

One important consequence of encounter and exchange is that the communication source exerts some influence over the receiver. *Influence can be defined as the discrepancy between (a) a person's attitude toward an object or situation, or his behavioral patterns, before his voluntary or involuntary participation in encounter and/or exchange and (b) his attitude or behavioral patterns after such encounter and/or exchange.* Influence may be either psychological or behavioral. The transfer from encounter and exchange to influence has been studied by many investigators. For example, Lemert (1969), following up Lazarsfeld's suggestion that press coverage renders status conferral, found that in experimental situations, the mentioning of a person's name in newspapers, without any evaluative statements, tended to increase the person's status in the minds of those who read the news item. Bateson (1951) suggests that a person's decoding behavior in itself tends to lead to his evaluation of the codes. Thus, there seem to be many occasions in which encounter and exchange lead to influence. In addition to the spontaneous relationship between encounter/exchange and influence, communication may take place solely for the purpose of wielding influence. In this chapter I will discuss some general issues concerning influence as a communication variable and, in the next two chapters, treat the topic in detail.

Influence as a theoretical concept has been extensively discussed in all disciplines of the social sciences. It is impossible to deal with all the viewpoints here. Therefore, I will select for discussion four divergent analyses which relate the concept of influence to human communication. In these four viewpoints the concept of influence is variously analyzed (1) as one of several media of social interaction (Parsons, 1963), (2) as a set of processes (Kelman, 1961), (3) as a psychological variable (Katz, 1960), and (4) as the consequence of interaction between a legitimating unit and the receiver (Lin, 1967).

Influence can occur at two levels. The receiver may be psychologically influenced or behaviorally influenced. I will briefly introduce these two levels of influence in this chapter, then treat them in detail in the next two chapters. One important consequence of analyzing the two levels of influence separately is to isolate possible answers to the crucial question, "To what extent do the two levels of influence overlap?" In other words, does the psychological influence induce behavioral changes? And does the behavioral influence induce psychological changes? The basic problems involved in the linkage between attitude and behavior constitute the topic for a discussion in another section of this chapter.

Four Paradigms of Influence

PARSONS'S SOCIAL ACTION ANALYSIS

The most general discussion of *influence* in the context of communication was offered by Parsons (1963), who defined it as the *medium through which a source transmits a positive assertion about an idea or practice on the basis of the intrinsic value of the idea.* To place influence in the proper perspective in his framework, Parsons discussed the generalized medium and a number of specialized media of social interaction. Language, he suggested, represents the generalized medium for social interaction. It is used to emit and transmit messages. In Parsons's view, special media may be categorized according to a typology constructed from the cross-classifications of two variables: sanction (whether the source makes positive or negative assertions about the idea or practice) and channel (whether the source intends to commit the receiver to the intrinsic value of the idea or practice, or simply to the situation). A positive sanction exists when the source advocates a certain change; a negative sanction indicates the source's negative feeling toward or belief about a certain change. An intentional channel represents the situation in which the source attempts to elicit the receiver's agreement on the intrinsic value of the effect. The situational channel represents the situation in which the source is only interested in the commitment of the receiver to the particular situation in which the effect takes place. A cross-classification of these two factors results in the typology presented in Table 4–1. Thus, influence, looked upon in this context, represents a specialized medium which exists when the contact between the source and the receiver originates with and is sustained by the source's attempt to elicit agreement from the receiver on the intrinsic value of the change.

Parsons then proceeded to suggest four types of influence: (1) *political influence,* which operates as generalized persuasion without power (that is, independent of the use of force or direct threat) for a group to achieve certain goals; (2) *fiduciary influence,* which occurs when the interest is the allocation and distribution of resources rather than the attainment of goals (for example, administration of the property interests of minors by trustees); (3) *influence through appeal to differential loyalties,* which concerns activating the commitments of individuals to particular collective activities;

and (4) *influence oriented to the interpretation of norms* (for example, the process of interpreting legal norms in the appellate phase of the judicial

TABLE 4-1. A PARADIGM OF SOCIAL SANCTIONS

	Channel	
Sanction	Intentional	Situational
Positive		
mode	Persuasion	Inducement
medium	Influence	Money
function	Integrative	Adoptive
Negative		
mode	Activation of Commitments	Deterrence
medium	Generalization of Commitments	Power
function	Pattern Maintenance	Goal-attainment

SOURCE: Adapted from Parsons, 1963.

process). While acknowledging that influence occurs at the interpersonal level, Parsons focuses on the types of influence which occur mainly at the collective level.

KELMAN'S ANALYSIS OF INFLUENCE PROCESSES

Kelman (1961) suggests a typology which focuses on three different processes by which influence can be imposed upon the receiver, each characterized by a distinct set of antecedent conditions and a distinct set of consequent conditions. He calls them compliance, identification, and internalization. *Compliance can be said to occur when a receiver accepts influence from a source (be it a person or a group) because he hopes to achieve a favorable reaction from the source.* The receiver does not adopt the induced behavior because he believes in its content, but because it is instrumental in producing a satisfying social effect. *Identification can be said to occur when the receiver adopts behavior derived from another person or group because this behavior is associated with a satisfying, self-defining relationship with this person or group.* It represents a way of establishing or maintaining the desired relationship with the other and the self-definition that is anchored in this relationship. Identification is similar to compliance in that the receiver does not adopt the induced behavior because its content, per se, is intrinsically satisfying. Identification differs from compliance, however, in that the receiver actually believes in the opinions and actions he adopts. Finally, *internalization can be said to occur when the receiver accepts influence because the induced behavior is congruent with his value system.* It is the content of the induced behavior that is intrinsically rewarding here.

Compliance occurs when, for example, an individual makes a special effort to express only "correct" opinions in order to gain admission into a particular group or social set or in order to avoid being tortured in a prison camp. Identification is said to occur when an individual buys a special brand of hair lotion because his favorite baseball player appears in a TV commercial advocating that brand or when a student participates in a demonstration because someone he really admires is leading the demonstration. It is internalization when an individual joins a peace demonstration because he feels it is congruent with his value system, specifically with his belief that all men should have an equal opportunity to live and to do so in peace.

Table 4-2 summarizes the various antecedents and consequents which

TABLE 4-2. SUMMARY OF DISTINCTIONS AMONG THE THREE TYPES OF INFLUENCE

	Compliance	Identification	Internalization
Antecedents			
1. Basis for importance of induction	Concern with social effects of behavior	Concern with social anchorage of behavior	Concern with value congruence of behavior
2. Source of power of influencing agent	Means of control	Attractiveness	Credibility
3. Manner of achieving prepotency of the induced response	Limitation of choice of behavior	Delineation of role requirements	Reorganization of means-ends framework
Consequents			
1. Conditions for performance of induced response	Surveillance by influencing agent	Salience of relationship to agent	Relevance of value to issue
2. Conditions for change and extinction of induced response	Changed perception of conditions for social rewards	Changed perception of conditions for satisfying self-defining relationships	Changed perception of conditions for value maximization
3. Type of behavior system in which induced response is embedded	External demands of a specific setting	Expectations defining a specific role	Person's value system

SOURCE: Adapted from Kelman, 1961.

define the three types of influence. As can be seen from the table, *three antecedent factors* determine the relative probability of occurrence for a particular type of influence: (1) *the importance of the induction for the receiver;* (2) *the power of the source;* and (3) *the manner in which the induced response is conditioned.*

Thus, compliance may result when (1) the receiver is concerned with the social effect of his behavior, (2) the source's power is based on his means of control over the receiver, and (3) the receiver's choice of behavior is limited. Identification may occur when (1) the receiver is concerned with the social anchorage of his behavior, (2) the source's power is based on his personal attractiveness to the receiver, and (3) the receiver's role perception is limited. Finally, internalization may take place when (1) the receiver is concerned with the value congruence of his behavior, (2) the source's power is based on his credibility, and (3) the receiver's concept of means-ends relationships is reorganized.

Consequences derived from the three influence processes in the receiver's attitude or behavior differ in terms of (1) *the subsequent conditions under which the induced response will be expressed or performed,* (2) *the conditions under which they will be abandoned,* and (3) *the type of behavior system in which the induced response is embedded.*

Thus, when a receiver adopts an induced response through compliance, (1) he tends to express or perform it only under conditions of surveillance by the source, (2) he will abandon the response if it is no longer perceived as the best path toward the attainment of social rewards, and (3) the response is only part of a system of external demands that characterize a specific setting. When a receiver adopts the response through identification, (1) he tends to express or perform it only under conditions that are salient to his relationship with the source, (2) he will abandon the response if it is no longer perceived as the best path toward the maintenance or establishment of satisfying self-defining relationships, and (3) the response is part of a system of expectations defining a particular role. Finally, when a receiver adopts the response through internalization, (1) he tends to express or perform it under conditions of relevance to the values that were initially involved in the influence situation, (2) he will abandon it if it is no longer perceived as the best path toward the maximization of his values, and (3) the response is part of an internal system.

As Kelman pointed out, these three types are not mutually exclusive. We can only define situations in which one type of influence dominates and determines the central features of a particular communication pattern. In fact, there is an underlying relationship among the three types of influence. Over time, for example, prolonged compliance behavior may lead to identification and even to internalization, or identification may evolve into internalization. The conditions under which these influences evolve into each other are still unclear and deserve research attention.

As mentioned before, while Parsons discusses influence as one of many specialized media of social interaction, Kelman analyzes in depth the subprocesses of influence. While Parsons suggests types of influence mainly at the collective level, Kelman hypothesizes processes of influence mainly at the interpersonal level. To further pursue the interpersonal level of influence, I will present another paradigm which focuses on psychological influence (attitude) and describes the basic functions attitude serves.

KATZ'S FUNCTIONAL ANALYSIS OF INFLUENCE

Katz (1960) proposed that psychological influence (attitude) should be analyzed in terms of the various functions it performs. Primarily concerned with the motivational bases of attitudes, he felt the need (1) to develop some generalizations about human behavior, (2) to avoid the error of oversimplification—attributing a single cause to given types of attitudes, and (3) to specify the conditions under which given types of attitude will change. Thus, he described four major functions of attitudes in terms of (1) their origins and dynamics, (2) their arousal conditions, and (3) the conditions under which they might change. The specifications are presented in Table 4–3.

TABLE 4–3. DETERMINANTS OF ATTITUDE FORMATION, AROUSAL, AND CHANGE IN RELATION TO TYPE OF FUNCTION

Function	Origin and Dynamics	Arousal Conditions	Change Conditions
Adjustment	Utility of attitudinal object in need satisfaction. Maximizing external rewards and minimizing punishments	1. Activation of needs 2. Salience of need satisfaction	1. Need deprivation 2. Creation of new needs and new levels of aspiration 3. Shifting rewards and punishments 4. Emphasis on new and better paths to need satisfaction
Ego Defense	Protecting against internal conflicts and external dangers	1. Posing of threats 2. Appeals to hatred and repressed impulses 3. Rise in frustration 4. Use of authoritarian suggestion	1. Removal of threats 2. Catharsis 3. Development of self-insight
Value Expression	Maintaining self-identity; enhancing favorable self-image; self-expression and self-determination	1. Salience of cues associated with values 2. Appeals to individual to reassert self-image	1. Some degree of dissatisfaction with self 2. Greater appropriateness of new attitude for the self 3. Control of all environmental supports to undermine old values
Knowledge	Need for understanding, meaningful cognitive organization, and consistency and clarity	1. Reinstatement of cues associated with old problem or of old problem itself	1. Ambiguity created by new knowledge of change in environment 2. More meaningful information about problems

SOURCE: Adapted from Katz, 1960.

The *adjustment* function of attitude is served when people strive to maximize the rewards and to minimize the penalties of their external environment, thereby satisfying utilitarian needs. The *ego-defensive* function concerns the mechanisms by which an individual protects his ego from his own unacceptable impulses and from the knowledge of threatening forces from outside and the methods by which he reduces the anxieties created by such problems—in short, how he handles internal conflicts. The *value-expressive* function of attitude is served when a person gives positive expression to his central values and to the type of person he conceives himself to be—thereby maintaining his self-identity and enhancing his self-image. The *knowledge* function of attitude concerns the standards or frames of reference an individual depends on to give meaning to the complexities and ambiguities of the world about him.

The arousal conditions for the various functions, according to Katz, relate to the excitation of some need in the individual or to some relevant cue in the environment. The conditions conducive to a change in attitude relative to each function occur when the expression of the attitude, or its anticipated expression, no longer gives satisfaction to the related need state.

The *two basic conditions for the arousal of existing attitudes* are the *activation of their relevant need states* and the *perception of the appropriate cues associated with the content of the attitude*. The specific arousal conditions for attitudes serving the adjustment function are (1) the activation of needs in the person and (2) the importance of satisfying such needs. To change attitudes which serve a utilitarian (adjustment) function, Katz feels that one of two conditions must exist: either the attitude and the activities related to it no longer provide the satisfaction they once did, or the individual's level of aspiration has been raised.

Attitudes serving the function of ego defense can be elicited by (1) any form of threat to the ego, (2) the encouragement given to their expression by some form of social support, (3) the building up of frustration in the individual, and (4) the appeal of authority. Three factors can help change ego-defense attitudes: (1) the removal of threat, (2) the ventilation of feelings (thus discharging inhibited impulses), and (3) the individual's acquiring insight into his own mechanisms of defense.

Two conditions for the arousal of value-expressive attitudes were specified by Katz: (1) the occurrence of the cue in the stimulus situation which has been associated with the attitude and (2) appeals to the individual to reassert his self-image. Two conditions are also relevant in changing value-expressive attitudes: (1) some degree of dissatisfaction with one's self-concept or its associated values and (2) dissatisfaction with old attitudes as inappropriate to one's basic values.

According to Katz, attitudes acquired in the interests of the need to know are elicited by a stimulus associated with the attitude and can be changed when the individual recognizes the inadequacies of the existing attitudes to deal with new and changing situations.

LIN'S ANALYSIS OF THE INFLUENCE STRUCTURE

While Kelman's typology defines the processes by which influence can occur within the receiver, influence can also be discussed in terms of the structural *interaction between the legitimating force and the receiver* (Lin, 1967). This relationship may be specified with a simplified classification of the legitimating units of ideas and practices and the units of receivers. The legitimating source may be a person, a group (defined as a subpopulation within a given population), or the system itself (administration). The receiver may also be a person, a group, or the system itself. By cross-classifying the legitimating source and the receiver unit, we arrive at the typology shown in Table 4-4.

TABLE 4-4. A STRUCTURAL TYPOLOGY OF INFLUENCE AS THE CONSEQUENCE OF LEGITIMATION

Unit of Receiver	Legitimating Unit		
	Individual	Group	Administration (of System)
Individual	Voluntary	Normative	Legalistic
Group	Persuasive	Collective	Referendum
Administration (of System)	Suggestive	Petitionary (lobby)	Authoritarian

This typology specifies the particular type of influence that occurs when a certain legitimating influence is exerted by a certain source—either an individual, a group, or the administration—and when the unit of the receiver is identified as an individual, a group, or the administration. This typology assumes, first, that the legitimating source and the receiving unit belong to the same system—an idiosyncratic system. Thus, when the legitimating unit is an individual, and the receiving unit is also an individual, these are understood to be the same individual. Second, it assumes that the magnitude of influence exerted by a legitimating unit is linearly related to the unit size involved; the larger the unit, the stronger the force. Presumably, the individual possesses the least binding power since the influence of an individual, acting as a normative singular unit, is relatively limited. The group, which may be any subsystem of the system defined in any way, has some binding power over the individuals in the group, although this binding may be consensual rather than legalistic. The administration, as the power unit of the system, has the greatest binding power over the groups and individuals in the system.[1]

When the legitimating unit is the same individual as the receiving unit, there is no external force involved, and the formation of attitudinal or behavioral change is said to be *voluntary*. When an individual initiates efforts to induce change in the group of which he is a member, the influence is defined as *persuasive*. The pressure is a weak one. When an individual attempts to change the system to which he belongs, the influence is only *suggestive*. It is generally a very weak one (for instance, suggestion boxes in organizations, letters to the president, etc.). When a group attempts to

1. Here I am discussing only those cases where the legitimation occurs before the receiving unit makes any changes. A model incorporating the posterior legitimation process is conceivable but not discussed here.

change an individual in the group, the influence is termed *normative*. While initial legitimation comes from the group, the individual, by and large, still has a great deal of freedom to determine the extent to which he is willing to change along the lines advocated by the group. When the group exerts influence on itself, it represents a typical *collective* decision situation in which the group determines its own extent of change. When a group exerts influence on the system of which it is a sybsystem, the influence is *petitionary* or *lobbying* (depending on the structure of the change process in the administrative unit); it represents some membership interest, but the extent of influence is determined, to a large extent, by the political-economic power the group has in the system. Finally, if the system itself exerts influence on one of its individual members, the influence is substantial and can be imposing, the limiting case being a law the individual is required to obey. When the system exerts influence on certain groups in the system, we have what can be termed the referendum influence; although the system has approved the change, such change can be administered only through a group decision or if the majority of the group concurs. When the system exerts influence on itself, it represents an authoritarian decision; it affects every member and group in the system automatically.

While this structural typology specifies, in a simplistic way, the extent of influence as a function of the unit of the legitimating source and the receiving unit, the effectiveness of the actual change that occurs may be measured against the effectiveness of the change intended by the communication source. In some cases, voluntary change is most effective and permanent; in other cases, authoritarian influence may be most efficient and economical. The structural typology, then, should help determine—for the various changes desired—which of the different influential structures would be most effective in bringing about change.

A SUMMARY OF THE PARADIGMS

The above discussion demonstrates the scope of the meaning of influence and shows how the concept can be approached from different perspectives. The four paradigms can be summarized in terms of the following differentiating characteristics:

1. *The framework of analysis.* Parsons's paradigm places *influence* in the larger context of *social interaction* and identifies it as *one of many specialized media* facilitating interaction. The other three paradigms focus on the *internal structure of influence.* Kelman is interested in the various influence processes differentiated on the basis of the situational-internalizational continuum, while Lin's paradigm explores different types of influence as consequences of coupling various legitimating units with the receiving units. Katz's paradigm focuses on attitudes and the conditions for attitude change—the dynamics of the psychological influence associated with the different functions performed by attitudes.

2. *The orientation of analysis*. The four paradigms focus on different components in the process of influence. Parsons's paradigm focuses on the *source* in identifying influence as a medium—on whether the source makes a positive or negative assertion about an idea or practice and whether the source is interested in transmitting the intrinsic value of the idea or practice or merely in the receiver's expression and performance in a given situation. Kelman and Katz, on the other hand, suggest paradigms which focus on the *receivers* in the influence process and on the conditions under which various types of influence may be aroused and changed. The *interaction between the legitimating unit and the receiving unit* is the main concern in Lin's analysis.

3. *The level of analysis*. While acknowledging that his typology applies to individuals, Parsons mainly discusses influence on the *societal and collective level*. Kelman and Katz, on the other hand, stress influence as it occurs on the *interpersonal and individual level*. Lin's typology is an attempt to *link the societal, collective, and individual levels*.

4. *The nature of analysis*. Katz and Parsons are interested mainly in the *functions* of different types of influence. For example, Parsons associates his four types of influence—political influence, fiduciary influence, commitment, and normative interpretation—with what he terms functional subsystems of the society (polity, economy, pattern maintenance, and integration). Katz's discussion is entirely concerned with the different functions attitudes serve. Lin's typology applies solely to the situation in which a *legitimation process* occurs. Kelman provides a *causal analysis* of the influence processes—the antecedents and consequents of each process.

These paradigms, diversified in their analytic framework, orientation level, and nature, clearly indicate the close relationship between influence and human communication. In fact, they suggest *influence as a subconcept of communication*; it concerns a set of particular communication situations involving a source, a medium, a receiver, and a message and concerning the *change as expressed or performed* by the receiver resulting from such communication. The difference between *expression* and *performance* can now be discussed more precisely.

Levels of Influence

Influence generally occurs at two levels. On the one level, human communication results in changes in the *receiver's psychological structure*. He may see, interpret, and evaluate things differently; he may rearrange his own hierarchy of values. The most important of the psychological influences to draw considerable research attention by psychologists and sociologists is attitude change.

An *attitude* is defined as a *relatively enduring organization of beliefs* about an object or situation predisposing a person to respond in some preferential manner (Rokeach, 1966b). Presumably most central and important in the psychological structure of a human being is a set of basic beliefs about himself which more or less define the person. These beliefs combine to assert the identity of the person. One interesting way to identify a person's beliefs is to ask the question, "Who are you?" Responses such as "I am a woman," "I am a Buddhist," or "I am a Nigerian" usually reflect what is considered to be central to the person and index his basic beliefs. Surrounding these basic beliefs are sets of attitudes. All attitudes are organized from subsets of beliefs. While beliefs may be very general ("I am a Christian," "I am a man"), attitudes are very specific ("I don't like birth control," "I love Steve McQueen"). A person has numerous attitudes—perhaps as many as there are objects and situations for him to encounter. Each attitude may be favorable or unfavorable, and there are different degrees, of course, of favorability and unfavorability. Each attitude also has an importance dimension to the person, as compared with other attitudes in each given situation. Thus, when a segregationist psychologist attends a national convention of psychologists, several attitudes are aroused in him by the occasion. He has an attitude toward his profession and toward his fellow psychologists, regardless of their color or religious background, but he also has a personal attitude toward certain minority groups. Thus, the particular occasion makes him assess his attitudes, all of which may come into play during his participation at the meeting. After assessing the social situation and his attitudes, he may decide that in this particular situation, his attitude toward his colleagues ranks higher than his racial attitude. Thus, during the meeting, he acts as a professional scientist would and treats his black colleagues simply as other psychologists. After the meeting, when he goes back to the environment of his daily life, he may rerank his attitudes toward his professional colleagues and other races and behave differently (that is, as he did at the meeting) when he faces blacks in his community. Thus, for every type of social situation a particular set of rank-ordered attitudes is activated in the individual. These rank-ordered attitudes form the basis of predispositions for his subsequent behavior patterns.

A change in attitude is said to have taken place if the position of a particular attitude in the rank-order is different from what it would formerly have been in the same type of social situation. Thus, the influence of a communication, in terms of attitude change, can be gauged by the discrepancy between a person's ranking of a specific attitude toward an object or situation in a given type of social situation before his participation, either voluntary or involuntary, in encounter and/or exchange and his ranking of the same attitude in a similar social situation after such encounter and/or exchange. Such a rigorous definition, however, is not used in most studies of attitude change. The less stringent definition of attitude change usually used in attitude change studies can be stated as follows: the discrepancy

between a person's attitude toward an object or situation before his participation, either voluntary or involuntary, in encounter and/or exchange and
his attitude after such encounter and/or exchange. The definition is relaxed
in that instead of measuring the discrepancy in the rank-ordered attitudes
in a given type of situation, it measures only the direction or magnitude of a
single attitude in a given situation.

Human communication and psychological influence (attitude change)
have been closely associated in the literature, mainly because if the change
is not generated within the person, such influence must come through some
communication process—involving a source, a message, a channel, and
a social environment. Different approaches to the study of attitude change
place different degrees of emphasis on the communication process. For
some (Hovland and his associates, for example), communication itself
provides the mechanism by which attitudes are changed. Thus, they
manipulate components of the communication situation (such as the source,
the message, the channel, the reference group, and so on) to achieve such
change. Other approaches (such as dissonance theory, social judgment
theory, etc.) stress the fundamental cognitive process within the individual,
and the communication situation is given secondary consideration. But,
there is no doubt that in all studies dealing with attitude change, communication elements are not only present but quite often provide crucial
clues for the control and manipulation of attitude change.

I mentioned earlier that influence generally occurs on two levels, the
first involving changes in the receiver's psychological structure. On the
second level, influence may be induced by communication to achieve
behavioral changes. Behavior is defined here as an *overt gesture, either
spoken or enacted/acted out, which can be immediately verified by other
individuals.* Voting, for example, is a form of behavior which can be verified
by many individuals, among them, a man's neighbors, who saw him drive
off to the polls, his wife, who was told which candidate he was going to
vote for, the voting officials, who observed him casting his vote, and so
forth. Of course, many attitudes and behaviors can only be measured
through a person's verbal response to test questions or items (opinions).
To avoid the confusion which arises from this problem, behavior must be
measured in a situation apart from attitude response measure where it can
be verified by individuals independent of the test personnel. In most studies,
however, both attitude and behavior are measured via opinion tests. Efforts
have been made to record actual behavior through such means as voting
records (to verify the presence of the individual at the polls), prescriptions
(to verify the prescriptions actually made by physicians and taken by patients),
and verification of the products a person claims to have bought. However,
such measures are available only when the behavior is so unusual or
atypical of daily behavior that specific records have been kept in the first
place. It is much more difficult to study behavior typical of a person's daily

life. Strict records are hard to come by and the average person's memory may not be very specific or long-lasting. It is vital, therefore, that studies of behavior be made as close to the time of the behavioral occurrence as possible if the behavior studied falls into a person's daily behavioral pattern.

A *behavioral change induced by communication* is said to have occurred if there is a *discrepancy between a person's behavioral pattern or specific behavior before his participation, either voluntary or involuntary, in encounter and/or exchange and his behavioral pattern or specific behavior after such encounter and/or exchange.* This definition also applies to the behavioral pattern or specific behavior which occurs only after encounter and/or exchange (from nonexistent to existent). Communication, again, constitutes the focal point in the study of behavioral change. Examples can be drawn all the way from political campaigns, advertising and marketing, the mass media, fashion choices, and innovation adoptions to movie choices, physical checkups, and participations in various social and community activities and functions. The main interest of the researchers who are concerned with behavioral change through communication is twofold. On the conceptual side, they are interested in mapping out the process by which communication induces behavioral change, either as that process exists now or as it should exist. The former emphasis is on the existing process; the latter is on the ideal, or optimal, process. On the practical side, they are interested in finding the best ways of communicating so as to induce behavioral change, again either through existing communication systems or through created communication systems. The two types of research overlap substantially, although the principal interests of the researchers and therefore the descriptions of their results differ.

Linkage Between Attitude and Behavior

One important *assumption* widely, if only implicitly, held by researchers in attitude change is that *there is a consistent linkage between attitude and behavior.* This assumption is quite crucial, for if it proved erroneous, the whole basis for focusing on attitude and attitude change, rather than directly on behavioral patterns and behavioral change, would be severely shaken. Recently, this problem has come into focus among social psychologists (Cohen, 1964; Festinger, 1964b). The discussion draws attention to two problems relative to the linkage of attitude and behavior: (1) there is extremely limited literature on the topic; and (2) there has been research evidence that such consistent linkage is not strong, and in some cases, does not exist.

During the thirties, La Piere (1934) did a series of studies in which he traveled extensively with a Chinese couple by car. Without letting his companions know, he kept a record of the hotels and restaurants they stopped at on the tour. Of the 250 hotels and restaurants they visited, only one place refused service. La Piere also observed that 40 percent of the places they visited gave them better than average treatment. After the trip, he wrote to the 250 hotels and restaurants inquiring whether they would accept Chinese guests. Over 90 percent of the 128 responding proprietors indicated that they would not serve Chinese. Similar results were obtained by Kutner et al. (1952) in a study of discriminatory behavior evaluated by telephone calls to restaurants which had served Negroes. In a review of the literature on behavioral changes following psychotherapy, Zax and Klein (1960) concluded that there was no adequate evidence to link verbal changes during therapy with subsequent behavioral changes in the family and community. In a recent summary of more than 30 studies dealing with both attitude and behavior, Wicker (1969) concluded that taken as a whole, the data suggest that "it is considerably more likely that attitudes will be unrelated or only slightly related to overt behaviors than that attitudes will be closely related to actions." Since such evidence is persistent over time and across subjects (races, jobs, organizations, etc.), the accusation that the evidence results from unreliable test measures and devices is not satisfactory. It is also unsatisfactory to conclude that there is actually no consistent linkage between attitude and behavior. The more acceptable thesis is that there are factors or variables which intervene between attitude and behavior. Suggestions about the *nature of the intervening variables* can be subsumed under the following categories:

1. *Social constraint, pressure, or incentive.* Warner and DeFleur (1969), in a study of college students' attitudes and behavior toward blacks, devised a test to measure the effect of two social variables (social constraint— whether the behavior involved public or private commitment, and social distance—whether the behavior indicated maintenance or reduction of social distance between the white subject and black) on the consistency between attitude and behavior. When the two social variables were taken into account, more consistency was found between the subjects' *attitudes* toward blacks and their willingness to *sign* a document stating their willingness to participate in various activities with blacks.

2. *Situational intervention.* Closely related to the social variables is the attitude the person has toward the situation. Rokeach (1966a) suggests that each person has two attitudes in a given situation: he has an attitude toward an object (be it an individual or an issue) and an attitude toward a situation. If the two attitudes are consistent, the person's attitudes and behavior will be consistent; but if his attitudes are inconsistent, the person will be constrained by the two inconsistent attitudes and exhibit a certain degree of inconsistency between his attitude and his behavior. The extent to which such inconsistency is exhibited is determined, of course, by the extent of the inconsistency of the two attitudes.

3. *Personal involvement.* Sherif et al. (1965) pointed to the dimension

they term ego-involvement. They say, in short, that consistency of attitude and behavior depends on the extent to which the individual is personally involved in the issue. In general, when ego-involvement is strong, consistency will also be strong and when ego-involvement is weak, consistency will also be weak since the person perceives no great need to carry out a specific behavior or action when he is only peripherally interested.

These factors suggest that multiple attitudes and behaviors are available to an individual in a given situation. A person feels as he does about the issue or behaves in a certain manner simply as a result of an evaluation of his attitudes and his behavioral alternatives in a given situation. In any given situation, and in fact at any moment, he is assessing and reassessing the rank-orders of these existing attitudes and available behaviors. Using a "least effort" formula—that is, by attempting to obtain the greatest benefit or utility at the least possible cost—he will assign top rankings to a particular attitude and a particular behavior and this attitude and behavior will prevail. In a different situation, a different pair of attitudes and behaviors may be selected. Thus, the *person usually chooses and acts, as a result of a continuous assessment of his needs and benefits in a given situation, in terms of a matrix of attitudes and behaviors.* These adjustments cannot be regarded as change or inconsistency. A change or inconsistency can be said to have occurred only when the selected pair of attitude and behavior varies across similar situations. A teen-age boy may exhibit one set of attitudes and behaviors toward minority group members during the academic year at college and another set of attitudes and behaviors toward minority group members during the summer when he is home with his family. There is no inconsistency involved because the different social situations call for reranking of his attitudes and behaviors. However, if he exhibits such different sets of attitudes and behaviors one year and the next year, both at home and at college, exhibits an identical set of attitudes and behaviors toward minority members, then we may say that a change of attitude or behavior or both has taken place.

The above discussion points to the need for research (1) to devise reliable measures for the ranking of attitudes and behaviors, (2) to select limited but salient situations and issues for study, (3) to construct or uncover ways of studying attitudes and behaviors over time and across situations, and (4) to determine the latent factors that must be activated for different individuals to assess and rank their attitudes and behaviors in given situations. When such research accumulates, it should demonstrate that attitude and behavior are usually consistent and it should reveal the underlying variables which cause an individual to re-evaluate his rank-ordered attitudes and behaviors.

Concluding Remarks

In this chapter, I have attempted to introduce the concept of influence as it is related to human communication. Influence is seen, through the four paradigms, as a subconcept of human communication. It concerns a set of particular communication situations which involve change in the receiver's attitude or behavior. While our knowledge about the linkage between attitude and change is still incomplete, studies on psychological influence (attitude change) and behavioral influence (behavioral change) have been extensive.

In the following two chapters I will discuss, separately and in detail, the psychological influence (mainly attitude change) and the behavioral influence of human communication.

5

The Psychological Dimension of Communication's Influence: ATTITUDE CHANGE

As Rokeach defined it (1966b), an *attitude is a relatively enduring organization of beliefs about an object or situation predisposing a person to respond in some preferential manner.* Attitude change, then, can be defined as a change of such organization of beliefs about an object or situation. This change can be demonstrated by the different preferential responses the person may exhibit toward the object or situation. This definition implies that to ascertain the extent of attitude change, we must measure the person's or group's attitude toward an object or situation at time one and again at time two. Comparing the degree of favorability of these two attitudes over time, we may then state whether an attitude change has taken place. However, the measurement of attitude change is complicated by the following factors:

1. As yet, we do not have a device with which to measure attitude and attitude change directly. The available measurements rely heavily on the person's or group's *verbal testimony*—that is, on *opinion*. Such opinion is elicited *either* by a questionnaire or by a personal interview schedule which contains items or scales (a number of items) with response categories such as (1) pro- or con-measurement, for example, "Are you for or against legalized abortion?", (2) most favorable to most unfavorable choices, such as the semantic differentials mentioned in Chapter 3, (3) sorting and ranking of statements, and (4) scalogram analysis, an analytic procedure by which statements can be assembled to measure varying levels of favorability (Kiesler, Collins, and Miller, 1969). It has been argued that opinion does not necessarily correspond with attitude and that opinion is only an index of a cognitively structured variable—the attitude. Thus, favorable opinions do not directly imply the existence of favorable attitudes to the same degree. Although some physiological tests, such as the galvanic skin response (see Chapter 3), vascular constriction in the finger, and pupillary dilation (Leiderman and Shapiro, 1964), have been tried, they cannot yet be appropriately interpreted (as to whether it is excitement or attitude that causes the response, and there are too many intervening variables such as the variability across people and across situations for consideration). Rokeach, along with

others, has suggested that an attitude is an implicit concept that can be measured only through opinions across objects and situations and the inter-action of the two types of opinions. Yet, in the literature in general, attitude change is still mostly measured by opinion change over time. McGuire (1968) feels that *it is currently impractical to separate attitude and opinion and that distinguishing between the two concepts in the future would not necessarily change the validity of the opinion data accumulated.*

2. In some cases, measurements are not gathered over time; only cross-sectional data are available. Thus, the sampled respondents are classified according to some social and psychological measurements and these measurement differences are correlated with attitude (opinion) measure-ment. Since there can be no causal linkage between the two sets of measure-ment (correlations do not provide evidence of a causal relationship be-tween the variables, and cross-section data gathered at one point in time do not permit processing *view*), it becomes difficult to ascertain, when a difference of attitude has been obtained among the different groups of respondents, whether the difference is (a) the result of the effect of these other measures on the attitude, (b) the result of the effect of the difference of attitude which led to the differences observed in these other measures, or (c) the result of the effect on the attitude of some unknown and un-measured variables. The most one can state with regard to such data is that attitude, as measured by opinion, covaries with some other variables.

3. Some psychologists argue that attitude itself is impossible to measure and that it should be considered only as a latent variable. It can be expressed in either opinion or behavior. The discrepancy observed between opinion and behavior provides no indication of inconsistency between attitude and behavior. Rather, it indicates only that some other intervening variables have set in (Campbell, 1963). One such intervening variable may be the situation itself, as Campbell and Rokeach have both pointed out. This approach makes the important assumption that a discrepancy among attitudes or between attitudes and behavior does not exist, since, according to this approach, behavior is but one indication of attitude. But since attitude is regarded as immeasurable, the arguments for and against this assumption are difficult to resolve. Furthermore, theoretically, no two situations are the same; the invisibility of attitude is measured always through different sets of intervening variables, such as the situations. Thus, it becomes im-possible to measure any real change in attitude.

Because of these and other complications, the measurement and indeed the definition of attitude and attitude change are not at all identical in the various studies reported in the literature. Fortunately, there is enough litera-ture focusing essentially on similarly defined variables and situations and on change of attitude (as measured by opinion) over time; a systematic body of literature on attitude change is available. In the following discussion of attitude change studies, I am assuming that *opinion,* up to now, is the best available measure of attitude, that data collected over time are reliable, and that any change in the measured opinion over time is, to a large extent, due to some manipulation which has occurred between the time of the attitude measurements.

To demonstrate the kind of data usually collected to study the phenomenon of attitude change, I will now describe a hypothetical study that is typical of this area of research. Suppose we were to study the effect of housing arrangement on white subjects' attitudes toward blacks. A substantial difference has indeed been found between the attitudes of whites who live in integrated housing and the attitudes of those who live in segregated housing. The former group showed far more favorable attitudes toward blacks (see Table 5–1). This finding shows that there is a relationship

TABLE 5–1. TIME 1: ATTITUDE TOWARD BLACKS

Housing	Attitude	
	Favorable	Unfavorable
Integrated	75%	25%
Segregated	25%	75%

between housing arrangement and attitude toward blacks. However, we cannot, on the basis of this finding alone, state that integrated housing led to the attitude change toward blacks. Such a finding may only indicate that those having more favorable attitudes toward blacks were more likely to move into integrated housing in the first place. Thus, the finding can also be interpreted to mean that favorable attitudes toward blacks affected the choice of housing arrangement. In order to ascertain that it was the housing arrangement rather than the attitude which was the antecedent variable, we would need another set of data which would reveal any difference in attitude among the two groups of residents—the whites moving into integrated housing and the whites moving into segregated housing—before they first moved into their respective housing arrangements. Suppose such a set of data were available to us and we found that just prior to their moving into their respective housing arrangements, their attitudes toward blacks were about the same (see Table 5–2). Then, we might conclude that the

TABLE 5–2. TIME 0: ATTITUDE TOWARD BLACKS

Housing	Attitude	
	Favorable	Unfavorable
Integrated	50%	50%
Segregated	50%	50%

housing arrangements did indeed affect the residents' attitudes toward blacks. But even at this point, it could be argued that it was not the housing arrangement per se, but rather some factors which became salient because of the housing arrangement, such as accelerated contact and exchange among the residents as the result of the spatial network, which made the difference. This does not negate the fact that the housing arrangement was responsible for creating the network for such contact and exchange, which in turn influenced the attitudes of the residents. Thus, we may conduct studies focusing on those specific aspects of integrated and segregated housing which play more important roles than other aspects in generating such influence.

In other studies, the manipulation may involve only one group of persons. For example, a study might focus on the effect of counterargument on attitude change. In one group, counterargument is introduced; in another it is not. If the two groups are composed of randomly assigned subjects, the first group is called the experimental group because it is exposed to the experimental message—the counterargument—and the latter group is called the control group. Comparisons of the two groups' attitudes toward a certain object or situation over time may also indicate the extent of the effect of the counterargument on the subjects' attitude change.

Numerous studies, making use of various strategies similar to the one proposed in the hypothetical case, have been conducted on attitude change. Some of the studies bear directly on the effect of human communication on attitude change. In one study, for example, the credibility (trustworthiness and expertise) of the communication source was manipulated to ascertain whether source credibility had any effect on the subjects' attitude change toward a certain object or situation. Other studies are more concerned with the cognitive structure which may explain such change. For example, a study may attempt to commit the subjects to certain boring tasks and then try to ascertain whether such negative-inducing behavior has created dissonance in the subjects and forced them to restructure their cognitive system so as to generate a more favorable attitude toward the task. The foci of the two approaches are drastically different. In the former type of study, researchers are more interested in the lower level of theoretical construction and concentrate on the variables that are immediately observable and manipulatable; in the latter, they are more concerned with a higher level of theoretical construction; they attempt to ascertain the basic explanation for attitude change and then try to derive working hypotheses from the higher-level statement and to test the lower-level hypotheses with empirical data. The advantages and disadvantages of the various theoretical approaches will be discussed later in Chapter 8.

In addition to the component approach[1] (the former variety) and the cognitive approach (the latter variety), discussed previously, there are other studies of attitudes which have still different foci. We will now discuss the major approaches to attitude change which have an important bearing on influence through communication.

1. The literature tends to call this approach the "behavioral approach." To avoid confusion with the term "behavior" as it is defined in this book, we use the term "component" instead.

The Component Approach

Basically, the component approach to the study of attitude change makes use of the communication model and attempts to study the effects the various components of communication may have on attitude change for the receivers. Typically, the study begins with a pretest that measures the subjects' attitudes toward an object (for example, a person) or a situation (for example, tooth brushing). Then, a certain aspect of the communication model (such as the source of the persuasive message) is manipulated in the experimental group. A postmanipulation test examines the attitudes of the experimental subjects as well as those of the control subjects, who did not receive the treatment (manipulation). The discrepancy observed between the two groups' attitudes toward the same object or situation over time is then attributed to the effect of the particular aspect manipulated. Although numerous isolated studies in attitude change have taken this approach, the research program at Yale after the Second World War under the guidance of Carl I. Hovland represents the most systematic, focused, precise, and fruitful effort in this area. Results of the research program have been published in a number of books (Hovland, Lumsdaine, and Sheffield, 1949; Hovland, Janis, and Kelley, 1953; Hovland et al., 1957; Janis, Hovland, et al., 1959; Rosenberg et al., 1960; Sherif and Hovland, 1961). In each of the studies, the focus was on one specific component (such as source, message, receiver, or reference group) as the subjects received messages with regard to a specific topic toward which their attitudes had been pretested before the communication took place. In the following, I will only discuss the best-known studies and their findings. For detailed descriptions of the program and the findings, the reader is referred to the original sources—both the above-cited books and summary texts (Cohen, 1964; Rosnow and Robinson, 1967; McGuire, 1968; Kiesler, Collins, and Miller, 1969).

SOURCE ANALYSIS

Source Credibility

Hovland and Weiss (1951) studied whether the credibility of the communication source is a factor in inducing attitude change among the receivers of a persuasive message in the direction of the opinion advocated by the source. They presented an identical message to two groups. In one, a communicator of a generally "trustworthy" character was used; in the other, the communicator was generally regarded as "untrustworthy." The topics and sources used appear in Table 5–3. The subjects' responses to opinion, information, and other items were surveyed before the communication, immediately after the communication, and a month after the communication. Four topics were used in the construction of the messages; each topic had alternate versions—a positive and a negative advocating position—based on essentially the same facts but arriving at opposite conclusions. Four versions of the eight possible versions (for the four topics) and the eight sources (four highly credible sources and four untrustworthy sources) were systematically combined, and each subject was asked to respond to one version for each of the four topics advocated by four sources. The subjects were college students. In the first questionnaire, administered to the subjects five days before the treatment messages, the subjects were asked to express their opinions on a number of topics, through which were scattered the selected four topics, and to evaluate the general trustworthiness of a long list of sources, including the ones to be used as the message sources in the treatment. The evaluation was on a five-point scale ranging from very trustworthy to very untrustworthy. The ratings obtained validated the source selections: the trustworthy sources were rated as very trustworthy or trustworthy by 81 percent to 94 percent of the subjects and the untrustworthy sources were rated as very trustworthy or trustworthy by only 21 percent to 1 percent of the subjects.

TABLE 5-3. SOURCES AND TOPICS SELECTED FOR CREDIBILITY STUDY

Topic	"High Credibility" Source	"Low Credibility" Source
A. Antihistamine Drugs: Should the antihistamine drugs continue to be sold without a doctor's prescription?	New England Journal of Biology and Medicine	Magazine A[1] (a mass circulation monthly pictorial magazine)
B. Atomic Submarines: Can a practicable atomic-powered submarine be built at the present time?	Robert J. Oppenheimer	Pravda
C. The Steel Shortage: Is the steel industry to blame for the current shortage of steel?	Bulletin of National Resources Planning Board	Writer A[1] (a widely syndicated anti-labor, anti-New Deal, "rightist" newspaper columnist)
D. The Future of Movie Theaters: As a result of TV, will there be a decrease in the number of movie theaters in operation by 1955?	Fortune Magazine	Writer B[1] (an extensively syndicated woman movie gossip columnist)

SOURCE: Adapted from Hovland and Weiss, 1951.

[1]The names of one of the magazines and two of the writers used in the study had to be withheld to avoid any possible embarrassment to them. These sources will be referred to hereafter only by the letter designations given.

Five days later, in a regular class situation, the substitute lecturer (the senior experimenter) asked the subjects to read "excerpts from recent magazine and newspaper articles on controversial topics." These contained the different combinations of sources and versions. As soon as the subjects finished reading, a second questionnaire was handed out, asking them, among other things, to recall the facts and to express their attitudes toward the topics. An identical questionnaire was administered four weeks after the communication treatment. The results, presented in Figures 5−1 and 5−2, showed consistently *greater change in the direction advocated by*

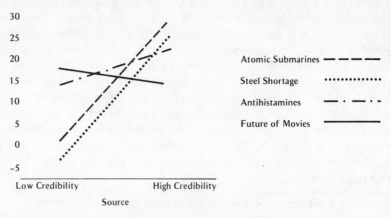

Figure 5−1. Net Change of Opinion in Direction of Communication for Sources Classified by Hovland and Weiss (1951) as "Low Credibility" or "High Credibility" Sources

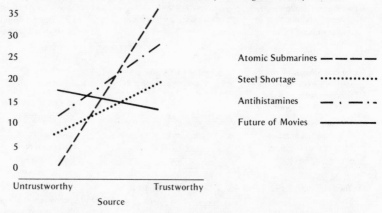

Figure 5−2. Net Change of Opinion in Direction of Communication for Sources Classified by Hovland and Weiss (1951) as "Untrustworthy" or "Trustworthy"

trustworthy sources than in that advocated by untrustworthy ones, with the exception of the "future of movies" topic. This trend was found both when the experimenter rated source classification and when the subjects' own pretest-rated classifications were used. There was no difference between the amount of factual information retained in the immediate questionnaire and the amount retained in the four-week-after questionnaire.

Sleeper Effect

The questionnaire administered four weeks later, however, showed a decrease in the extent of agreement with the high credibility source but an increase of agreement in the case of the low credibility source (Figure 5–3). The difference in attitudes toward the two groups—high credibility source and low credibility source—was nullified. This phenomenon, called the "sleeper effect,"[2] was not due to the subjects' forgetting the source, since

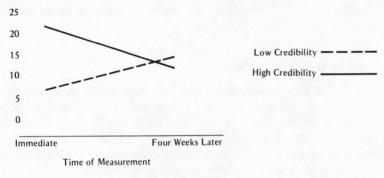

Figure 5–3. The "Sleeper Effect"
Adapted from Hovland and Weiss (1951)

retention of the sources was about the same for all groups. Rather, the effect was believed to be due to a dissociation between the source and the message in the minds of the subjects over time. To test this hypothesis, Kelman and Hovland (1953) conducted a study in which they reminded the subjects of the sources of the specific messages three weeks after the message treatment and retested them again. They found that the test immediately after the treatment achieved a differentiation of attitudes toward the topics because of the high and low credibility sources. Furthermore, the delay period of three weeks did not regenerate the sleeper effect because the sources were reinstated: that is, *when the subjects were reminded of the linkage between the messages they had read and the sources which presented the messages, the differentiation persisted among the groups even after three weeks.* Dissociation of source and message could therefore be avoided or eliminated if the linkage between the specific source and the message was reinstated.

Amount of Change Advocated

Hovland (1959) also suggested that source credibility has a differential effect depending on the different amounts of change advocated. When there is *some ambiguity about the credibility of the source, the greater the attempted change, the higher the resistance.* When the *source has high perceived credibility, the greater the change advocated, the greater the success.*

Recent studies (for example, Berlo, Lemert, and Merz, 1970) have indicated that source credibility is a multidimensional concept. In addition to the dimension of trustworthiness, there are probably other dimensions such as dynamism and expertise. Studies (for instance, Kelman and Hov-

2. First found by Hovland, Lumsdaine, and Sheffield (1949).

land, 1953) have shown that *trustworthiness is more important than expertise in persuading subjects* and that a *relevant source is more effective than an irrelevant source in inducing attitude change* (Aronson and Golden, 1962). More research is needed to specify the effectiveness of various dimensions of source credibility for different types of topics and different receivers.

MESSAGE ANALYSIS

Another component of the communication system concerns the message transmitted. The message is probably also the most complicated component in the system. In addition to the meaning contained therein, the organization of the message may vary along many dimensions. For example, the message can present only the favorable argument that the source is advocating or it can present both favorable and unfavorable arguments. If both sides are presented, it must be decided which argument should be presented first. Should a conclusion in favor of the source's position be presented or should it be left to the subjects (receivers) to decide? Would the inclusion of a fear-appealing or threatening element enhance the effectiveness of the message? How can the communication be made to have a long-lasting effect when the same subjects will be confronted with counterarguments in the future? Such questions have generated exciting studies on the role of the message component in inducing influence (attitude change).

One-Sided Versus Two-Sided Message

Hovland, Lumsdaine, and Sheffield (1949) conducted a study among American soldiers as to whether they thought there would be a quick end to the war with Japan after the surrender of Germany in 1945. After measuring the subjects' opinions, they argued in one experimental group that it was going to be a long war, stressing the strength of Japan (one-sided message). In another, while still stressing that it was going to be a long war, they presented material on Japan's strengths and weaknesses and the United States' advantages (two-sided message). In the control group, they presented no message at all. Another opinion measure was made after the presentation. A comparison between the pretest and posttest opinions of the experimental subjects and the control subjects showed that *both the one-sided and the two-sided messages were effective in inducing change* in the soldiers' attitudes in the direction of a longer war. However, in investigating the initial positions of the soldiers as to the length of the war, they found that the *two-sided message was more effective with those who initially disagreed with the position advocated* (those who expected a short war), while the *one-sided message was more effective among men who initially agreed with the position advocated* (those who expected a long war). They found, also, that the *two-sided message was more effective with the better-educated men.* But when the two factors—initial position and educational level—were considered concurrently, they found that the two-sided message was more effective with better-educated men, regardless of their initial position on the issue, and that the one-sided message was more effective with those of the less-educated men who initially sided with the position advocated. In other words, *as between the educational level and the initial attitude, the educational level is the more important determinant of the effect of one-sided or two-sided messages on attitude change.*

Further studies (Hovland, Janis, and Kelley, 1953; Lumsdaine and Janis, 1953) found that a *two-sided message is more effective in the long run if the subjects are exposed to subsequent counterargument,* regardless of the initial position the subjects held, or, if the subjects initially favored the position advocated, regardless of whether they are exposed to subsequent counterargument. The two-sided message is less effective than the one-sided message if the subjects favored the position advocated and are not exposed to subsequent counterargument. That the two-sided message "immunizes" the audience against future counterargument was attributed to the fact that the two-sided message presents the opposite point of view and thus builds up the subject's resistance to that point of view when he is confronted with it again. The inoculation phenomenon will be discussed in a later section.

A recent study (Jones and Brehm, 1970) showed that the persuasiveness of a one-sided message would be reduced more than would that of a two-sided message when the audience had been made aware, before the message was transmitted, that there were two plausible sides to the issue.

Stating a Conclusion Versus Not Stating a Conclusion

Hovland and Mandell (1952) conducted an experiment in which they presented identical messages, with one variation, to two groups of subjects; in one group, the message contained a conclusion, and in the other, no conclusion was drawn. The message dealt with current economic issues and the conclusion presented to one group stated that it was desirable to devaluate American currency. They found that the message with a conclusion was more effective than the one without. A later study (Thistlewaite, de Haan, and Kamenetsky, 1955) qualified this by finding that the *message with a conclusion was more effective in changing the attitudes of the less intelligent subjects than those of the more intelligent.* Other factors, such as the complexity of the argument, familiarity of the topic, and so forth, have also been found to contribute to the differential effects of the conclusion.

Order of Presentation

The organization of the argument(s) in the message provides another interesting line of investigation. Studies have focused on two questions: (1) whether the climax of the argument should be presented at the beginning or at the end, and (2) when two different views are presented, which view has the advantage, the first view presented (the primacy effect) or the second view presented (the recency effect).

Hovland and Mandell (1952), after a series of studies on both questions, concluded that neither order of presentation has a substantial advantage over the other. More important, for different audiences, other factors such as attention, learning, and acceptance will contribute to making one order of presentation superior to the other. With regard to the primacy versus recency issue, they pointed out (Hovland et al., 1957) that the so-called law of primacy, first suggested by Lund (1925), does not hold true in general, that primacy occurs when the audience is asked to make a public commitment in favor of the first viewpoint between presentation of the first and the second viewpoints, and that primacy may occur if the second view presented by the same source contradicts the first view just presented. However, this last effect disappears if the audience is warned of the fallibility of the first viewpoint, if activities intervene between the two presentations, or if different sources present the two viewpoints.

When the message contains only one viewpoint, *it is desirable first to arouse the subjects' needs and then to present information that may satisfy such needs.* This order is more effective in inducing attitude change than presenting the information first and arousing the needs second (Cohen, 1964). It is also preferable to first present information that is highly desirable to the subjects and then to present the less desirable information. Because of the forgetting function, recency is more likely to take effect if attitude change is measured after a period of delay. Cohen (1964) summarized the findings on primacy and recency and pointed out that there is no universal principle of primacy in persuasion. Either primacy effect or recency effect depends on a number of other factors such as time of measurement, similarity of issues, contiguity of presentations, number of separate issues, earlier positive experiences with the communicator, interpolated activity, warnings against premature commitment, encouragement toward commitment, ambiguity inherent in the sequence of communications, and arousal of needs before presentation of information.

Types of Appeals

Whether emotional appeals enhance a message's effectiveness in inducing attitude change was tested among college students by Janis and Feshbach (1953) in an experiment in which they presented a 15-minute talk on dental hygiene. Three versions of the message were used, each of which contained essentially the same information but a differing amount of fear-arousing material. The strong fear-appeal version emphasized the frightful consequences of tooth decay and its relation to cancer, blindness, and other ills. The moderate fear-appeal version presented the same dangers in milder form, excluding the statements on the relation between tooth decay and cancer and blindness. The minimal fear-appeal version contained more neutral material and fewer painful predictions. The subjects were quizzed before and after the message on their tooth-care practices. Results showed that the *minimal fear-appeal message was most effective in inducing changes in tooth-care practices in the direction recommended by the message, followed by the moderate fear-appealing message and the high fear-appealing message.* Two factors were thought to have caused the ineffectiveness of the high fear-appeal message: (1) anxiety aroused by the frightening appeal might have caused inattentiveness to the message and a desire to forget the information received; and (2) the unpleasant message might have induced hostility toward both the source and the message itself. However, analyses of the data showed that retention of information was similar for all three groups and that the extent of aggressiveness toward the source was about the same for all three groups. One plausible explanation was that the unpleasant message had created defensive avoidance. When the audience was exposed to a strong threat but not relieved by subsequent information in the message, they tended to ignore the message and thus to minimize the importance of the threat (Janis and Terwilliger, 1962).

RECEIVER ANALYSIS

Hovland, Janis, and Kelley (1953), after citing a number of studies, concluded that different types of receivers tend to be influenced to different degrees. They called these consistent individual differences in susceptibility to influence "persuasibility." Evidence suggests that different people show different degrees of persuasibility, but are there personality or social traits which can account for such differences?

Self-Esteem

Janis and Field (Hovland and Janis, 1959) found that *high persuasibility was related to low self-esteem as measured by feelings of inadequacy, social inhibitions, and test anxiety.* A later study of institutionalized mental patients conducted by Janis and Rife confirmed the relationship. Cohen (1959), defining self-esteem as the value an individual places on himself, found that *persons of low self-esteem tended to be more susceptible to influence from persons of higher self-esteem than vice versa and to be less active in attempting to exert influence.* He suggested that persons of low self-esteem are characterized by expressive defenses which sensitize them to environmental stimuli and make them vulnerable to the influence of external events, while persons of high self-esteem, who use avoidance defenses, are able to repress, deny, or ignore challenging experiences stemming from the environment and to maintain a stable self-image at a high level. Thus, he hypothesized that threatening appeals are more likely to be rejected by those of high self-esteem than by those of low self-esteem. Leventhal and Perloe (1962) confirmed Cohen's hypothesis.

Authoritarianism

Similar to the *relationship between self-esteem of the audience* and the *perceived self-esteem of the sources,* Powell (1965) found that *high authoritarian (dogmatic) subjects were influenced more by the source of the mes-*

sage than were low authoritarian subjects. In other words, the more dogmatic person tends to associate the information with its source in evaluating the information, while the less dogmatic person tends to evaluate the information on its own merits, independent of the source. Since the sources used in most persuasion studies are of the self-assured type or are credible sources in reality, the more dogmatic persons thus show higher susceptibility to influence.

Cognitive Variations

Cohen (1957), in his study of how an effective message should be arranged (need arousal first and then information, or information first and then need arousal?), found that his subjects saw these communications as differing in the degree to which they were ambiguous and lacking in cognitive clarity and reasonableness. He hypothesized that while a subject's need for cognitive clarity would make little difference in the acceptance of the information where the communication was clear (need-information order), it would make a great deal of difference where the communication was ambiguous (information-need order). The experiment confirmed his hypothesis. *Subjects with a high need for cognitive clarity changed their attitudes in the direction of the position advocated to the same extent, whether the order was need-information or information-need. Subjects with a low need for cognitive clarity who received the need-arousal material first changed their opinions, but similar subjects who received the information first changed less.* Kelman and Cohler (1959) identified subjects as to strong and weak needs for cognitive clarity and within each category they further identified subjects as to cognitive style. The "sharpeners" were those who emphasized unique distinguishing details. The "levelers" were those who operated with a limited set of cognitive categories and tended to ignore distinguishing details. They found that the sharpeners showed greater acceptance of the position advocated than the levelers, and among those with a high need for cognitive clarity, the sharpeners showed even greater acceptance than the levelers. Baron (1963) added a third variable to the experimental situation—ambiguity of the message. His data showed that sharpeners changed their attitudes more than levelers did where the need for cognitive clarity was strong, but that where the need was weak, the effect was reversed (levelers showed more attitude change than sharpeners); the effect of different needs and styles is greater where the message is more ambiguous. Further studies along these lines are needed to specify the relationship between cognitive variations among subjects and their persuasibility.

Other Factors

Other factors mentioned which may be related to persuasibility include perceptual dependence, other-directedness, social isolation, richness of fantasy, sex, psychosexual conflict, and ego-defensiveness. These data and suggestions demonstrate that the specification of personality and psychological traits for persuasibility is no simple task. Assuming that such relationships do exist, they will be very complex ones. How to weave all the factors together to achieve a viable theory of persuasibility traits remains the difficult and important task.

REFERENCE GROUP ANALYSIS

The audiences receiving persuasive messages are not isolated elements. They are members of social groups and have referent persons in their minds when they evaluate the input information. In fact, the experimenter, or the source of the experimental message, is also evaluated in terms of whether he has any relevance to the subjects—whether he is a positive, negative, or neutral referent. Singer (1961), for example, found that the experimenter's saying "good" or "right" affected the subjects' attitudes differently, depending on whether the subjects agreed or disagreed with the statements producing such remarks. Similar results were obtained by Hildum and Brown (1956) and Scott (1957, 1959a, 1959b).

Group Membership

Rhine (1958) conducted an experiment in which some subjects made responses after hearing the responses of three confederates who were supposed to be fellow students, while other subjects made their responses in private. The results showed that the *subjects who heard the confederates' responses adopted a similar attitude more readily than those who responded in private.* Kelley and Volkhart (1952) found that persons who were most strongly motivated to retain their membership in a group and who therefore depended most upon approval from the group were less likely to accept messages advocating positions opposed to the norms and values of the group than were other members in the group. Kelly and Woodruff (1956) studied a situation in which subjects who were exposed to a message contrary to their group norms "learned" that other members of their group had approved the position advocated. They found that these subjects, as compared with those who had not heard that their group members had approved of the message, were more likely to change their attitude toward the position advocated.

Group Decision

How the decision is reached in a group situation seems to affect a person's attitude toward the position advocated. Lewin and his associates (1943), in an experiment conducted during the Second World War, tried to persuade housewives to eat unusual foods, such as beef hearts, kidneys, and sweetbreads. Some groups of housewives listened to a lecture on the nutritiousness and cheapness of these meats and were given recipes for their preparation. Other groups of housewives participated in a discussion, in the course of which the same positive information was provided. Following the discussion in the latter groups, the housewives were asked to indicate by a show of hands whether they intended to serve the unfamiliar meats. When, after a period of time, the same housewives were questioned again, it became apparent that more of the discussion group subjects (32 percent) than of the lecture group subjects (3 percent) were serving the meats. In another study, they tested the same procedure among mothers who had just had their first child and who were being discharged from a state hospital with a persuasive message (in either a lecture or a discussion situation) to feed their babies cod-liver oil and orange juice. The data again confirmed that the *group discussion was far superior to the lecture approach in inducing attitude and behavior change among the mothers.* Later studies by others (Mitnick and McGinnies, 1958; Pennington, Haravey, and Bass, 1958) confirmed the greater effectiveness of discussion over lecture in inducing attitude change.

Group Pressure

In an interesting study, Asch (1951) set up an experiment to test whether a person's decision or perception could be changed under group pressure. In the experimental situation, the subjects were first exposed to a line flashed on the screen and then to three lines of different lengths shown on the screen. They were then asked to indicate which of the three lines was identical to the single line shown previously. Since the three lines varied substantially in length, the evaluation was not a difficult one. However, all but one of the subjects were actually confederates of the experimenter and the real subject was seated near the end of the row. As each person was asked to report his judgment, the confederates all gave a wrong answer. Thus, the subject was confronted with a situation in which pressure was exerted by the group, even though the formation of the group was entirely artificial. The data showed that *about 40 percent of the subjects yielded to group pressure and modified their judgments in line with those of the confederates.* Asch found that the extent to which a subject yielded or showed independence was related to the perceived unclearness of the stimulus, to the closeness of the three reference lines to each other, to whether the opposition was unanimous, to the size of the group in opposition (the optimal size being four or five), and to individual differences among the subjects. To separate the effect of normative influence (where the subject gives the wrong answer not because of wrong perception but because he goes along with the group) from that of informational social influence (where he gives the wrong answer because he believes it to be the true answer), Deutsch and Gerard (1955) conducted an experiment in which they found that subjects who believed they were members of a group made more errors (conformed more) than those who did not participate in the task as members of a group. This result illustrates normative social influence. Among those who committed themselves to certain responses either in public or private (they were asked to announce or to write down their own judgments), normative social influence was reduced. *Future researchers should set up genuine groups whose members interact or know each other well, so that the group norms and pressures are realistic and pervasive among the group members. Also, direct testing of the relationship between group properties and attitude change is lacking;* most past research has focused on perceptual or information problems.

INOCULATION ANALYSIS

As with the question of how attitudes can be changed by the manipulation of various components in a communication situation, the topic of resistance to persuasion has also drawn considerable research attention. Early evidence as to the possibility and feasibility of building up a person's resistance to subsequent persuasive messages was provided by Janis, Lumsdaine, and Gladstone (1951). They showed that people who had been forewarned of the difficulties involved in building and testing an atomic bomb were less influenced by the subsequent message that Russia would soon have large numbers of A-bombs after its first exploding one than were members of a control group that had not received such forewarning. Subsequent studies have demonstrated that such resistance is analogous to that provided by medical inoculation; just as we develop the resistance to disease in a person raised in a germ-free environment by pre-exposing him to a weakened dosage of a virus so as to stimulate, without overcoming, his defenses, so can we develop the resistance to persuasion in a person raised in an "ideologically" or attitudinally clean environment by pre-exposing him to weakened forms of counterarguments or to some other belief-threatening material strong enough to stimulate, but not so strong as to overcome, his defenses against belief (McGuire and Papageorgis, 1962; Cohen, 1964). McGuire and Papageorgis conducted a series of investigations into the nature and extent of various types of inoculation. In one experiment (1961), different experimental groups were exposed to the following types of inoculations: (1) counterargument versus no counterargument, (2) refutational defense versus supportive defense, and (3) active participation versus passive participation in the defense training (that is writing versus reading arguments). They found that a *subsequent persuasive message was more effective in the absence of counterarguments. Furthermore, the refutational defense conferred more resistance than the supportive one. Finally, active participation (writing) was less effective than passive participation (reading the defense) in building up resistance to future persuasive messages.* In another experiment (1961), they found a generalized immunization effect. *Through exposure to prior defense, a person would not only be resistant to strong doses of the specific counterarguments refuted but to alternative counterarguments against the belief as well.* McGuire, in another experiment (1961a), further showed that a passive defense is superior to an active defense in developing resistance to attacks by familiar counterarguments, but that an active defense is superior in protecting the person against novel counterarguments. In addition, a double defense (both active and passive) is superior to either one alone in developing resistance when the counterarguments that have been refuted earlier are used again in the later attack. The supportive argument, however, is not useless. On the contrary, McGuire argues, when the person is stimulated by the refutational argument, he is motivated to absorb and digest the supportive argument. The supportive material, once assimilated, becomes a potent force in increasing resistance to later persuasion. This argument was supported in an experiment (McGuire, 1961b). McGuire (1962) found that defenses conferred resistance to immediate attacks, but that the resistance conferred by supportive defenses fell off more rapidly than the resistance provided by refutational defenses. No appreciable resistance remained from a supportive argument two days afterward, while resistance was still found one full week after a refutational defense. Resistance to the counterarguments explicitly refuted fell off more rapidly than did resistance to novel counterarguments; and there was greater resistance to novel counterarguments two days after a refutational defense than immediately afterward. These findings, striking as they are, may be limited to the topics used in the experiments. The topics used were mostly truisms in the culture. *Controversial issues may generate different patterns of response* (Cohen, 1964).

In summary, researchers employing the component approach seek to isolate the important components in the communication situation which exert influence on the receivers (their attitudes toward the position advocated in the message on the selected topic). For each component, specific characteristics are tested for their relationship to attitude change. For the past two and a half decades, this approach, generally called attitude change research or persuasion research, has drawn considerable attention from researchers; studies based on it will undoubtedly continue to grow in both quality and quantity. Two other approaches to the problem of attitude change, to be discussed in the next section, have quite different orientations. They have also generated much attention and numerous research efforts. I will again summarize the more significant and interesting studies. After the discussion, I will try to compare the differences as well as the similarities among the three approaches and to ascertain whether there is a convergent point for the three approaches.

The Social Judgment Approach

Another important approach to the study of attitude change is the social judgment approach suggested by Sherif and Hovland (1961). They argue that a *person makes a judgment as to how close or how far the position of a persuasive message is relative to his own position on the issue.* Attitude change may result from such evaluation. The amount of attitude change is determined by the degree of discrepancy between the person's originally held position and the position advocated in the message. *When the persuasive message is within the receiver's range (latitude) of acceptance, the person tends to accept the position advocated and to change his attitude in the direction of the new position.* The process by which the persuasive message is anchored in the receiver's evaluative scheme is called assimilation. If, on the other hand, the *persuasive message falls outside the receiver's range of acceptance, the person will tend to change his attitude away from the position advocated.* This pulling-away effect is called *contrast.* Figure 5−4 shows the assimilation and contrast effects. The theory also postulates a number of variables which affect the judgmental process. These variables include: (1) internal factors like motivation, learning, and attitude, (2) social factors such as instructions given to the subjects and demand made upon the subjects, and (3) the ego-involvement of the person in the issue (an ego-involving attitude being defined as a social value the individual strongly identifies with and incorporates into himself). Most of Sherif's work focuses on the ego-involvement variable. According to Sherif and Hovland (1961), a person's attitude toward any topic consists of three regions: the region of acceptance, the region of noncommitment, and the region of rejection. As his ego-involvement in the issue increases, the breadth of his region of rejection also increases. However, the theory does not specify that the region of acceptance is affected by the extent of ego-involvement. Thus, as ego-involvement in the topic increases, the region of rejection increases, the region of noncommitment decreases, and the region of acceptance is assumed to remain constant. From these general principles, certain predictions about attitude change can be made (Kiesler, Collins, and Miller, 1969, p. 248): (1) When the persuasive message falls within a person's region of acceptance, his opinion or attitude will change in the direction of the advocated position. (2) When it falls within his region of rejection, he will not change his attitude. In fact, his original position will be reinforced and if there is any attitude change, it will be away from the advocated position. (3) As the discrepancy between his original stand and the position advocated increases, there will be greater attitude change provided that the advocated stand does not fall within the region of rejection. (4) For messages which advocate positions that are within the region of rejection, increased discrepancy will produce decreased attitude change.

In an experiment conducted by Hovland, Harvey, and Sherif (1957), the topic selected for investigation was prohibition, the study being made in Oklahoma shortly after a referendum there had decided in favor of prohibition. Three groups of subjects were selected: 183 subjects were chosen from Women's Christian Temperance Union groups, the Salvation Army, and strict denominational colleges to represent the extremes on the "dry" side; extremist "wet" stands were represented by 25 acquaintances of the experi-

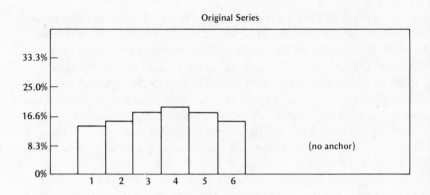

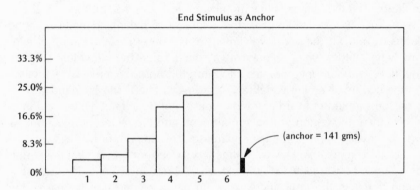

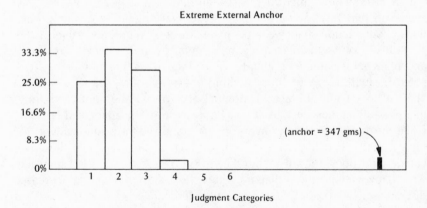

Figure 5–4. Assimilation and Contrast Effect Graph
Adapted from Kiesler et al. (1969)

menters; while an additional 290 subjects were selected for their moderate views on the issue. The subjects were first asked to place each of nine statements on prohibition into one of three categories (regions of acceptance, noncommitment, and rejection) and then to state their own positions. One to three weeks later, the subjects listened to a tape recording of a 15-minute-long message. On this, the religious, health, and financial aspects of the prohibition issue were discussed. A moderately wet message was presented to wet, dry, and moderate subjects. A wet message was presented to extremely dry subjects and a dry message was presented to both wet and moderate subjects. The subjects were then asked to estimate the position advocated in the message, to indicate their responses to the source (in terms of the source's fairness and impartiality), and to state their preferred position as well as their regions of acceptance and rejection. The data showed that *subjects with extreme positions used broader categories for rejection than for acceptance and that their category for rejection was wider than the rejection category of more moderate subjects.* Furthermore, those with extremely wet stands judged that the moderately wet message advocated a drier position than it did, while those with extremely dry stands believed that this same message advocated a much wetter position than it did—confirmation of the contrast effect. The dry subjects showed stronger contrast than the extremely wet subjects. On the other hand, those whose own positions were close to that advocated by the message judged it more accurately. The findings also showed that the closer the message was to the subject's own position, the more favorably disposed he was toward the communicator.

The attitude measures showed that for those exposed to the wet message, the net percent of change in the direction advocated was 4.3 percent for the extremely dry subjects and 28.3 percent for the moderate subjects. For those exposed to the dry message, the net percent of change was 4.0 percent for the extremely wet subjects and 13.8 percent for the moderate subjects. In each case, approximately twice as many extreme subjects as moderate subjects remained unchanged by the message.

Similar results were obtained in a study of political attitudes made just prior to the 1960 presidential election (Sherif, Sherif, and Nebergall, 1965, p. 175).[3]

3. Some questions have been raised about these studies (Kiesler, Collins, and Miller, 1969, pp. 253–263). The most critical comment focuses on the composition of the subjects. That the subjects were not randomly assigned to the experimental conditions but instead came from different natural groups created the problem that many extraneous variables, such as education, intelligence, motivation, and involvement, might differ among subjects from different natural groups—such as the respondents from the Salvation Army and those from colleges. However, such a predetermined condition is extremely difficult, if not impossible, to create in an experimental situation. Another critic questioned the assumed relationship between the initial judgment and the eventual attitude change. Since such a relationship was only assumed in the experiment, there was nothing in the data (1) to show that the subjects had indeed used their judgments to evaluate the message or (2) to determine subsequent attitude change. Thus, the causal relationship between social judgment and attitude change was considered not proven. Again, such criticism can easily be applied to experiments derived from other theories. Its generality has implications for many psychological experiments, not just for the social judgment theory.

In sum, the two variables studied in the social judgment approach are the person's involvement in the issue and the discrepancy between his originally held attitude and the advocated position. *The higher the involvement, the broader the region of rejection. The greater the discrepancy, the greater the change, provided the advocated position does not fall within the region of rejection.* Berkowitz and Goranson (1964) showed that *induced attitude is more important than discrepancy in predicting change.* When a subject was previously induced to like her partner she minimized the difference between her and her partner's positions and when the subject was induced to dislike her partner, she overestimated the difference between their scale positions, regardless of the objective discrepancy between herself and her partner. Other studies (Manis, 1960; Zavalloni and Cook, 1965; Selltiz, Edrich, and Cook, 1965; Ward, 1965) confirmed the general statement of the theory—that greater involvement and greater discrepancy generate greater change. However, numerous qualifications and modifications have also been discussed in order to justify later findings.

Many of them concern measurement problems. It was found, for example, that mid-scale displacements are more complicated than anyone initially realized. Also, displacement effects have been shown to be continuous rather than restricted to certain portions of the response dimension (but for a detailed discussion of various inconsistent findings and theoretical problems connected with the social judgment theory, see Kiesler, Collins, and Miller, 1969, pp. 264–297).

The Cognitive Approach

Another group of social psychologists, following the lead of Kurt Lewin, have investigated attitude change in terms of the psychological structure. According to Gestalt psychology, a person perceives, thinks about, and charts his environment as a whole and is examining his relationship with his environment all the time. Therefore, he acts and reacts according to a set of rules by which the things in his universe are organized in a systematic manner. The process of organizing one's environment and one's relationship with it is called cognition. These social psychologists feel, then, that for a person to live comfortably in his environment, he must feel cognitively consistent. That is, he is constantly striving for consistency and trying to fit incoming information into his existing cognitive system. When any incoming information does not fit into his cognitive system, he is then said to be in a dissonant, incongruent, or unbalanced state. In these circumstances, it is a natural tendency for him to reorganize his cognitive structure, reject the incoming information, misinterpret the information, or do something so as to restore the consistency, balance, or congruity of his cognitive system, even though the structure of the cognitive system will now be different from what it was before he confronted the information. If this assumption is valid, then attitude change is one phenomenon which can be explained by it. Since attitude change is induced by the introduction of a message which advocates a different position from the one a person holds, this confrontation with the message typically puts the person into a cognitively dissonant state. If the theory about the cognitive system is valid, it should be able to explain the process and consequences of attitude change. This route of reasoning has led to many fascinating studies and to different strategies in the study of attitude change. I will discuss the variations of the cognitive approach in studies of attitude change and compare their similarities and differences. These variations include: (1) *the balance model,* initially proposed by Heider, (2) *the strain toward symmetry model,* proposed by Newcomb, (3) *the principle of congruity,* suggested by Osgood and Tannenbaum, and (4) *the cognitive dissonance model,* pioneered by Festinger.

THE BALANCE MODEL

Heider (1946) proposed to study situations in which one person (P) was engaged in some contact with another person (O) and with a nonhuman object (X)—whether an idea, a physical object, an event, or so forth. When P develops a liking or dislike for both O and X, and furthermore, when O is known (to P) to like or dislike X, then a triangular relationship has been established. These relationships, as they exist in P's cognition, can be represented in the following diagrams (the solid lines indicate liking and the broken lines indicate disliking):

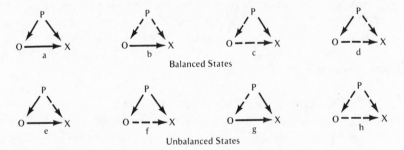

Balanced States

Unbalanced States

The first four diagrams (a, b, c, d) represent what Heider called the balanced states; the relationship among P, O, and X, as they exist in P's cognition, is a balanced one, for the patterns of liking and disliking in each state do not create conflicting interests in P. The next four diagrams (e, f, g, h) represent the unbalanced states, since the relationships among the P, O, and X in each situation create conflict in P. In simple terms, when the triangular relationship involves an odd number of likings (one or three), the state is balanced, but when the triangular relationship involves an even number of likings (zero or two), it is unbalanced. The implication of this specification of balanced and unbalanced states is that *when the relationship is a balanced state, P tends to maintain his cognitive system and to resist or be resistant to change, but that when it is an unbalanced state, P tends to do something that will restore his cognitive system to a balanced state.* In the latter case, attitude change may be one way to restore to balance P's attitude toward O or X. However, there are many alternatives: (1) P may dissociate himself from X; (2) P may dissociate himself from O; (3) P may misinterpret the relationship between O and X—he may perceive either a change in the O-X relationship or a dissociation in the O-X relationship. Because of the various alternatives available to P when confronting an unbalanced state, the only way to test whether P's attitude toward O may change is to block all other potential alternatives in the experimental situation. The situation is further complicated by the fact that the model does not specify different kinds of associations (for example, Cartwright and Harary, 1956, suggested the absence of relationship), nor does it show the magnitude of relationship.

In a further extension of Heider's balance model, Cartwright and Harary (1956) attempted to give more precision to the relationships. They improved the basic model by (1) handling asymmetrical relationships, thus extending the model from an intrapersonal to an interpersonal model (for example, PLO; ODLP), (2) incorporating a multipersonal network situation, (3) distinguishing the absence of, as well as negative, relationships, and (4) defining different degrees of balance for the whole configuration or network. Using graph theory, they attempted to formalize the balance model by specifying the degree of imbalance and the optimal manipulation (change of relationships)—the minimal pairs of relationships that must be changed —needed to restore the network to a balance network. Further mathematical developments along these lines have been made (Cartwright and Harary, 1970). However, few experiments utilizing the various properties have verified or confirmed precise predictions.

STRAIN TOWARD SYMMETRY MODEL

Newcomb (1953) proposed a "strain toward symmetry" model in which the relationships of liking and disliking extended to a group of people on a given topic. He suggested that *a strain toward symmetry exerts force upon persons connected with one another by a given criterion* (members in a social club, brothers in a fraternity, etc.) *to communicate with one another so as to achieve harmony as a group on the topic.* He tested the hypothesis in a number of longitudinal studies (Newcomb, 1956) of college students living in a house. The data revealed a tendency for those who were attracted to one another to agree on many matters, including the way they perceived themselves and their ideal selves and whether they attracted other group members. These similarities tended to increase over time.

Newcomb was more interested, however, in the relationship between interpersonal attitudes and interpersonal communication. His model predicts that *as two people's attitudes toward each other, called co-orientation, strive toward harmony, the frequency of their communication will also increase. It is not clear if Newcomb also believed that increased communication would induce the two people to develop more harmonious attitudes.* He did say that interpersonal attraction induces such attitudinal changes; however, this proposition has been contradicted or qualified by other studies (Kiesler, 1963; Kiesler and Corbin, 1965; Kiesler, Zanna, and De Salvo, 1966) which have shown that under certain conditions, such as commitment to continue in the relationship, lowering the attraction between A and B may increase the influence of A over B (Kiesler, Collins, and Miller, 1969).

Rosenberg and Abelson (1960) tested the idea of a least-effort solution to an unbalanced situation. They created three unbalanced situations in two studies. Each situation involved three elements: high sales volume, modern art, and the manager of a rug department. Each subject was asked to play a role and to assume a favorable or an unfavorable attitude toward each of the elements, and each was assigned relationships among the elements; for example, displays of modern art reduce sales volume (a negative relationship); the manager plans to mount such a display in the rug department (a positive relationship); the manager in his capacity as rug department manager has increased the volume of sales (positive relationship). While the relationships were the same for all subjects, the attitudes of the subjects toward these three elements were varied. Thus, in all situations, the structure of relationships was an unbalanced one. Potential solutions to each of the situations were then suggested to the subjects. One of the three solutions involved one relationship change, while the two other solutions involved two or three relationship changes. The data showed that the *subjects indeed tended to choose the solution requiring the least number of relationship changes in the situation.* In addition, the researchers found that the *magnitude of such change was greatest when the solution maximized potential gain* (sales increase) *and minimized potential loss* (sales decrease).

The balance model, after several important revisions and improvements, still awaits further specifications before it can be meaningfully and definitively tested in experiments. Such specifications, however, may reduce its simplicity advantage and when it becomes a powerful theory, perhaps it will lose its advantages over other more complex models.

THE PRINCIPLE OF CONGRUITY

Osgood and Tannenbaum chose to investigate another type of cognitive situation. *If a person has a favorable attitude toward another person and he also has an unfavorable attitude toward an idea, but the other person ex-*

presses a favorable opinion about the idea, then, according to Osgood and Tannenbaum (1955), *the person is in an incongruous state.* Because he strives for congruence, something has to be changed in his cognition. According to the principle of congruity, *this person will change his attitudes toward both the other person and the idea. He will decrease his liking for that person, but at the same time also decrease his antipathy toward the idea.* Finally, the two attitudes will reach a compromise point where his cognition is again congruent. Furthermore, *the extent to which this person will change his attitude toward the person or the idea will be inversely related to the degree of his original liking or disliking of the person or idea.* For example, if he initially liked the person much more than he disliked the idea, then the change in his attitude toward the person will be much less than the change in his attitude toward the idea.

Thus, the principle of congruity concerns a person's attitudes toward an idea and toward a source (person) who asserts certain attitude change toward the idea. To measure the changes in the model, Osgood and Tannenbaum utilized the semantic differential which Osgood developed and which was discussed in Chapter 3. The semantic scale has seven points, ranging from $+3$ to -3. If a person rates President Nixon a $+2$ and if he rates legalized abortion a -3, and if he is told that President Nixon has come out in favor of a legalized abortion bill, then we say that this person is in an incongruent state. This incongruity (presented in Figure 5–5) is caused by an

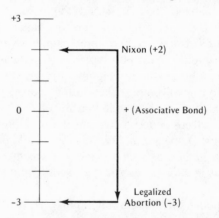

Figure 5–5. The Incongruent State According to the Congruity Principle

associative bond between the source and the idea. Incongruity may also occur, although to a lesser extent, if there is a dissociative bond between the source and the idea (President Nixon has come out against a legalized abortion bill). Osgood and Tannenbaum developed a simple mathematical formula to calculate the changes the person has to make in his attitudes toward the source and the idea. Let the rating of the source be denoted as S, that of the idea as I, and the relative magnitudes of difference between the source rating and the idea as D_S and D_I. The attitude changes of the person toward the source (AC_S) and toward the idea (AC_I) are computed from the following:

$$AC_S = \frac{|\ I\ |}{|\ S\ | + |\ I\ |} \cdot D_S \qquad AC_I = \frac{|\ S\ |}{|\ S\ | + |\ I\ |} \cdot D_I$$

where $D_S = I - S$, and $D_I = S - I$

Thus, the attitude change toward President Nixon of the person under discussion would be:

$$AC_S = \frac{|-3|}{|\ 2\ | + |\ 3\ |}\ (-5) = -3$$

And the attitude change toward legalized abortion would be:

$$AC_I = \frac{|+2|}{|\ 2\ | + |\ 3\ |}\ (5) = +2$$

Thus, the person achieves congruity in his cognition when he shifts his rating of President Nixon downward for three points on the scale and his rating of legalized abortion upward two points on the scale. The final congruent position of his attitudes converges at -1, as presented in Figure 5–6.

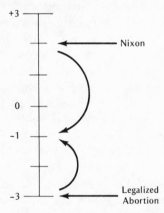

Figure 5–6. The Congruence Position Reached According to the Congruity Principle

In the dissociative bond situation—President Nixon condemns legalized abortion—the formulas would be the same except for the computations of the D's. Now the D's become the absolute (positive) distance between the two ratings from the zero point ($D_S = D_I = \Big|\ |\ I\ | - |\ S\ |\ \Big|$).

$$AC_S = \frac{3}{2+3}\ (1) = +0.60 \qquad AC_I = \frac{2}{2+3}\ (1) = +0.40$$

The final congruent position of the person's attitudes now becomes a $+2.60$ toward President Nixon and a -2.60 toward legalized abortion. The rationale behind this phenomenon—that his attitude toward legalized abortion changes in a positive direction—is as follows: because President Nixon makes a negative statement about legalized abortion, his original negative attitude toward legalized abortion is justified and supported. This confirmation of his attitudes toward both President Nixon and legalized abortion relaxes his defense mechanism against the idea and "eases" his resentment against the concept, even though he is still quite firm in his negative attitude toward legalizing abortion.

The principle was put to a test in an experiment run by Tannenbaum (1953). Using bogus newspaper articles to present the assertions of pretested pairs of a source (Chicago Tribune, Senator Taft, and "labor leaders") and an object (abstract art, accelerated college programs, and legalized gambling), he found that the principle predicted the directions quite well. However, predictive power was improved with two additional modifications. He found that his subjects consistently changed their attitudes more toward the objects than toward the sources. Apparently, the subjects thought the sources more important than they did the objects. This adjustment was also suggested by Rokeach and Rothman (1965), who modified the congruity formula by incorporating into it the magnitude of importance of the sources and ideas. Another consistent variation that Tannenbaum found in his data which was not explained by the principle was that when the two initial attitudes were at or near the opposite extremes, an associative bond, instead of bringing the two attitudes toward each other, would be rejected as false. Tannenbaum found it necessary to correct this type of response which contradicts the predicted outcome of the congruity principle and called it "correction for incredulity." For example, if the message states that Pope Paul is for legalized abortion and if the subject rates the Pope very favorably and legalized abortion very unfavorably, the subject may simply reject the message.

Another problem with the principle arises when two positively (or negatively) rated attitudes are associatively bound. Kerrick (Osgood, 1960) found that in this situation the compromise of attitudes did not occur. Instead, he found a summation effect; the two attitudes were both more favorably (or unfavorably) rated as a result of the associative assertion than they were alone. Similar results were obtained by Fishbein and his associates (Fishbein and Hunter, 1964; Fishbein, 1965; Triandis and Fishbein, 1965). One explanation for this contradiction of the principle of congruity may be that the latter applies to situations where incongruent relationship occurs. When the assertion does not create any incongruity in the situation, as in the case of an associative bond between two positive or negative attitudes, the assumption of the principle of congruity is violated and therefore does not apply.

THE COGNITIVE DISSONANCE MODEL

Festinger (1957) proposed a theory of cognitive dissonance which has had an important impact on attitude change research. He was interested in the relationship between two cognitive elements in a person. Cognitive elements are defined as bits of knowledge, or opinions or beliefs, about oneself, about one's behavior, or about one's surroundings. According to Festinger, *two or more elements are in a dissonant relation if, considering the elements alone, the obverse of one would follow from the other.* The most often cited and researched condition concerns two such elements — for example, an attitude and a behavior. If a person believes that smoking may cause lung cancer and yet continues to smoke, a dissonance is created. When a dissonance occurs within a person, *Festinger feels the following are the consequent hypotheses:*

1. *The existence of dissonance creates psychological tension or discomfort and will motivate the person to reduce the dissonance and achieve consonance.*

2. *When dissonance exists, not only will the person attempt to reduce it, but he will actively attempt to avoid situations and information which would increase dissonance.*

Thus, the theory consists of two portions for empirical testing: the first portion concerns *ways of reducing dissonance* and the second concerns *ways of avoiding situations and information* which would increase the dissonance. The magnitude of dissonance, remaining a largely unsolved quantification problem, is roughly defined as a function of two things: (1) the importance of the elements and (2) the weighed proportion of the elements which are in a dissonant relationship (Kiesler, Collins, and Miller, 1966, pp. 194–196).

Festinger recognized *three means of dissonance reduction:* (1) *the person may change a cognitive element related to his behavior*—for example, he may undergo a behavioral change or a denial or distortion of the behavior; (2) *the person may change a cognitive element related to his environment,* including both the physical and psychological environment; or (3) *the person may reduce dissonance by adding new cognitive elements to one cluster or the other or to both.* Numerous studies have applied the dissonance principle to attitude change. However, most of the studies have been designed in such a manner that *instead of attempting to identify the conditions under which each of the ways of dissonance reduction might occur, the researchers investigate whether a specific way of dissonance reduction would occur if other potential ways were experimentally blocked off.*

Many direct empirical studies have been made to test the *hypothesis concerning the avoidance of dissonant situations and information.* The general conclusion is that *the evidence fails to support the hypothesis.*

Because of the greater flexibility allowed by the first hypothesis and the generally unfruitful results from the testing of the second hypothesis, the literature on dissonance theory usually gives much greater attention to the first hypothesis data while only briefly mentioning the failure to confirm the second hypothesis. Our discussion will therefore focus on the available data concerning dissonance reduction. But the reader is reminded that the *dissonance theory is handicapped by unfruitful attempts to confirm one of its two basic hypotheses.* I will now describe two major areas of research concerned with applying the principle of cognitive dissonance reduction to attitude change.

Justification of Choice Over Alternatives: Postdecision Studies

According to Festinger (1957), *conflict occurs before a person makes a decision on a certain issue and when he is faced with alternatives or choices. Dissonance occurs only after a person has made, and when he is trying to justify, a decision.* Thus, ideal situations in which dissonance can occur and in which to study dissonance reduction are when a person has made a decision, when the decision is important, when the chosen course is not very attractive, when the unchosen alternative(s) is attractive, or when the chosen and unchosen alternatives are not similar (Kiesler, Collins, and Miller, 1969, p. 201).

One of the earliest and best-known experiments to test the postdecision area of the dissonance theory was conducted by Brehm (1956). In this experiment, the subjects were first asked to rate eight objects of approximately equivalent price in terms of the objects' attractiveness to them. The objects included such things as a toaster and a silk screen print. Then, each subject was assigned to one of two conditions. In one condition, the subjects were given what they had chosen. This group served as the control group. In the other condition, each subject was told that he could choose between two objects. The experimenter evaluated the initial ratings of the objects by the subjects and manipulated the objects offered the subjects to choose from. Half of the subjects had rated the two objects presented as about equally attractive to them. The other half of the subjects had initially rated the two objects presented quite differently (one high and the other low). Thus, the experimenter created a high dissonance in the first group of subjects, who confronted a decision between two equally attractive objects, and a low dissonance in the second group of subjects. After each subject had made his choice, the selected object was given to him. It was expected that the high-dissonance group, to whom both alternatives were attractive, would experience much more dissonance than the low-dissonance group, for whom one object was attractive and the other was not. The subjects were then asked to read bogus research reports on four of the objects. Each of the reports discussed both good and bad aspects of the objects. For half the experimental subjects, these research reports dealt with objects not involved in the choice. For the other half, two of the reports were about objects involved in the choice. It was expected that providing information on the choice objects would reduce the dissonance. Finally, the subjects were asked to re-rate the attractiveness of the eight objects.

Brehm expected that the experimental design would allow the dissonance to be reduced in one of two ways: (1) by increasing the perceived attractiveness of the chosen object or (2) by decreasing the perceived attractiveness of the unchosen object. He predicted that the high-dissonance group subjects would indicate more of both (1) and (2). The results are shown in Table 5–4, with the first column indicating the initial ratings,

TABLE 5–4. POSTDECISION CHANGES IN ATTRACTIVENESS OF ALTERNATIVES

	N	Initial Rating	Rating Change	Corrected Rating Change
No Research Reports				
Low dissonance	33			
Chosen		5.98	.33	.38[b]
Unchosen		3.54	− .14	− .24
Total change[a]			− .47	− .62[b]
High dissonance	27			
Chosen		6.19	.20	.26
Unchosen		5.23	− .66[c]	− .66[c]
Total change			− .86[c]	− .92[c]
Research Reports				
Low dissonance	30			
Chosen		6.00	− .30	.11
Unchosen		3.47	.07	.00
Total change			.37	.11
High dissonance	27			
Chosen		6.05	− .04	.38[b]
Unchosen		5.07	− .64[c]	− .41[b]
Total change			− .60[b]	− .79[c]
Gift Only	30	5.19	− .40[c]	.00

SOURCE: Adapted from Brehm, 1956.

[a]Total change in the direction of dissonance reduction. A minus sign under total change indicates a reduction of dissonance.
[b]Statistically significantly different from zero change (p < .05).
[c]Statistically significantly different from zero change (p < .01).

the second column containing the net change between the second rating and the initial rating, and the third column presenting the "corrected rating change." This third measure was necessary because the objects initially differed in attractiveness and there might have been differential statistical regressions. Thus, the "corrected rating change" represents the raw change score minus the mean change of items not involved in the choice but rated approximately the same on the initial rating. In a sense, they were the standard deviation scores. As can be seen in Table 5–4, there was significant dissonance reduction in three of the four experimental conditions. After reading the research reports on the choice objects, high-dissonance subjects showed significantly more evidence of dissonance reduction than did low-dissonance subjects. With no research reports on the choice subjects, high-dissonance subjects also tended to show greater dissonance reduction than did low-dissonance subjects, though the difference was not significant. Subsequent studies (Ehrlich, Guttman, Schönbach, and Mills, 1957; Brehm and Cohen, 1959a; Deutsch, Krauss, and Rosenau, 1962; Brock, 1963; Walster, 1964) generally supported the following findings: (1) *dissonance reduction occurs only when the decision made is a commitment and important, or* (2) *when the chosen and unchosen alternatives are equally attractive, and* (3) *similarity among alternatives does not affect the amount of dissonance reduction as predicted.* Thus, studies in the area of postdecision justification generally confirm two of the three predictions made by the cognitive dissonance theorists.

Justification of Forced Compliance: Postbehavioral Studies

In postdecision studies, the subject is given a choice among the alternatives and thus in theory he has a free choice. What happens when he is forced to behave in a manner contradictory to his beliefs or attitudes—in short, when he is given no choice? This area is usually called the forced compliance dissonance. Again, the basic procedure in experiments is to ask the subject to state his attitudes and beliefs on a number of issues. Then, he is asked to become involved in a task which is either low on his attitudinal scale or unusually boring and tedious. It is assumed that the subject is confronted here with a dissonance situation since his behavioral involvement is not justified either by his attitude or by the behavior's attractiveness. A certain stimulus, such as differential amounts of reward or pressure of various kinds (money, etc.), is then introduced into the situation. When the reward or pressure is high, it is hypothesized, the reward or pressure will justify the unpleasant or unliked behavior; therefore the dissonance will be reduced. When the reward or pressure is low, it is hypothesized, the behavior will remain unjustified; therefore, the subject will be forced to justify his behavior by changing his attitude—the only way the subject can reduce his dissonance.

Probably the best-known experiment in this area was that conducted by Festinger and Carlsmith (1959). In this experiment, the subject was asked to perform an extremely dull and tedious task—putting spools in trays and turning pegs for one hour. After the task, the subject was requested to tell the next person (actually a confederate of the experimenters) who would perform the same task that the task was a pleasant one. If she agreed to do it, she was paid. Half the consenting subjects were paid $1.00 and the other half $20.00. Other subjects serving as the control group performed the task and were dismissed. On a later occasion, totally unrelated to the experimental situation, the classes involving the subjects were asked to respond to questionnaires regarding their latest participation in psychological experiments and to describe how enjoyable the experiments had been. According to the hypothesis, the subjects receiving the high reward ($20.00) would rate the task as less enjoyable than those receiving the low reward ($1.00). The data confirmed the differential effect, with a *greater number of the low-reward subjects than of the high-reward and control groups rating the task more enjoyable.*

Cohen (1962) extended the basic experiment by varying the levels of reward ($.50, $1.00, $5.00, $10.00) and by requesting his subjects to write an essay (contrary to their private views on the issue) "in favor of the actions of the police in handling a campus riot." The data confirmed that *the smaller the reward, the greater the dissonance reduction* (in changing the subjects' private views about the police action).

Other investigators (Brehm and Crocker, 1962; Brehm, 1962c) studied the effect of rewards on hunger and thirst. The data showed that the greater the dissonance induced by the performance and the lower the reward, the less the amount of food or water ordered and consumed. It has also been found that the more negative the character of the person or persons inducing the subject to perform the discrepant act, the greater the attitude change (Smith, 1961; Weick, 1964; Zimbardo, Weisenberg, Firstone, and Levy, 1965; Kiesler and De Salvo, 1967); that the less "coerced" the subject is to perform the act, the greater the subsequent attitude change (Brehm and Cohen, 1959b; Brehm, 1962b, pp. 84–88; Aronson and Carlsmith, 1963; Freedman, 1965) that greater perceived choice in performing the discrepant act leads to greater dissonance and greater predicted attitude change toward consonance with the act (Brehm and Cohen, 1959b; Davis and Jones, 1960; Brock, 1962; Brock and Buss, 1962; Cohen and Latané, 1962, pp. 88-91; Hall, 1964); and that the more negative the behavior the person performs is, or the more negative the information about the dissonant situation, or the greater the amount of effort the person must expend to perform the discrepant behavior, the greater the dissonance will be (Aronson and Mills, 1959; Brehm and Cohen, 1959b; Brehm, 1960; Aronson, 1961; Cohen and Zimbardo, 1962; Gerard and Mathewson, 1966).

Other Relevant Research

Personality correlates with the degree of dissonance have also been studied. For example, Bremel (1962, 1963) and Kiesler and Singer (1963) found that high self-esteem subjects tended to experience higher dissonance than did low self-esteem subjects. Gerard (1961) found that subjects whose ability had been rated high experienced more dissonance in compliance than did subjects of low ability, and that in order to reduce that dissonance, they became more attracted to the group and modified their behavior in the direction of the group's on a subsequent series of trials.

Controversies Over the Dissonance Theory

While numerous researchers have designed various experimental conditions and claimed confirmation of certain aspects of the dissonance theory, many investigators have also raised important questions and made severe criticisms of the theory and the studies. In general, the controversy

relates to three problems: *the limitations of the applications of the dissonance theory, the gap between the theory and the empirical data, and
the failure to confirm the hypothesis on information avoidance.*

1. Limitations of the dissonance theory: A number of researchers
(Janis, 1959; Rosenberg, 1960; Elms and Janis, 1965; Janis and Gilmore,
1965; Rosenberg, 1965; Elms, 1967) have proposed theories of incentive
effects with predictions contrary to those of dissonance theory. They argue
that a larger incentive increases a person's motivation to think up all the
good arguments he can and at the same time to suppress the negative arguments, and that this in turn increases the chances of acceptance of the new
attitude position (Janis and Gilmore, 1965, pp. 17–19). While definitive
empirical data for the counterhypothesis are lacking, Zimbardo (1965)
and others have introduced an additional variable to resolve the conflict
—the effect of differential effort. The prediction is that the greater the effort
expended in a counterattitudinal task, the greater the dissonance aroused.
In other words, dissonance theory loses its predictive power over the effects
of incentives if the degree of effort remains uncontrolled. If higher-payment
subjects work harder at the task, the theoretical sources of dissonance
compete with one another (Kiesler, Collins, and Miller, 1969, p. 214).
Other proposed intervening variables on the effects of incentives on dissonance reduction include (1) extraneous rewards, (2) attention effects,
(3) selective retention effects, and (4) improvisation factors (Hovland, Janis,
and Kelley, 1953, pp. 233–234). Most of these factors remain unexplored.

Another limiting factor, proposed by Carlsmith, Collins, and Helmreich
(1966), concerns the commitment of the subjects. They argue that writing
counterattitudinal essays does not in and of itself produce dissonance.
Rather, it merely indicates the intellectual ability of the subject to perform
a task which runs counter to his beliefs. In the experiment they conducted,
they found a negative relationship between incentive and attitude change,
as predicted by the dissonance theory, under the face-to-face condition,
but a positive relationship under the anonymous condition.

Still another proposed limiting factor of the dissonance theory concerns
the degree of perceived choice in performing discrepant behavior or tasks
(Linder, Cooper, and Jones, 1967). It was found that dissonance and dissonance reduction occur only under the free-choice conditions. Under
no-choice conditions, the results were in the opposite direction (although
not significantly so). Interestingly, they utilized essay writing as the task
and yet produced the dissonance effect, whereas Carlsmith et al. argue that
essay writing should not arouse dissonance.

The empirical evidence indicates some limiting and intervening variables
which qualify the conditions of the dissonance theory. However, specific
and precise descriptions and evidence of the relationships between these
variables and the dissonance effect and among these variables themselves
are thus far incomplete and quite unclear.

2. The gap between the theory and the data: Questions have been raised as to whether the empirical data obtained are indeed derivations of the dissonance theory. Alternative theoretical propositions have been offered to explain the empirical data. One such alternative was suggested by Bem. In a number of studies (Bem, 1965, 1967; Jones, 1966), Bem and his associates gave subjects (observers) information about one "subject" in a dissonance experiment, for example, that the "subject" was paid a certain amount of money for performing a dull task and for telling another person it was actually fun. Bem then asked his subjects to evaluate that "subject's" opinion of the task. Bem's observers rated the "subject" who was paid less as being more favorable to the task. These interpersonal replications of the dissonance experiments (including both the postdecision and forced compliance types) were offered as evidence by Bem that the same process went on for the subjects in the dissonance experiments. That the subjects told themselves, "I did it for 50 cents, I guess I did like the task," is not, according to Bem, the result of an aversive motivational state (dissonance) but, rather, the result of a passive process by which the person infers his own attitudes from his behavior. Thus, Bem argues that people learn to label their own internal states and those of others by reference to overt behavior.

However, Bem's studies were criticized by Jones et al. (Jones, Linder, Kiesler, Zanna, and Brehm, 1968). These researchers contended that Bem's observer-subjects were not behaving according to his hypothesis of self-perception, but were merely judging differential hypothetical subject self-selection (Jones et al., 1968, p. 249). They suspected that Bem's observers could be thought of as ignoring the possible systematic effects of the dissonant act itself and as assuming that the positive attitude inferred from the low-payment condition existed prior to the payment or performance of the dissonant act. These researchers replicated Bem's results with the procedures Bem utilized. Then, they provided the observers with the pretest scores of the "subject" (the initial attitude of the "subject"); the result did not reproduce Bem's effect. Their effort, however, only raised questions concerning the experimental design of some of Bem's research (dealing with the postdecision type). Since many of the original dissonance experiments in the forced compliance area did not pretest the subjects' initial attitudes toward the task they were to perform, these researchers could not refute Bem's results in that area. They also admitted that they could only state that Bem's experiments in some cases did not test his alternative explanation of dissonance phenomena but that they could not rule out the possible validity of Bem's theory itself. Thus, Bem's alternative to dissonance theory remains untested.

3. Failure to confirm the avoidance of dissonant information: One of the two original hypotheses forwarded by Festinger states that when dissonance exists, not only will the person attempt to reduce it, but he will actively attempt to avoid situations and information that would increase the dis-

sonance. As we mentioned earlier, empirical studies time and again have failed to confirm the hypothesis (Cohen, Brehm, and Latané, 1959; Mills, Aronson, and Robinson, 1959; Adams, 1961; Rosen, 1961; Canon, 1964; Freedman, 1965; Freedman and Sears, 1966; Mills, 1966). Failure to confirm the hypothesis, however, does not negate the hypothesis itself. Researchers (for example, Mills, 1966) have proposed that under some circumstances perhaps the hypothesis can be confirmed. This topic provides an important challenge to dissonance theorists. Unless they can specify the intervening variables inducing the confirmation of the hypothesis (the only one of the two original hypotheses which provides a statement for direct empirical tests), the dissonance theory will suffer.

Criticisms of the Dissonance Theory

Kiesler, Collins, and Miller (1969) listed a host of criticisms (pp. 232–237) that have been voiced relative to the theory and empirical evidence of the dissonance theory. Some of these criticisms are:

1. It is extremely difficult, if not impossible, to make precise, quantitative measurements of the degree of dissonance. We have not devised measures to quantify a person's cognitions before he arrives at the experiment, to ascertain the importance of each of these cognitions, to obtain more information about what is and what is not a cognition, or, lastly, to determine the relevance of each of these cognitions for the experimental situation (p. 232).

2. How will dissonance be reduced? Researchers tend to block off alternatives in their experiments in testing specific consequences of dissonance. But the whole problem of what the person might have done had alternative avenues of escape not been blocked off is unexplored (p. 232).

3. The question of individual differences requires further consideration. Researchers have just begun to explore the personality and cognitive traits which induce varying degrees of dissonance and alternatives of dissonance reduction, yet preliminary results show that individual differences play an important role in the results of dissonance experiments.

4. Precise predictions are impeded by the difficulty of measuring a cognitive element's resistance to change. Central to the dissonance theory is the relative degree of resistance to change among the cognitive elements, since the theory hypothesizes that the cognitive element with the least resistant potential will be the one that will undergo change. Yet we do not know how to measure precisely the relative resistance to change of the cognitive elements.

5. How do we measure the importance of an element? The importance of the cognitive elements for each person also needs further study. Rokeach has specified the various types of elements in a person's cognitive system, ranging from the central beliefs, to values, to the peripheral attitudes. Future research incorporating the magnitudes of the cognitive elements would enhance the evaluation of potential dissonance.

6. Are the alternative modes of dissonance reduction an either-or proposition? In most experiments, the subjects could either change their attitude in the direction advocated or reject the communication. Objection has been made to this dichotomization (Sherif, Sherif, and Nebergall, 1965) and suggestions offered that other alternatives, such as distortion of the information, are just as valid.

7. How can one specify when one cognition "psychologically implies the obverse" of the other? We need direct measures to ascertain whether the two cognitive elements are in fact regarded as the obverse of one another. This problem is complicated, moreover, because subjects show individual differences, such as differences in degree of self-esteem. Such differences imply that cognitive elements, perceived as obverse by one subject, may not be so perceived by another.

8. Can the dissonance theory be disproved? It has been contended that many empirical data supporting the dissonance theory can be explained away with different propositions. Again, this points to the gap between the theory and the data. Since the one hypothesis which has gathered an enormous amount of supportive data ("The existence of dissonance creates psychological tension or discomfort and will motivate the person to reduce the dissonance and achieve consonance") is in itself very flexible and loose, an almost infinite number of designs and alternatives can be offered and have been offered as proof. Instead of blocking off alternatives and forcing a specific reduction alternative designed by the experimenter, one needs to ascertain the conditions under which a certain alternative would be chosen by the subjects over other alternatives to reduce the dissonance created.

COMPARISONS OF THE COGNITIVE MODELS

All the cognitive models have been developed upon the following working *assumptions:*

1. *An individual develops and maintains a balance among his various cognitive elements or states.* Thus, it is assumed that there is a unidimensionality to the cognitive structure. All cognitive elements are perceived as either compatible or not compatible. The models do not apply to areas where compartmentalization or multidimensionality of the cognitive structure is contemplated.

2. *A person perceiving any stimulus as linked and perceiving it further as cognitively different from existing cognitive elements feels unpleasant and painful tension.*

3. *These psychological tensions lead to attempts to reduce the perceived differences among the cognitive elements.*

4. *Reduction of the cognitive differences in turn reduces the tension and thereby restores the person's balance of cognitive elements or states.* The extent of the reduction is a function of the magnitude of the tension.

Based upon these assumptions (or axioms, as some call them), the different cognitive models generate theories applying to various conditions and circumstances. Although the results derived from these cognitive models may look superficially different or even contradictory, such differences can usually be resolved as the conditions and circumstances of the various proposed theoretical approaches are specified. I will now compare the conditions and circumstances which tend to differentiate the various cognitive models as they are applied to the study of attitude change. As shown in Table 5–5, the discussion will focus on differences in substance, rather than on differences in degree, such as the extent of the perceptual or psychological differences among the cognitive elements in each model. It has been suggested, for example, that while slight inconsistency among the elements is considered in Heider's balance model, in Newcomb's co-orientation model, and in Osgood's congruity principle, only elements perceived as "obversive" of one another are considered in the dissonance theory. Such a distinction would induce arguments from disciples of each theoretical position and finally lose its usefulness when borderline cases are presented as counterevidence.

TABLE 5–5. COMPARISONS OF THE COGNITIVE MODELS

Characteristic	Heider's balance model	Newcomb's co-orientation model	Osgood's congruity model	Festinger's dissonance theory
Levels of analysis	Intrapersonal	Interpersonal	Intrapersonal	Intrapersonal
Cognitive elements considered	Source, object	Source, object	Source, object	Two or more objects
Assumed assertion between elements	Yes	Yes	Yes	No
Reduction strategy studied	Perceived attitude discrepancy leading to own attitude change	Perceived attitude discrepancy leading to own attitude or behavioral change	Perceived attitude discrepancy leading to own attitude change	Behavioral change leading to attitude change
Tension reduction route	Selection among alternative attitudes	Selection among alternative attitudes and behaviors	Compromise	Justification
Precision	Low	Low-moderate	High	Low
Flexibility	Moderate	Moderate	Low	High

1. *The models differ in the intra- or interpersonal dimension.* While Heider's model, Osgood's principle, and Festinger's theory focus on the psychological and cognitive structure within an individual, Newcomb's model specifically emphasizes the co-orientational aspect. Newcomb's model thus is an interpersonal one.

2. *The cognitive elements considered by the models are also different.* Heider's model, Newcomb's model, and Osgood's principle all take into

consideration a person's attitude toward *another person* and his attitude toward *an object (idea).* Festinger's model concerns a person's evaluation of *two objects.* Although the first three models could incorporate objects only, the theoretical discussion, as well as the empirical evidence, focuses on one or more sources and one object or idea.

3. *Three of the four models assume some assertion between the cognitive elements.* In Heider's model, for example, the person or source has a certain attitude, either positive or negative, toward the object, as well as toward the person in question. Newcomb's model postulates a similar assertion, although the assertion differs in degree and in that it is multidirectional. Osgood's congruity principle also assumes some binding, either associative or dissociative, between the source and the idea. Festinger's model, on the other hand, does not assume an explicit linkage between the cognitive elements. For example, the discrepant behavior is not explicitly presented to the subject as something that negates his initial attitude, even though such a relationship is strongly implied.

4. *The reduction strategy devised or considered also differs among the models.* For Heider, Newcomb, and Osgood, the strategy is that since there is perceived *attitudinal discrepancy,* certain attitudinal change will take place. For Festinger, the strategy is that since there is *discrepancy between the initial attitude and the behavior,* there will be certain attitudinal change. Such attitudinal change will take place, however, only if other channels of escape have been blocked off or ruled out; this blocking principle is assumed or used in all four models.

5. *The method of tension reduction also differs from model to model.* Heider sees that change results from a process of *selection* among several alternative attitudes for the person in question. The person thus may change one or more of several attitudes—he may either actually change or distort his perception—to restore the balance state. Newcomb followed the method proposed by Heider, but added behavioral changes as other alternatives. For Newcomb, the person in question may disengage himself from the attitudinal configuration to strive toward symmetry. The congruity principle asserts the principle of *compromise* among attitudes in the reduction and elimination of the *incongruence.* It assumes that all attitudes involved will undergo change—toward a compromise position. The dissonance theory sees the *justification* of the discrepant cognitive element —mostly the behavior—as the solution. The person in question will change his attitude to better suit his behavior. This attitudinal change results from an effort to justify the behavior or decision the person has opted for.

6. *In terms of precision of measurement, Osgood's congruity formulas are the most rigorous.* The formulas provide precise measurement as to the prediction of the model. Newcomb's model and other modifications of his model, such as the work of Cartwright and Harary (1956, 1970), are also precise, although the solution may not always be unique. That is, their

model and their mathematical formulas may result in several minimal ways by which the attitudinal configuration can eliminate its imbalance; attitude changes of several different minimal sets of persons may be equally effective in reducing or eliminating the group imbalance. Heider's model is rather low in precision; the degree of attitudes is not involved. The same can be said about the dissonance theory; the degree of dissonance still poses a strong challenge to many researchers in the field.

7. *The greater the flexibility a model usually shows, the less its precision.* Because of the rigid prediction of the congruity principle, the principle is very inflexible—either the prediction is confirmed or it is not confirmed. For Heider and Newcomb, because several alternatives are posed, the failure to predict one solution does not necessarily imply the failure of the model. Other alternatives may be present and tested. The dissonance theory is probably the most flexible of all cognitive models of attitude change. Since the theory specifies the basic process of the change, all possible routes associated with the cognitive elements as perceived by the person in question may be considered as hypotheses of the theory. The research efforts have dealt with monetary rewards, incentives, forced compliance, decision-making, and numerous other factors. Any of these may be brought into the hypothesis or blocked off from the experimental design.

It should be clear by now that any discussion of the results derived from the various congitive models would be completely meaningless unless the basic differences in the models' assumptions, structures, reduction strategy and method, and so forth are established. But even when these differences are considered, the results are still difficult to compare, for such differences almost prohibit any direct comparisons. The important task now is to integrate the various theories of cognition with regard to attitude change and to specify the various conditions and constraints, as forwarded by each of the theories, under which attitude change does or does not occur.

Comparisons Among the Component Approach, the Social Judgment Approach, and the Cognitive Approach

On the surface, the three approaches to the study of attitude change differ drastically and the results in many instances seem rather contradictory. For example, the component approach indicates that the greater the perceived credibility of the source, the more attitude change will result, while the dissonance theory predicts that the lower the perceived self-esteem of the source, the greater the dissonance and therefore the greater the subsequent change. The social judgment theory states that the greater the discrepancy between a person's attitude and the position advocated in the message, the less the attitude change. Dissonance theory, on the other hand, hypothesizes that the discrepancy actually induces dissonance and thus possibly attitude change. Is it true, then, that the various approaches have resulted in mutually incompatible findings? The answer is a necessary no. Researchers using these intrinsically different approaches apply different concepts, use different methods and measurements, test in different experimental conditions, and produce different results. Just as the various models of the cognitive approach focus on different aspects of the cognitive process and produce different results, so do the three general approaches to attitude change differ in many respects. It has been pointed out by Campbell, for example, that different theoretical language has been used to discuss the different approaches, thus magnifying the differences among the approaches (1963).

Aside from such obvious terminological differences, there are several *fundamental differences* among the various approaches which provide crucial clues for the assessment of the different results as well as for the potential integration of the various approaches to the study of attitude change in the future.

1. *Level of theorization:* A theory consists of several levels or propositions. The highest level specifies some simple but crucial relationships among a limited number of concepts which may not have any empirical equivalence. On the lower level, the propositions specify derived relationships among the concepts from the highest level of theoretical statements which may have empirical equivalence. On the lowest level of theoretical propositions, the statements specify relationships among empirically verifiable variables. Thus, the variables and the relationships can be directly tested in the empirical and observable world. It is also on the lowest level of theoretical propositions that both the inductive and deductive approaches of theory building converge. More discussion on theory building and other related topics will appear in the final chapter of this book. Here, I merely want to point out that the three approaches to the investigation of attitude change differ drastically on the level of theorization. *The cognitive approach represents a very high level of theorization* in that it is abstract concepts that are discussed in the theory—the cognitive elements and their relationships and the possible consequences of relationship disruption (dissonance). *The theory itself is not subject to empirical testing.* Further derivations from the theory are necessary before empirical examination of the theory becomes possible. Thus, for example, the lower level of statements must include some concepts or variables such as forced compliance, postdecision, and so forth. *The component approach,* on the other hand, *exists on a low theoretical level.* Most of the variables discussed in the approach can be easily operationalized and submitted to testing. Thus, a fear-appealing message can be constructed from empirical data and then used

as a variable to test its effect on attitude change. Likewise, source credibility (for instance, trustworthiness or expertise) can be empirically and directly constructed and used to test its effect on attitude change. *The social judgment approach is somewhere in between in its theorization level.* While it involves some concepts such as social judgment, it develops specific rating and rating methodology to operationalize the concept and empirically focus on the intermediary variables such as ego-involvement and discrepancy.

Because the various approaches address themselves to different levels of theoretical discourse, each confronts different sets of problems. For example, the cognitive approach inevitably faces the problem of whether the lower levels of derived propositions and hypotheses actually represent true tests of the theory. Furthermore, it is difficult to formulate propositions that might refute the theory, because the concepts are abstract and the relationships have such broad alternative implications. The component approach, on the other hand, suffers in that it is unable to move up toward higher levels of propositions and theorization. Recently, Weiss (1962) undertook to remedy this shortcoming by attempting to build a Hull–Spencer–type behavior theory for the component approach. Although the analogy is far from complete and verification is only just being initiated, the attempt certainly points to the urgent need for research in this area of the component approach because of its so-far low level of theorization. Unfortunately, the social judgment approach, being in the middle somewhere, is plagued by problems of both kinds. On the one hand, it lacks a consistent abstract level of concepts of involvement and scale extremity. On the other hand, the specific empirical scaling methodology, a Thurston scale, has also met with strong criticism. However, such intermediary theoretical statements are probably most difficult ones; since the social judgment approach attempts to bridge the gap between abstract theory and empirical data, its indifferent success in achieving this goal is not surprising and should not be used to downgrade its important position in theorization.

2. *Area of focus:* The focuses of the approaches also differ. *The cognitive theories are concerned foremost with the phenomenon of cognitive dissonance and consonance.* From this concern for cognitive dissonance and consonance, various consequences are derived. When other potential consequences are experimentally blocked off, one of the derived consequences of cognitive dissonance is attitude change. Thus, the approach is a *divergent one, starting with a fundamental theoretical statement and enumerating an almost infinite number of consequences from the statement.* *The component approach,* on the other hand, *focuses on the phenomenon of attitude change* and asks what conceptual factors would lead to attitude change. Thus, the approach is a *convergent one; it looks for the various potential causal or interdependent factors that would lead to attitude change.* As McGuire (1968) pointed out, the cognitive approach focuses

on the independent variable and the component approach focuses on the dependent variable. Because of the divergent approach of the cognitive models, attitude change is but one of the many possible outcomes or dependent variables. Other outcomes include some behavioral change, dissociation between cognitive elements, distortion of the cognitive elements, and so forth. It has so happened that most of the cognitive research deals with attitude change, while all other potential outcomes are blocked off experimentally. The component approach also considers cognitive elements such as information increment and statements about beliefs. But such consideration is one of the numerous independent variables studied. The component researchers are not yet prepared to state that the cognitive consideration is the most important among the variables studied.

3. *A priori assumption:* The basic assumption of the cognitive approach is that cognitive dissonance is intolerable and thus induces possible attitude change. The component approach operates more under the learning assumption: cumulative experience and learning account for changes. The social judgment approach assumes that a person evaluates incoming messages in terms of his reference groups or reference attitudes. Whether cognitive dissonance is indeed intolerable and thus leads to possible attitude change has been questioned (McGuire, 1968). Questions have also been raised as to whether the judgment effects really were necessary to explain the empirical findings in the social judgment approach and to explain changes due to nonlearning situations. In this sense, the models with a priori assumptions only operate within the boundary where the assumptions are held true. Outside this boundary, the approach has specified nothing and may not apply.

4. *Measurements and methodology:* McGuire (1968) points out some measuring and methodological differences between the component approach and the cognitive approach. The component approach tends to control extraneous variables such as age, sex, and education by way of covariance, taking these factors into account after the experiment. The cognitive approach tends to control the extraneous variables by way of elimination, holding these variables at a constant level while the experiment is being conducted. The component approach, because of its focus on the dependent variable—attitude change—usually employs an elaborate and precise measurement of attitude, while it is less rigorous about the measurement of the independent variables. The cognitive approach, on the other hand, focuses on the measurement of the independent variable—the cognitive elements and their relationship—rather than on the measurement of the dependent variable—attitude change. These methodological differences derive directly from the differential theoretical orientation of the two approaches, as discussed in Chapter 1.

On the surface, the component approach seems most appropriate for discussion in a book on human communication, because it focuses on the various components of human communication situations. This argument has its merits. It would be foolish, however, for human communication researchers to ignore the contributions of the cognitive and social judgment approaches. Insofar as the ultimate goal of scientific exploration is to integrate observable data within parsimonious and highest-order theoretical statements, we cannot ignore the potential routes to such integration, and the cognitive and social judgment approaches certainly provide important clues, if they do nothing else, in our search for such theoretical integration. They become more meaningful to us when we realize that in most of the situations created in experiments, these two approaches utilize various aspects of human communication as means of manipulation or control. The initial link between these approaches and eventual human communication theories has been established both on theoretical and empirical grounds.

6

The Behavioral Dimension of Communication's Influence: DECISION AND ACTION

While the literature on the psychological influence of human communication is concentrated under the rubrics of persuasion and attitude change and can easily be found in psychological journals and books, the literature on the behavioral influence of human communication is scattered throughout many social, psychological, and other disciplinary journals and books, and cannot be easily retrieved. The diffuseness of the literature stems primarily from the problem of defining behavior and behavioral change.

Behavior, in contrast to attitude, can be defined as an *overt gesture indicating a person's preference and commitment in some observable activity.* The gesture may involve social or economic investment (such as voting for a certain candidate in an election or buying a specific brand of detergent), time and physical allocation (participating in a political demonstration, going to a fraternity party, or watching a football game on television), or any of a number of other forms. While most of the behavioral indicators can easily be distinguished from attitudes, there is a thin line of demarcation between the two concepts mainly due to the problem of measurement. While, ideally, behavior should be measured by the actual gesture, many cases do not permit such direct measure. More often than not, the measure of the behavior has to rely on the testimony of the person in question—on his expressed description of his gesture or activity. Since in many cases, attitude is also measured along with opinion, it is not entirely possible to distinguish between an opinion representing an attitude and a gesture representing a behavior. Even the public-private distinction loses its usefulness when some gestures are committed for private purposes only and are not intended for public observation (participating in a revolutionary movement, engaging in courtship, working for a particular religious, political, or personal goal). Such difficulty, however, does not eliminate the overwhelming advantage of distinguishing between an attitude and a behavior. While an attitude is a predisposed psychological concept, behavior primarily concerns a gesture that is at least theoretically observable to potential eyewitnesses. The evidence in research literature consistently shows that attitude and behavior do not correspond in a one-to-one relationship; the consistency and inconsistency between the two are influenced by many social, psychological, and other factors. Thus, separate discussion of the two types of influence—attitude and behavior—is warranted.

Indicators of Behavioral Influence

Although behavioral activities are theoretically observable, studies of the influence of human communication on behavior are complicated by several factors. First, there is the problem of finding indicators of behavioral change. Since a person is continuously involved in behavioral activities, to study where the change takes place and how such change comes about is not a simple matter.

Usually, indicators of behavioral change can be classified into *three types*, each associated with a distinct type of behavioral commitment. The first type of behavioral change indicator mainly concerns *patterns of habits*. Such behavioral changes involve a person's daily life and his almost continuous commitment to such behaviors. One such habitual commitment is mass media consumption (TV viewing, radio listening, newspaper and magazine reading, etc.). Another is shopping for essential goods (groceries, household and personal necessities, etc.). Still another involves entertainment (attending movies, buying records, attending musical and sports events, going camping, etc.). All these activities are almost constantly in our minds and require our commitment almost continuously.

A second type of indicator of behavioral change focuses on behaviors which only require our *periodical attention and commitment*. These activities do not occur weekly, monthly, or even annually, but when they do occur, observations can be made rather easily (except where such behavior is not open to observation for certain ritualistic, moralistic, legalistic, or cultural reasons). Voting behavior is one such activity; buying a car, a house, or other things requiring a large investment represents another. A university or corporation buying or renting a computer system is still another example. And now that birth control methods are so widespread, family planning may be regarded as another form of behavior requiring our periodical commitment.

Still a third type of indicator of behavioral change comes from consideration of *events which are new* and unaccustomed or unfamiliar to the person who makes the commitment. Presumably as soon as he commits himself, the behavior will no longer be new and will involve a rather long-lasting commitment for him. A farmer's adoption of hybrid seed corn is one example. A physician's prescription of a new drug is another. A school's adoption of more flexible scheduling or of team teaching or a nation's decision to administer a new six-year compulsory education system are other examples.

These different indicators of behavioral change, ranging from habitual behavioral commitment and periodical behavioral commitment to innovative behavioral commitment, provide different data sources for those who are investigating human communication's influence on behavior. In general, different groups of researchers focus on different types of indicators. As a result, *investigations of the first two types of indicators—the habitual and periodical behaviors—fall into the research tradition of mass communication, while those of the third type—the commitment to new ideas and new practices—form the research tradition of diffusion and adoption of innovations.* This distinction does not mean that all behavior can easily be categorized into one camp or another. In fact, more than a few types of behavioral indicators have been studied by researchers in both the mass communication and diffusion traditions. This overlap results mainly from the definition of innovation. Many diffusion researchers define any practice or idea which in itself represents something the person has not previously committed himself to as an innovation for the person. Thus, buying a particular brand of cigarettes for the first time is regarded as the person's adoption of an innovation; the same is true when a woman first tries the contraceptive pill, even though she may have used other birth control methods before. On the other hand, it can be argued that since he has smoked other brands of cigarettes and she has used other birth control methods, their change in preference does not constitute any innovativeness. The former classification rests on the specific item itself; the latter argument focuses on the type of items involved. Also "newness" can be defined at different levels: an idea or practice or thing can be new to a person in terms of awareness (he did not know about it before), attitude (he did not like it before), or behavioral commitment (he did not use it before). As a consequence, researchers in both traditions—mass communication and diffusion —feel it is legitimate to conduct studies of behavioral changes which have similar degrees of newness to a person.

Another difficulty regarding the distinction between the two research traditions concerns their theoretical contributions. While the research strategies and theoretical assumptions employed by researchers in the two traditions differ (E. Katz, 1960), the findings from the two camps point to a converging theory in the end. And this theoretical convergence focuses eventually on the potential effects of various communication channels on behavioral change. Thus, the distinction between the traditions necessarily lies in the different types of indicators focused on and the disciplinary biases of the researchers rather than in any theoretical deviation. In the following pages, I will first discuss the contributions of the two research traditions to the study of behavioral change and then consider the theoretical convergence of the two traditions.

Before we embark, however, one note of caution is necessary regarding the mass media, which, although this book is presumably concerned only with human communication, have been mentioned before as communication channels. The question now becomes whether mass media should be considered as part of human communication and, if so, why. This question can be resolved by the empirical examination of the pervasiveness of mass media in our daily lives (here "mass media" is used inclusively to indicate media available for mass consumption, such as television, newspapers, radio, mass-circulated magazines, and movies; it excludes specialized forms of the media such as closed-circuit television, trade and professional journals, periodicals, newspapers, newsletters, and others [DeFleur, 1966]). Since our lives are so interwoven with our use of mass media, the mass media are in effect a mere extension of our biological senses and organs. Thus, it is almost the consensual view of scholars and students in human communication that mass media (usually regarded as part of mass communication) fall under the heading of human communication. In fact, many interesting and significant theoretical considerations, to be discussed in detail below, focus on the differential contributions of the mass media and interpersonal exchange to affecting behavioral changes.

As mentioned earlier, the distinction between mass communication research and diffusion research is more a matter of disciplinary emphasis and methodology than of theoretical considerations. Katz (1963) and others have compared the two research traditions in terms of the following differential characteristics:

1. *Diffusion research focuses on the receiver, while mass communication research focuses on the source.* The diffusion study typically analyzes the social and personal characteristics that determine the relative earliness when a person commits himself to an innovation. Mass communication research, on the other hand, traces the effects of specific sources and channels of information and influence.

2. *Diffusion research derives mostly from sociology, while mass communication research originates mainly in individual psychology.* Thus, diffusion research focuses on the interactive patterns among members of a social system, while mass communication focuses on the source-receiver relationship analysis.

3. Because of the differences mentioned in 2, the *sampling strategy differs for the two traditions.* Diffusion research, to study the interactive patterns, tends to use saturation sampling or snowball sampling methods. Mass communication research, to study the effects of a particular medium, relies on representative sampling in a social system.

4. *Mass communication research operates on the initial assumption that mass media play a crucial role in behavioral change.* Diffusion research has no such presupposition.

Thus, the two traditions, with different orientations and assumptions, employ different strategies and focus on different types of behavioral change. As we shall soon see, however, they have converged on the theoretical path and now find themselves complementing each other in the search for a communication framework of behavioral change.

Effects of Mass Communication

During the 1920s and 1930s, three factors contributed to extensive research interest in the effects of the mass media (Lazarsfeld and Menzel, 1963). One was the fast rise and popularization of radio. Radio not only disseminated the news much more rapidly than the printed media, but invested daily events with a much greater sense of realism (live broadcasts, for example). The rise of radio, in effect, coincided with the decline of the newspaper in the United States during and after the 1930s (DeFleur, 1966). The direct impact of radio on the general public was dramatically illustrated by Orson Welles's dramatization of an invasion of America by hostile forces from Mars on October 30, 1938. Although the broadcast began with the announcement that the play was based on H. G. Wells's *War of the Worlds,* the technique of on-the-spot reporting caused a panic of major proportions in many communities across the country. Homes were deserted, streets jammed with traffic, congregations gathered in churches to pray, telephone switchboards were overwhelmed with calls to police stations and newspapers for clarification and further information, and accidents increased. Another powerful demonstration of radio broadcasting's impact in inducing mass behavioral commitment occurred during World War II when Kate Smith, a well-known vocalist, made 65 separate sales talks for war bonds during an 18-hour marathon rally over a radio network on September 21, 1943. The effort netted $39 million worth of bonds for the government.

With the arrival of television in the 1950s, popular fears concerning the massive impact of the mass media continued to rise. The frequency and intensity of dramatic depictions of violence and crime on TV programs, viewed by young and old alike, continue to this day to inspire apprehension among both the general public and the Congress. The major questions have been: (1) do such programs induce violence and crime in society, and (2) do such programs affect the behavioral patterns of certain segments of the population (for instance, children)?

The second factor that contributed to extensive research interest in the effects of the mass media was the large *advertising investment in the mass media,* especially as exemplified by commercial sponsorship in the United States. Even in the 1930s, advertising expenditures per year for newspapers in the United States reached over $750 million. The figures went up during the 1950s to over $3 billion per year for newspaper advertising, $1.25 billion for television advertising, $750 million for mass-circulation magazine advertising, and over $500 million for radio advertising (Schramm, 1960, p. 292). The figures continued to rise in the 1960s: in 1968, for example, about $4 billion for newspaper advertising, $2 billion for television advertising, $1.5 billion for periodicals, and $1 billion for radio advertising (U.S. Bureau of the Census, 1970).

The logical conclusion from such figures is that the mass media must be quite effective in inducing consumers of the mass media to change their behavioral patterns and commitments.

The third factor that aroused research interest in the mass media was the *use made by authoritarian governments and agencies of the mass media for political and ideological propaganda and brainwashing.* The apparent success with which Hitler monopolized the mass media to unify Germany behind the Nazi Party and to exert enormous influence throughout Europe convinced many that the politicalization of the mass media could mean that governments would henceforth have the power to completely indoctrinate their populations with devastating ideologies. The extensive and exclusive use of the mass media by government dissemination agents in the Soviet Union and China (Inkeles, 1958; Yu, 1964; Liu, 1971) further reinforced the belief that mass media were effective brainwashing apparatuses when controlled by authoritarian governments or interests.

However, acceptance of such an all-powerful hypodermic-needle model of the mass media gradually decreased as more and more research efforts were made to ascertain the extent to which mass media actually exerted influence over human behavior. The turning point came in 1948 with a study of how voters had behaved during the 1940 presidential election (Lazarsfeld, Berelson, and Gaudet, 1948).

THE ERIE COUNTY STUDY

To study how the voter makes up his mind in a presidential campaign, Lazarsfeld, Berelson, and Gaudet (1948) conducted a social survey in Erie County, Ohio, during the 1940 presidential election campaign. One unique method utilized in the survey was the panel method. They sampled every fourth house in the area and included 3,000 respondents in their sample, which approximated the county population as to age, sex, residence, education, telephone and car ownership, and nativity. From this poll of 3,000, four groups of 600 respondents each were selected by stratified sampling. Each group was closely matched to the others and constituted a miniature sample of the whole poll and of the county itself. Of these four groups, three were interviewed twice; all groups were interviewed in May, and one of the three each in July, August, and October; these three groups also served as the control groups. The fourth group—the panel—was interviewed once each month from May to November (see Figure 6–1). Thus, one of the functions of the control groups was to test the effect that repeated inter-viewings might have on the panel group. With the panel method, the respondents' time of voting decisions could be detected precisely and possible changes in voting intentions could be studied in a dynamic way.

| Group | \multicolumn{7}{c}{Date of Interview} |
	May	June	July	August	September	October	Election Day November
Control A	X		X				Δ
Control B	X			X			Δ
Control C	X					X	Δ
Panel	X	X	X	X	X	X	Δ X

Figure 6-1. The Study Design of the Erie County Study

The findings of this survey, first of all, confirmed many already-known principles. For example, most people were exposed to a multitude of channels in receiving information about an event. More of the educated people attended to more of the mass media; people paid attention mostly to statements with which they already agreed or in which they were already quite interested. It was also found that delay in coming to a decision was principally caused by two factors: (1) the person was not interested in the election, or (2) the person was under cross-pressures from several groups to which he belonged.

The more significant findings concerned changes in voting decision and the sources of influence behind such change. During the six months of the survey (from May to November), 51 percent of the panel respondents did not change their voting intentions and actually did, on election day, what they had originally intended to do (either voted for their preferred candidate or did not vote at all). Another 28 percent had no vote intention in May but later acquired one, and 15 percent changed their minds during this period but eventually voted for the candidate they had initially preferred. Therefore, *only 8 percent of the respondents actually changed their voting intentions*—that is, switched from one candidate to another—between the time they were surveyed in May and the time they actually cast their ballots in November. In other words, once they had decided for whom they would vote, very few people changed their minds.

Furthermore, an analysis of the sources which exerted influence on those who did change their minds showed that *the mass media* (radio, newspapers, etc.) *had almost no effect. These people were much more likely to have been influenced by their families, friends, and co-workers.*

These two findings—that few people changed their minds and that interpersonal influence was most effective—led the researchers to study the "opinion leaders." At about midpoint in the campaign, the respondents were asked these two questions:

1. "Have you tried to convince anyone of your political ideas recently?"

2. "Has anyone asked your advice on a political question recently?"

All those people who answered "yes" to either or both these questions—21 percent of the entire group—were designated opinion leaders (Lazarsfeld, Berelson, and Gaudet, 1948, p. 50). Contrary to previous assumptions, these opinion leaders were found not to be particularly concentrated in the more educated classes or in the more prestigeful positions in the community, but were almost evenly distributed throughout every class and occupation. They were, however, more interested in the election than the others and were considerably more exposed to mass media.

Based on these findings, the researchers proposed a two-step flow hypothesis of communication: ideas often flow from radio and print to the opinion leaders and from them to the less active segments of the population (Lazarsfeld, Berelson, and Gaudet, 1948, p. 151). This hypothesis has since —over the last two decades—become the focal point for research in mass communication. It has two important dimensions: (1) for the first time, the all-powerful hypodermic-needle model of mass media was systematically and empirically negated; that is, it was shown that mass media do not, after all, exert much influence in changing human behavior; and (2) persons who serve as the relayers or gatekeepers of communication—the opinion leaders—deserve much greater research attention because of their potential conversion power.

THE NEW JERSEY STUDY

Following up the discovery of the opinion leadership in the Erie County study, another member of the Columbia University Bureau of Applied Social Research conducted a case study in a small town in New Jersey to identify types of opinion leaders in terms of a number of characteristics (Merton, 1949). In this study, a sample of 86 residents were asked to mention people to whom they turned for help or advice in making various types of personal decisions (ranging from choice of a job, to educational plans for self and children, to selection of books, plays, or furniture). A total of 379 people were mentioned and 57 (15 percent) were named four or more times. These 57 persons were designated as the opinion leaders, or influentials. Thirty of these influentials were subsequently interviewed. From evaluations of their orientations toward the community, two types of influentials were identified: the local and the cosmopolitan. The locals typically were born locally, were interested in meeting many townspeople, intended to stay there, and were more likely to be interested in local politics. The cosmopolitans, on the other hand, were more typically new arrivals, were more selective in their choice of friends and acquaintances, were more concerned with national political issues, and were more likely to be exposed to national magazines and public affairs broadcasts. *The influence of the locals seemed rooted in whom they knew; the influence of the cosmopoli-*

tans seemed rooted in what they knew. The data also suggested that (1) people in each influence stratum were more likely to be influenced by their peers in this structure than by people in other strata; (2) despite the great concentration of interpersonal influence among relatively few individuals, the bulk of such influence was widely dispersed among the larger number of people in the lower reaches of that structure; (3) there appeared to be a chain of influence such that people in each influence stratum were more likely to regard as influential people who were in the stratum immediately above their own than they were informants in other strata, either farther above or anywhere below themselves; and (4) influentials each had a specialized sphere of influence—they were opinion leaders only on specific topics.

While the small number of respondents in this study prevented any statistical analysis, the observations made were significant on several accounts: (1) the study represented a further step in identifying types of opinion leaders and paved the way for more extensive and rigorous studies; (2) it confirmed several important findings with regard to the characteristics of the opinion leaders from the 1940 Erie County study; and (3) it advanced several interesting hypotheses relative to the influence structure, in particular, the chain of influence.

THE DECATUR STUDY

Continuing their systematic investigation of the interpersonal influence, the Columbia group (Katz and Lazarsfeld, 1955), in a survey of female respondents in Decatur, Illinois, sought out people who had recently changed their opinions or who had otherwise made new decisions in four very different fields: marketing, fashion, public affairs, and movie going. In interviewing a cross-sectional sample of 800 women in the community, the researchers asked them to name (1) the people whom they believed to be trustworthy and knowledgeable about matters of public concern; (2) the people who actually influenced them to change their opinions on some matter of current concern; and (3) the people with whom they most often talked about what they heard on the radio or read in the papers. They were likewise asked to identify those whom they themselves had influenced on recent specific occasions. About two-thirds of the designated opinion leaders and followers, in the follow-up survey, confirmed such interactions and about four in five of those who confirmed the interactions also confirmed the designated roles, either as opinion leaders or as followers.

The findings from this survey generally confirmed the findings of the Erie County study—namely, that *personal influence rather than the mass media accounted for most of the changes in opinions.* Furthermore, the opinion leaders were more likely to be interested in the topics, to be situated in socially advantageous positions (marketing leaders tended to come from large households; movie-selection leaders tended to be single women; fashion leaders tended to be young, single women; and public affairs leaders tended to be better educated), to be gregarious and accessible, to have contact with information sources outside their immediate circle (such as mass media and cosmopolitan and specialized sources), and to appear and to exert influence at every social-class level.

From the Erie County study to the Decatur study, the Columbia research effort crystalized the significance of the two-step flow hypothesis of communication. From the mid-1950s, however, the hypothesis began undergoing several necessary modifications resulting from further studies on personal influence and opinion leadership.

THE ELMIRA STUDY

Another study conducted by the Columbia group (Berelson, Lazarsfeld, and McPhee, 1954) of a presidential campaign contributed to the initial modification of the two-step flow hypothesis. During the 1948 presidential election campaign, the researchers surveyed the community of Elmira, New York. A probability sample of 1,029 respondents was selected based upon dwelling units within the community. Again, the panel technique was used and groups of respondents were interviewed in June, August, October, and November.

In general, the data confirmed the Erie County study's findings that people tended to discuss the issue with those who agreed with their views, that such discussion took place mostly among people of similar social, occupational, age, and political characteristics, and that a change of voting intentions was most likely to occur under the influence of other persons—mainly family members, friends, and co-workers.

However, *their data on the opinion leaders presented some interesting results.* While the opinion leaders were found, more often than the followers, to be consistent supporters of their respective party's position on all possible issues, to belong to organizations, to know workers for the political party, and to be exposed to the mass media, *they were also more likely than the followers to have sought information and advice from yet other persons.* This finding necessitated a modification of the two-step flow hypothesis. Instead of the ideas flowing from the mass media, through opinion leaders, to the general public, the data suggested a *multi-step flow of communication: ideas flow from the mass media, through several relays of opinion leaders who communicate with one another, to the ultimate followers.*

SOME RECENT STUDIES OF THE
TWO-STEP FLOW HYPOTHESIS

Several studies have attempted to test the two-step flow hypothesis. So far, direct confirmation of the hypothesis has not occurred. Several conceptual and methodological problems relative to the test of the hypothesis will be discussed in a later chapter. Here, I will merely cite some attempts to verify the hypothesis, even though these studies did not focus on behavioral change as the dependent variable.

Van den Ban (1964), in a study of agricultural innovations among farmers in three rural communities in the Netherlands, found that farmers usually heard for the first time of the existence of a new method through the mass media, but that the decision to adopt an innovation was mainly influenced by personal contacts. Furthermore, people sought advice from others of similar socioeconomic status only for new ideas, but not for badly needed information. When they badly needed some information, people usually sought advice from those of higher socioeconomic status.

Troldahl (1966) specifically set up a field experiment to test the two-step flow hypothesis. In a before-after, experimental-control design, he placed an experimental message containing recommendations for the care of lawns, shrubs, flowers, and other plants in a monthly agricultural newspaper sent to the experimental group subscribers. Measures of the respondents' beliefs about the topics were obtained from personal interviews conducted five weeks before and one week after the experimental message was transmitted. The two interviews were successfully conducted with 55 percent of the respondents in both the experimental and control groups. The data neither confirm the original hypothesis nor Troldahl's modified hypothesis —that information flows in one step (direct from the mass media) but that influence flows in two steps.

Failure to confirm the two-step hypothesis also occurred with the data gathered by Arndt in a marketing study (1968). He found that the opinion leaders were more influenced by the impersonal source (direct-mail letter) than were the nonleaders. However, the opinion leaders were more active communicators, both as transmitters and as receivers of word-of-mouth communications. Arndt found, as did Troldahl, that opinion sharing between the opinion leaders and the followers was extensive, indicating a two-way communication flow between the opinion leaders and the followers.

Although the two studies by Troldahl and Arndt focused on attitude change rather than on behavioral change, they have been the only direct tests of the two-step hypothesis so far. The failure of their data to confirm the two-step flow hypothesis, while disheartening, points to several theoretical and empirical problems, without clarification of which further development of theoretical statements about the roles of mass media and interpersonal structure in inducing behavioral change cannot be carried very far. A more detailed discussion of these problems will appear in Chapter 8.

It is now well established that the focus of mass communication research has shifted during the last three decades from the study of the effects of mass media to the investigation of interpersonal influence and the effectiveness of mass media in bringing the initial information to the audience (see Chapter 2).

THE EFFECTS OF TV ON CHILDREN

As mentioned earlier, fears about the impact on children of the violence, sadism, and crime depicted on the TV screen have been voiced ever since television was first introduced into the home. The history of home TV is still too short for its long-term effects to have been studied; nevertheless, a number of extensive studies have been made in England, Japan, Australia, Germany, France, the United States, and Canada, and the results, with only a few exceptions, are similar cross-culturally.

The best-known study of television's effects on children was conducted by Himmelweit, Oppenheim, and Vince (1958) in England. Working with two matched samples (as to sex, age, intelligence, and social background) of 1,854 children aged 10 to 11 and 13 to 14 (those who were in television households and those who were not), they were able to gather a large amount of data about the children's and their families' characteristics as well as about the children's viewing habits. Similar methodology was used in studies conducted in other countries (Schramm, Lyle, and Parker, 1961; Maccoby, 1963).

In general, the data showed that *television viewing does not hurt children's eyesight, their school performance, or their interest in classroom work. Nor does television viewing interfere in any significant way with the children's reading of books.* Only a small portion (about one in five) of the children were occasionally frightened by violent programs.

Furthermore, *viewing crime and violence on television has not been positively associated with actual violent, delinquent, or aggressive behavior among children.* Studies (Maccoby, 1963) have only been able to show that viewing violence or crime inspires aggressive acts with toys and imitation of such acts in games and plays. In fact, one recent study (Feshbach and Singer, 1970) has found that children who viewed TV longer tended to show less aggressiveness. However, further studies are needed to ascertain positively the potential effect on children of the crime and violence portrayed on TV. It is difficult to predict, for example, what long-term effects TV programs will have on behavior, for the accumulated effect of television may not emerge until a day when the real environment provides appropriate cues that trigger hidden or even unconscious aggressive impulses stimulated by viewing TV over time. Furthermore, experimentally measuring the behavioral effect of TV viewing is a far cry from reality because actual crime and violence cannot be tolerated in any laboratory or experimental situation.

Heavy viewers of TV programs that depict crime and violence have been found to have fewer friends, to have poor relationships with their parents, or to possess an aggressive personality. These findings again support what is known about the mass media's effects—namely, that TV viewing may be effective for those who do not have peer-group support, who lack group-norm sanction, who lack a warm and stable relationship with their parents, who have low intelligence, or who are emotionally maladjusted. *When such social and psychological support breaks down, the mass media may be effective in inducing changes in a person's behavior* (Klapper, 1960).

TV DEBATE AND VOTING DECISION

After the Nixon and Kennedy dramatic television debates in full view of a nationwide audience during the 1960 presidential campaign, the common belief was that the TV confrontation had been the prime cause of the downfall of one candidate and of the victory of the other. But was the TV debate effective in inducing change in voters' intentions? It was estimated (Katz and Feldman, 1962) that at least 31 survey studies were made of the series of four debates between Kennedy and Nixon. Several studies specifically attempted to assess the effect of the debates on the images of the two candidates and on the voting intentions of the TV viewers (Kraus, 1962). For example, Deutschmann (1962) undertook a before-after survey relative to the first debate and found that those who had already made a party choice were more likely to expose themselves to the debate or to talk about it. Of those who did get into conversations about the debate, only 11 percent talked to persons with views contrary to their own, while 47 percent talked to persons with the same views as themselves, and 42 percent talked to groups of mixed opinions. These findings are similar to those in the voting studies mentioned earlier, that is, that people who decide early show more interest in and are more likely to expose themselves to messages on the issues and that people tend to discuss politics with those who already agree with their views. The study also found that there was less change in vote intention among those who had talked about the TV debate (19 percent of them changed) than among those who had not (30 percent changed). All in all, while the debates probably improved the image of Kennedy, a very small number of persons changed their voting intentions, and among those who did change, the percentage of shifts to each candidate was about equal. In other words, the viewers overwhelmingly continued to support the candidate of their pre-viewing choice. This finding was supported by other studies (Ben-Zeev and White, 1962; Carter, 1962; Lang and Lang, 1962; Kraus and Smith, 1962; Tannenbaum, Greenberg, and Silverman, 1962).

POTENTIAL EFFECTS OF TV ON
BEHAVIORAL COMMITMENT

Some recent studies have pointed to the direct impact of TV on behavioral commitment. As part of a program to recruit patients to use the facilities of the Planned Parenthood Center of Buffalo, two TV spots were constructed and broadcast alternately on a systematically rotated basis (Hutchinson, 1970). One message, using an informative and instructive approach, depicted a hypothetical patient's visit to the PPC and her use of the PPC services. Another message, using an emotional appeal approach, presented testimonies made by former patients. During the broadcasts, the 23 PPC clinics in the city showed a dramatic increase in the number of new patients who listed public information as a factor influencing their decision to come to the clinic over the same period the year before when no such TV campaign was conducted. In addition, the information message was much more effective than the testimonial message in inducing potential users to call the clinic for additional information (each message had a different calling number) and in inducing them to actually make appointments to visit the clinics.

It seems clear that *given predisposed motivations, TV messages based on information and instruction can be made effective in inducing behavioral commitment.*

SUMMARY OF THE PRINCIPLES
OF MASS COMMUNICATION

We may summarize the major findings of these and other studies on mass communication. The reader is reminded that all the studies discussed so far have been conducted in the more developed countries, mostly in the United States. Other studies made in the less developed countries have uncovered important differences and will be brought into the discussion at a later point in this chapter.

1. *Once a decision is reached, behavioral changes do not occur often.* When such changes do occur, they are more likely to be due to pressures from other persons than from the mass media. Furthermore, the most influential people tend to be close to the person in question in his social and physical network—like family members, friends, and co-workers. The mass media are relatively ineffective, mainly because of people's selective exposure, selective retention, and selective perception (interpretation) (Klapper, 1960). Thus, people tend to avoid information in the mass media that challenges their beliefs, attitudes, or behavior. On the other hand, interpersonal communication facilitates immediate feedback and immediate response to feedback, and the reward in interpersonal communication is immediate and personal (Lazarsfeld and Menzel, 1963). Thus, *in getting people to change their behavior, personal influence is much more effective than mass media influence.* Derived from these data was the two-step flow hypothesis, which has since been subjected to some modifications. Confirmation of the hypothesis has been hampered by some conceptual and methodological problems. These problems will be discussed in Chapter 8.

2. The extent of attention to and interaction with other persons and the mass media is positively related to a person's interest in the topic under dis-

cussion and to the degree to which these persons or media share his views.

3. Behavioral commitment to a topic also induces a person to engage in more extensive discussion with others and to seek greater exposure to the mass media carrying information about the topic.

4. Opinion leaders, either defined by the self-designated method or the sociometric choice method, tend to exhibit the following characteristics:

a. They appear in all social, occupational, and economic levels in in a social system.

b. They are interested in the topics on which they are opinion leaders.

c. They are more likely to be exposed to the mass media and to impersonal sources outside their own social circles.

d. They tend to hold strategic or advantageous social positions which facilitate their receiving information on topics on which they exert influence. For example, being in a large household facilitates a housewife's being an opinion leader on grocery shopping (Katz and Lazarsfeld, 1955).

e. They are accessible and gregarious.

f. They tend to be similar to their followers in social, economic, and occupational characteristics. However, they also tend to be slightly, but not much, better off than their followers in socioeconomic status.

g. They are social norm supporters rather than deviants. Thus, in the more developed countries, such as the United States, opinion leaders are prone to change simply because the social norm is in favor of change. However, in the less developed countries, where traditional and conservative norms prevail, the opinion leaders tend also to be less prone to change (Marsh and Coleman, 1956).

h. There may be two or more types of opinion leaders. One classification concerns the leaders' orientation to the local community. The locally oriented opinion leaders accumulate their influence by the local personalities they know and by their participation in local activities; the cosmopolitan opinion leaders gain their influence mainly through their participation in and awareness of activities outside the community. Another classification deals with formal and informal opinion leadership (Lowe and McCormick, 1956). Formal leaders represent experts with whom the followers do not have direct contact, while informal leaders are those to whom the specific followers have direct access through personal contact. Informal opinion leaders seem to have greater influence with the less educated and the older, formal leaders, with the moderately educated and the younger.

i. There is a positive relationship between the range of the opinion leaders' expertise and the extent of their local orientation. That is, the more local opinion leader tends to be polymorphic, specializing in a wide range of issues, whereas the more cosmopolitan opinion leader tends to be monomorphic, specializing in one narrowly defined area.

j. Opinion leaders who deviate from the existing norms may emerge when the traditional opinion leaders fail to relate the group to the larger social system. Eisenstadt (1952, 1955) discussed the emergence of such younger opinion leaders among new immigrant groups in Israel when the traditional opinion leaders in these groups could not cope with the difference between their group norms and the norms of the new, larger social system.

Diffusion of Innovations

Diffusion is defined as the process by which a new idea or practice spreads among members of a social system. The diffusion of innovations consists of several crucial elements: (1) the innovations, (2) the channels of transmission, (3) the spread over time, and (4) the members of a social system among whom they spread. My definition of "innovation" deviates from the traditional definition in that it refers to a new practice only, whereas the traditional approach also includes a new idea (Rogers, 1962; Katz, 1963; Rogers and Shoemaker, 1971). Researchers, on the basis of their findings and conceptual considerations, have concluded that the diffusion of new ideas and information flow are identical processes having similar structural and dynamic properties. I have treated the topic of information flow (especially diffusion of news) extensively in the encounter phase of human communication (Chapter 2); all the findings there apply to the diffusion of new ideas. Hence, my discussion here focuses only on the diffusion of innovations.

The defining characteristic of diffusion studies, as distinguished from other communication studies, is their narrow focus on the communication process of *new* practices. The newness of the practice is a perceptual phenomenon within the potential adopters rather than an objective characteristic of the practice itself. Thus, an old practice in one social system (that is, the use of washing machines in the United States) may be an innovation in another (Tibet, for instance).

The process of innovation diffusion can be a long and arduous one. There was a 40-year time lag between the first success of the tunnel oven in the English pottery industry and its general adoption (Carter and Williams, 1957); more than 14 years elapsed before hybrid seed corn was completely diffused among Iowa farmers (Ryan and Gross, 1943); more than 50 years were required for U.S. public schools to adopt the idea of the kindergarten (Ross, 1958), and five to six years for them to adopt modern math (Carlson, 1965); more than 30 years passed from first to complete adoption of chemical fertilizers in a small Colombian village (Deutschmann and Fals Borda, 1962); 10 to 15 years were needed for discoveries in the social sciences to make an impact on the scientific community and on public affairs (Deutsch, Platt, and Senghaas, 1971).

Social scientists have long been interested in discovering the factors which facilitate or hinder the diffusion process and the adoption process. Empirical investigations of innovation diffusion were conducted by anthropologists, rural sociologists, medical sociologists, education researchers, and others as far back as three decades ago (Katz, Levin, and Hamilton, 1963). However, it is only during the past 15 years that diffusion of innovation has become generally important and popular as a research area in the United States. Several factors contribute to the growing interest in this research tradition.

One source of stimulation was the Soviet Union's successful launch of the first man-made satellite in 1957. The launch, considered by many North Americans to be an indication of an important technological innovation gap between the U.S.S.R. and the United States, called attention to the problems of innovation diffusion in educational systems as well as in industrial technologies. Federal money thereafter became readily available for large-scale investigations into the process by which educational and technological innovations are diffused.

A second factor contributing to the popularization of diffusion research was the realization that diffusion research and mass communication research came up with strikingly similar findings (E. Katz, 1960). The convergence of the mass communication and diffusion research traditions marked the beginning of a concerted effort among mass communication and diffusion students to systematically integrate the available findings (Rogers, 1962) and to construct general principles of innovation diffusion and mass communication, focusing on the effect of human communication on aspects of behavioral change.

A third factor relates to the rapid increase in the number of newly independent countries around the world over the past 15 years. The primary interest of the developing countries has been modernization. American social scientists and their counterparts in the developing countries realized the applicability of the diffusion principles to the development and modernization process. With financial and organizational assistance from U.S. agencies and private foundations, delegations of American diffusion researchers have appeared in almost every corner of the earth, compiling data, giving advice, and training students. The last five years have seen a rapid growth in the number of competent diffusion researchers, mostly trained in the United States, in the establishment of diffusion centers and programs, and in research and training activities around the world. These programs and activities were concerned initially with agricultural innovations but have now been extended to health and family planning.

Diffusion research typically focuses on *two levels of analysis:* (1) *the aggregate diffusion rate over time* and (2) *the individual adoption process.* The diffusion rate is defined as the proportion of potential adopters in a social system who have adopted the innovation within a given time. The adopter unit can be an individual, a group, or a social subsystem. The adoption process is defined as the process by which an adopter unit becomes behaviorally committed to the innovation. For a given innovation, different diffusion rates may be found in different social systems.

When the diffusion rate of an innovation is faster in one social system (or subsystem) than in another, the research usually examines the social, political, economic, and population indicators that might explain the differential diffusion rates.

The individual adoption process can be studied more easily by classifying people in terms of their relative earliness or lateness in adopting the innovation. For example, one classic classification specifies five types of adopters: (1) the innovators—the small group of people who adopt the innovation first, usually defined as less than 3 percent of the total potential adopter population; (2) the early adopters—the minority of people who adopt later than the innovators but earlier than the majority of potential adopters, usually consisting of the next 14 percent of the adopter population; (3) the early majority—approximately the next 34 percent of the adopter population, whose acceptance of the innovation indicates that half the population in the system has adopted, (4) the late majority—the next 34 percent of the population, who adopt relatively late, and finally, (5) the laggards, composed of the last 16 percent of the adopter population, who either adopt the innovation last or do not adopt it at all. A recent study (Loy, 1969) confirmed that innovativeness should be regarded as a continuous variable, people in each category having distinctive social-psychological characteristics.

The diffusion and adoption processes are generally taken as the dependent variables, factors to be explained in terms of other variables. The independent, or explaining, variables usually considered include: (1) the characteristics of the innovations, (2) the sources and channels of information and influence, (3) the social structure of the adopter population, and (4) the characteristics of the potential adopters themselves.

In the following, I will describe some typical studies of innovation diffusion by early sociologists, rural sociologists, education researchers, medical sociologists, and communications researchers. Then, I will summarize the major findings relative to the differential diffusion rates and to the adoption process.

THE PEMBERTON STUDIES

Pemberton (1936, 1937) was one of the earliest sociologists who attempted to study the diffusion phenomenon on an empirical basis. Following Chapin (1928), Pemberton wanted to find empirical evidence for the S-shaped curve of the diffusion of cultural and sociological traits. In one study (1936), he studied the adoption of the postage stamp as a part of the culture of independent European and North and South American countries (at that time, 37 countries were included). The cumulative distribution of the adoptions is plotted in Figure 6-2. The data not only proved that the diffusion rate was S-curved, but also that the curve approached the normal distribution.

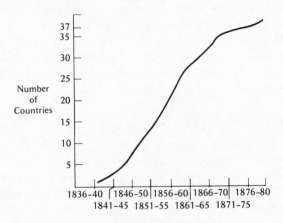

Figure 6-2. Cumulative Distribution of Postage Adoption
in Europe and North America, 1836-1880
Adapted from Pemberton (1936)

In another study, Pemberton (1936) investigated the adoption of compulsory school laws by the states in the United States. The overall diffusion curve did not follow the S-shape. In fact, there were two bulges instead of the one expected from an S-shaped curve or normal distribution. A further analysis of the data, however, led him to discover that the diffusion rates for Northern and Southern states differed, many Southern states with large Negro populations having been quite reluctant to enforce the compulsory school laws. By separating the 31 Northern and Western states from the 17 Southern states, Pemberton found two S-shaped curves. The adoptions among the Northern and Western states occurred between 1847 and 1907, while those among the Southern states occurred between 1891 and 1927. The former adoption curve occurred over a much longer period of time than the latter curve and there was an approximate 40-50-year difference between the average adoption dates of the two curves. The social factor, racial consideration, accounted for the deviation of the overall curve from being S-shaped or normal.

In three other studies (1937), Pemberton investigated the effect of social crises on the curve of diffusion. He found that both the total membership (per 10,000 population) and the state organization membership affiliated with the National Congress of Parents and Teachers in the United States cumulated in an S-shaped curve except during the period of World War I and the Great Depression. During these two periods, the adoption rate dropped and deviated from the expected rate of a normal distribution. However, as soon as the crisis was over in each period, the adoption rate not only resumed its growth but actually caught up with the original expected normal curve shortly and resumed its original adoption rate.

During this series of studies, Pemberton made *three important contributions to diffusion research:* (1) he was the first one to apply empirical data to verify a *theoretical and mathematical model of diffusion;* (2) he was the first to explain empirical deviations from the expected curve in terms of the *intervention of social variables;* and (3) he was the first to explain empirical *deviations* from the expected curve of diffusion in terms of *social crises* and to discover the *resumption of the growth rate following the crises.*

THE HYBRID SEED CORN STUDY

Probably the earliest and best-known empirical investigation of the diffusion of agricultural innovations was conducted by Ryan and Gross (on the diffusion of hybrid seed corn) in two Iowa communities in 1941 (1943). In the original plan, all 323 corn-growing farmers in the two communities were designated as respondents. However, since 64 families indicated that they had started farming after hybrid seed corn was introduced into the communities, the remaining 259 constituted the respondents. The researchers found that all but two of their respondents had adopted hybrid seed corn by the time of the investigation and that there was an average lag of five years between the farmers' first hearing about the hybrid seed corn and their adopting it on their farms. Among the major findings of the study were the following:

1. Early adopters took more time than late adopters did in deciding to switch completely to the new corn on their farms. The researchers felt that the early adopters served as the community laboratories and that they did not take the innovation at its face value. However, successful innovation by the early adopters provided concrete evidence of the hybrid corn's usefulness and inspired confidence in the late adopters who therefore more quickly reached complete adoption decisions.

2. The mass media (journals and radio) and impersonal sources (salesmen) were effective in transmitting the information, while nearby personal sources (neighbors) were most effective in inducing behavioral commitment. Forty-nine percent of the farmers indicated that they had initially heard about the innovation from salesmen, 15 percent heard about it from neighbors, 11 percent through farm journals, and 10 percent through radio advertising. However, 46 percent of the farmers identified their neighbors as having been most influential in inducing their adoption, 32 percent identified the salesmen as most influential, while less than 3 percent considered farm journals and radio advertising as influential.

3. The effect of interpersonal sources and/or channels for both information and influence increased over time. Among early knowers and early

adopters, the salesmen served as the most effective source for both information and influence. Among late knowers and late adopters, however, the effectiveness of salesmen decreased and that of neighbors increased dramatically. During the final years, salesmen and neighbors were about equally effective for the isolates who were the latest knowers and adopters.

4. The adoption curve deviated from the normal distribution. In plotting the cumulative curve of adoptions among the farmers over time, Ryan and Gross found that the overall adoption distribution was four years less than expected from the normal curve, that the frequency of early adopters was greater and that of the late adopters was less than expected, and that there was a greater concentration of adoptions in the modal year and the two following years than expected. The researchers felt that the intense pressure of economic gain and frequency of social interaction probably accounted for the observed diffusion rate.

THE SAUCIO STUDY

Deutschmann and Fals Borda conducted a study of the adoption of six farm practices in Saucio, an Andean village of Colombia, in 1961 (1962). The study was significant on several counts: (1) Although a number of diffusion studies had been conducted outside the United States by that time (Australia: Emery and Oeser, 1958; Wilkening et al., 1962; Mexico: Myren, 1962; the Netherlands: van den Ban, 1957 and 1961), this study represented one of the earliest efforts (another was Rahim, 1961, in Pakistan) to apply the knowledge obtained through American diffusion research to rural areas in a developing country; (2) it was also one of the earliest studies conducted by an international team of researchers involving substantial contributions by the nationals of a developing nation—the study was conducted under the auspices of the Programa Interamericano de Información Popular in Costa Rica (a research outpost of the Department of Communication at Michigan State University) and the Department of Sociology of the National University of Colombia; and (3) it was one of the first diffusion studies in which several innovations, rather than a single innovation, were the focus of investigation.

In the study, advanced sociology students from the National University interviewed 71 of the 79 local farmers concerning the history of their adoptions of six farm innovations (spray guns for fungicides and insecticides, chemical fertilizers, animal feed, seed potato, and vaccination of poultry for chicken cholera). The adoption rates ranged from 100 percent to 15 percent for the innovations. An index of innovativeness for the farmers was constructed from their adoptive behaviors relative to the six innovations, using the Guttman scaling analysis (the coefficient of reproducibility was a high .95, indicating that the adoption behaviors relative to the six innovations formed a unidimensional scale quite well).

Their data, while confirming many diffusion findings from U.S. data, also showed interesting differences. The major findings were:

1. Interpersonal sources were most effective for both information transmission and influence transmission. Only 17 percent of the respondents identified the mass media either as the initial source of information or as a supplementary source of information relative to the six innovations. This finding points to the relationship between the developmental level of the social system and the effectiveness of mass media as information sources. *In the developed countries, mass media are powerful tools in transmitting information; in the rural, less developed areas, they are not at all effective.*

2. A large number of farmers decided to adopt as soon as they initially heard about the innovations. The no-delay decision was made by almost half the farmers in adopting one or more of the six innovations. In the U.S. studies, five stages were identified from the initial awareness to the final adoption: awareness, interest, evaluation, trial, and adoption (North Central Rural Sociology Subcommittee, 1955). The researchers attributed the difference to cultural characteristics; for instance, in some cultures, authoritarian sources were received without questioning. The inadequacy of applying the five-stage adoption process to developing countries was subsequently demonstrated again by Rogers (1965).

3. The innovativeness of the farmers, as measured with the innovation scale, was highly correlated with adoption leadership, size of farm, years of education, earliness of awareness, mass media exposure, and cosmopolitan orientation. Most of these correlations held true in U.S. studies (Rogers, 1961).

4. Early adopters were more likely to be exposed to mass media of all types (radio, newspapers, books) than were late adopters, although the level of exposure was generally low for all.

5. In a tentative attempt to construct a theoretical model of innovativeness, the researchers identified two fundamental motivating forces: ability to understand and economic ability. The ability-to-understand factor consisted of such variables as years of education, literacy, and age (younger). The economic-ability factor included variables such as size of farm, account keeping, and willingness to go into debt to increase potential profit in the future. However, this model has yet to be further tested.

THE CARLSON STUDY

In the field of education, the adaptability of school systems to change was investigated extensively by a Columbia University group under the leadership of Mort from the 1920s to 1950s (Ross, 1958). The data, collected in more than 200 studies, consistently showed that school "adaptability" to new educational devices was related to the school system's level of expenditure per student. The studies, however, did not trace specific innovations. Carlson (1965), applying diffusion research methodology, conducted a survey to investigate the adoption of six educational innovations (modern math, programed instruction, team teaching, foreign language laboratories, foreign language instruction in elementary grades, and accelerated programs in secondary schools) in the school systems of Allegheny County, Pennsylvania, and of the state of West Virginia. Interviews were conducted with 61 of the 68 Allegheny County school superintendents and 46 of the 55 West Virginia school superintendents. Data were collected relative to the dates of adoption of the innovations, the characteristics of the superintendents (personal, communication habits, position in the social structure of superintendents in the area), and the characteristics of the innovations as rated by experts and the superintendents.

In this study, *mean expenditure per child was not found to be related to the innovativeness of the school systems.* Instead, the position of the superintendents in the social network among the superintendents seemed to play a major role in the communication and adoption of the innovations. It was found that when asked to name those persons from whom they would seek advice relative to new educational practices, the late adopters tended to name the slightly earlier adopters. Opinion leadership (measured in terms of the friendship network), and professional status (education, professionalism, prestige, and opinion leadership score, which was derived from the frequency of nominations by fellow superintendents) were all related to earliness of innovation adoption.

THE DRUG STUDY

A more extensive investigation of the interpersonal network and its effect on innovation adoption was made in a study of physicians conducted by Coleman, Katz, and Menzel (1957, 1959, 1966). In a survey of physicians specializing in a medical area in which a recently introduced drug was used, they obtained data from 216 physicians in four Midwest communities. The researchers also studied interpersonal relations in detail, mapping out a number of networks, ranging from friendship to professional advice. To validate the verbal testimony of the doctors about actual adoption of the drug, prescription records in local pharmacies were systematically searched. They found that more personal sources than printed sources were mentioned as the initial source of information about the drug. The most frequently mentioned source was the detailmen (cited by 57 percent of the physicians), followed by drug-house mail (18 percent).

Once the information reached the community of physicians, however, it was the interaction among the physicians that accounted for the diffusion of the drug in the community. At first, the new drug was passed on primarily between doctors who regarded each other as professional conversation partners. Then, it was passed on primarily between doctors who were friends and who were intensely involved in these friendship relations. In the third phase, the influence at last reached doctors who were relatively isolated. And in the final phase, individual adoptions occurred without reference to the interpersonal relationships of the doctors concerned (Lazarsfeld and Menzel, 1963).

The most important contribution of the study concerns the *differential adoption rates among physicians inside or outside the various interpersonal networks*. The better-integrated doctors, measured on all network indices, showed earlier adoptions as well as a much faster rate of adoption, while the less well-integrated physicians adopted the new drug at an almost constant rate. The data suggested to the researchers two distinctive adoption models. For the integrated physician group, the model predicts that the adoption rate is a function of the interaction between the adopters and the nonadopters at a given time. This model can be represented by the differential equation:

$$\frac{dX}{dt} = kX(N - X) \tag{1}$$

where X is the number of adopters at time t, N is the total potential adopters, and k is a constant coefficient. For the less well-integrated, or isolated, physicians, the adoption model predicts that the adoption rate is a simple function of the number of nonadopters at a given time, represented by the differential equation:

$$\frac{dX}{dt} = k(N - X) \tag{2}$$

Thus, the two models would predict the two different adoption curves, as shown in Figure 6-3.

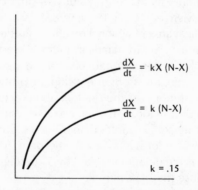

Figure 6-3. Diffusion Rates for the Interactive and Isolated Members
Adapted from Coleman, Katz, and Menzel, 1966 (p. 98)

Solving the two equations and letting X = 1 and t = 0, we find:

$$X = N(1 - e^{-kt}) \tag{3}$$

$$X = \frac{Ne^{kt}}{N + e^{kt} - 1} \qquad (4)$$

When k is greater than or equal to 0 and less than or equal to 1, the function X in equation (3) is a logistic function, with a quick acceleration of increase early in the time period, and the function in (4) is a monotonic increasing function with approximately a constant growth rate. The fast acceleration in the early periods of the first model was thought by the researchers to be accounted for by the chain-interactions among the integrated physicians. Their data bore out quite well the predicted curves for both the integrated and the isolated groups of physicians. The differential adoption curves could not be obtained by any of ten other individual variables. The important role of the social network in the diffusion of medical innovations was again confirmed by Becker (1970).

THE THREE-NATION STUDY

Rogers and his associates (Rogers, Ascroft, and Röling, 1970) conducted a large-scale cross-cultural study of the diffusion of agricultural and health innovations in Brazil, Nigeria, and India. The main data came from 1,307 peasants in 20 Brazilian villages, 1,142 peasants in 18 Nigerian villages, and 680 peasants in 8 Indian villages. The study was intended to ascertain the factors which determined the success on both the village level and the individual farmer level of innovative programs. The major findings were:

1. The success of village programs of agricultural change was most significantly related to the extent of contact between change agents (professionals who influence innovation decisions in a direction deemed desirable by a change agency) and their local clients.

2. The innovativeness of individual peasants was also found to be related to, among other variables, the extent of their contacts with change agents.

3. Change agent contact and opinion leadership in the village were more highly interrelated in the more modern villages, less highly interrelated in the more traditional villages. This finding reinforced earlier findings that the social climate in the more developed areas promotes change more strongly than does that in the less developed areas.

4. Field experiments confirmed that the efficiency of radio forums in diffusing innovations was much greater than that of either (1) literacy-reading classes or (2) community newspapers, whether the cost was measured for peasant-receivers or for change agencies. This finding suggests that the combination of mass media and interpersonal communication can provide an important influence strategy in the diffusion of innovations in the developing countries.

THE IMMUNIZATION STUDY

A series of studies conducted in Central America (Lin and Hingson, 1969;

Lin, 1971; Lin, Hingson, and Allwood-Paredes, 1971) examined the acceptance of disease-preventive inoculations among rural populations. Personal interviews were conducted with both adopters and nonadopters (the lady of the house for all households). The major findings were:

1. The diffusion rates were associated positively with the extent of effort invested by local disseminators (health officials, teachers, and priests) and with the socioeconomic level of the community, and negatively with the degree of isolation of the community from major roads and towns.

2. Mass media were more effective in transmitting information to early knowers, but personal sources were more effective in informing late knowers.

3. Adopters, as compared with nonadopters, were relatively higher on all socioeconomic indicators. In addition, they had greater access to information sources (both mass media and personal) and tended to learn about the immunization program through the mass media rather than through personal sources.

4. People took differential amounts of time to decide whether or not to accept the inoculations. The decision period varied from the instantaneous (upon becoming aware of the program, the person immediately decided to participate), to protracted (a time lag between the date of initial awareness and the date of decision to participate), to infinite (no decision was made to participate). Different types of decision-makers apparently represented different types of persons (Lin, 1971). The theoretical distinctions between the different types of decision-makers are not yet clear. The data suggest that the protracted decision-makers tend to possess modern personality traits, whereas the instantaneous decision-makers possess traditional personality traits. Thus, the protracted decision-makers took more time to assess the pros and cons of a commitment. Also, the protracted decision-makers seemed to be less integrated in the local community than the instantaneous decision-makers. Thus, the protracted decision-makers took more time to verify the information and assess the opinions of their local friends and opinion leaders. Further studies are being conducted to test out alternative theoretical propositions.

SUMMARY OF THE PRINCIPLES OF INNOVATION DIFFUSION

After having given a few examples of typical diffusion studies, I shall now discuss some major findings. These can be discussed in terms of the two major processes (the aggregate diffusion rate and the individual adoption process) and the major factor in both processes—the social structure within which the diffusion takes place.

Differential Diffusion Rates

Most of the diffusion rates have been found to be S-shaped, beginning slowly, increasing with a gradually accelerating rate, and finally tailing off slowly again. Some early studies also found that the cumulative diffusion rate approached the normal curve (Pemberton, 1936). The empirical finding is explained in terms of the assumption that there are two independent forces at work—the force in favor of the innovation and the force against the innovation. In the early stage, the unfavorable force in the social system is strong; therefore the diffusion is slow. As the favorable force gathers strength, the diffusion rate begins to accelerate. Finally, when the favorable force becomes the dominant force, only a few units in the social system have by this time not become adopters and therefore the diffusion rate is forced to slow down again (Pemberton, 1936). This interpretation went well with the assumption of the normal curve, which represents a combinatory expansion of two variables in the binomial form $(a+b)^n$. Some later studies (Rogers, 1957; Rogers, 1958; Beal and Rogers, 1960) also found the cumulative diffusion rates to approach normal. The normal curve diffusion rate had an additional attraction for diffusion researchers—it provided a means of standardizing the adopter categories. Rogers (1958) defined the five types of adopters (innovators, early adopters, early majority, late majority, and laggards) in terms of the standard deviations of the normal curve. Thus, the innovators were defined as those whose adoption time fell at least two standard deviations to the left of the mean adoption time, which constituted the first 2.5 percent of the area under the normal curve. The early adopters were defined as those whose adoption time fell between the first and second deviations to the left of the mean adoption time, which constituted the next 13.5 percent of the area under the normal curve. The areas one deviation to the left and to the right of the mean adoption time, each constituting 34 percent of the area, became the early majority and the late majority. Finally, those whose adoption time fell at least one deviation to the right of the mean adoption time became the laggards. These classifications are presented in Figure 6-4.

However, several studies (Ryan and Gross, 1943; Dimit, 1954; Beal and Rogers, 1960; Deutschmann and Fals Borda, 1962; Coleman, Katz, and Menzel, 1966; Lin and Hingson, 1969) have found that the cumulative diffusion curves deviate significantly from the normal curve. It seems that the extent of *deviation from the normal curve observed in cumulative diffusion rates can be explained by several important factors.* One factor is the *extent of interaction among the adopting units* in a social system. The normal curve is based on the assumption that the occurrences of the events are independent of each other, that they represent a total chance (random) noninteractive behavior among the events. When Pemberton (1936) studied the diffusion of postage stamps and of organizational memberships in the PTA, he might well have expected the diffusion curves to approach the normal curve, since a nation considering the adoption of postage stamps and a group thinking of joining the PTA were probably not under much pressure from other adopters. However, when the diffusion occurs in communities where interpersonal communication is frequent and important, as was the case with the farmers in the two Iowa communities and the physicians in the same specialized field in the four Midwestern communities, the assumption of the normal curve is violated. In fact, the interaction among the farmers and among the physicians was found to be very strong. Thus, when Coleman and others (1966) proposed two models, one for the interactive physicians and another for the isolated physicians, the data fitted quite well. The interactive model deviates significantly from the normal curve in that the acceleration rate is high soon after the diffusion begins, indicating that word-of-mouth communication among the adopting units starts right away after some physicians have tried the new drug.

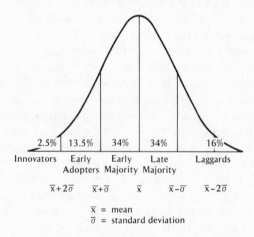

Figure 6-4. The Standard Deviations of a Normal Curve as Used in the Categorization of Adopters

The second factor which may account for the deviation of the cumulative diffusion curve from the normal curve relates to the *relative economic gain represented by the adoptive behavior.* When an innovation represents a genuine and significant economic improvement over the existing practice, the pressure upon nonadopters increases over time because the relative economic loss is increasingly painful to bear. The hybrid seed corn represents such an innovation. Thus, it was observed that it took a much shorter time for the late adopters to decide on complete adoption and that there was an abnormally high concentration of adopters around the modal adoption time.

A third factor may account for the deviation of a diffusion curve from a normal curve—*the authoritarian intervention.* Deutschmann and Fals Borda (1962) found that the innovations that were experimentally introduced into the community in Colombia by one of the authors showed an accelerated diffusion curve, not different from that found by Ryan and Gross in Iowa. Furthermore, even for other innovations, many Colombian farmers decided to adopt as soon as they heard about the innovations. This no-delay decision-making was described by one of the authors as a cultural trait—a tendency to have complete trust in authoritarian sources. Other studies in developing countries (Rahim, 1961; Lin and Hingson, 1969; Lin, 1971) also found substantial numbers of these instantaneous decision-makers receptive to agricultural and mass immunization campaigns in India and Central America. The adoption curves found here also deviated substantially from the normal curve. These findings indicate that even mass media and impersonal sources constitute effective persuasive forces when they reach the potential adopters in developing countries. That the authoritarian intervention accelerates diffusion rates should bring comfort to many who are responsible for planning change in the developing countries.

Finally, the *perceived characteristics of an innovation* also contribute to the variation of the diffusion curve from the normal curve. Fliegel and Kivlin, in a series of studies in Pennsylvania and India (Fliegel and Kivlin, 1966a; Fliegel and Kivlin, 1966b; Kivlin and Fliegel, 1967; Fliegel, Kivlin, and Sekhon, 1968), had both farmers and judges rate characteristics of farm innovations. The judges were farmers and agricultural change agents in the Pennsylvania county. The ratings of the innovation characteristics were then correlated with the adoption rates of the innovations. They found that for farmers in Pennsylvania, economic payoff and relevance to their specialty were important predictors of diffusion rates, while for the Indian sample, social approval was the most important attribute for predicting the diffusion rate of an innovation.

Other studies have confirmed the effect on the diffusion rate of the relative advantage of the innovation over the practice it supersedes, especially in a crisis situation (Wilkening, 1953; Mulford, 1959; Sutherland, 1959), of the compatibility of the innovation with potential adopters' values and experiences (Graham, 1956; Lionberger, 1960; Yeracaris, 1961), and of the relative ease with which the results can be communicated (Graham, 1956). Rogers and Shoemaker (1971) have also suggested that the divisibility (or "trialability") of the innovation (the extent to which an innovation can be tried on a limited basis) and the communicability (or observability) of the innovation (the extent to which the results of an innovation can be shown to others) might affect the diffusion rate.

Other dimensions of innovation characteristics deserve study. One is perceived terminality, which is defined as the point in time beyond which adoption of the innovation becomes relatively valueless or useless. Another is the "gatewayability" of the innovation, defined as the extent to which the adoption of the innovation facilitates the eventual adoption of other innovations. These and other characteristics should be evaluated in terms of the differential magnitude of their influence on the diffusion rate of innovations. Such influences may vary across cultural and social boundaries.

The Individual's Innovativeness

The innovativeness of an individual, usually measured by the earliness of his adoption of an innovation relative to other individuals in the social system or by the number of innovations he has adopted relative to those that others have adopted, is associated with several psychological and social traits. Rogers (1962; Rogers and Shoemaker, 1971) summarizes a number of such traits as follows:

1. Earlier adopters tend to be younger than later adopters. However, when the adoption of an innovation requires substantial experience and knowledge about the class of practices to which the innovation belongs, older persons may become more innovative.

2. Earlier adopters tend to have higher social status than later adopters. Education, one index of social status, is important, especially when the diffusion takes place in developing countries.

3. Earlier adopters have a more flexible financial management conception and assets than later adopters. Such flexibility is reflected in higher income, a commercial (rather than subsistence) economic orientation, larger-sized land ownership, and a more favorable attitude toward credit (borrowing money).

4. Earlier adopters have more specialized operations than later adopters. Specialization tends to lead to interest in and knowledge about innovations, thus contributing to early adoption.

5. Earlier adopters have greater empathy than later adopters. Empathy is the ability of an individual to project himself into the role of another person.

6. Earlier adopters are less dogmatic than later adopters.

7. Earlier adopters are more change-oriented than later adopters.

8. Earlier adopters use more information sources, more mass media, and more impersonal sources, and use them more frequently, than later adopters.

9. Earlier adopters tend to be closer to the original source or disseminators (change agents) of the innovation than later adopters.

10. Earlier adopters tend to have more external or cosmopolitan orientation than later adopters.

11. Earlier adopters tend more to be opinion leaders than later adopters.

12. The *earliest* adopters tend to be considered deviants relative to the existing norms in the social system.

A person's adoption of an innovation does not necessarily imply his permanent commitment to the particular practice he has adopted. In fact, *discontinuance of adoption occurs with regularity.* Discontinuance has been associated with several factors. One finding is that *those who are later adopters also tend to be the ones to discontinue adoption* (Johnson and van den Ban, 1959). As described above, the later adopters tend to be traditionally oriented, poorer, less exposed to mass media and impersonal sources, farther away from the original sources and disseminators of the innovations, less educated, more likely to be doubters, and so forth. All these factors may contribute to the improper adoption and use of the innovation.

Another reason for discontinuance of adoption is simply that the *practice adopted is superseded by another innovation.* Thus, the discontinuance of adoption of one innovation may simply indicate that another innovation has been adopted in place of the older practice. This substituting behavior, of course, goes on all the time. However, in contrast to the previous factor, which shows the tendency of later adopters to abandon the innovation for reasons such as improper use, the persons who substitute new innovations for old innovations should show a different pattern of social and psychological traits. They should possess the characteristics of the earlier adopters, being more affluent, educated, cosmopolitan, and so forth, and thus more prone to change. But more empirical data are needed to verify these characteristics.

Interpersonal Influence and Diffusion

Diffusion research reveals that interpersonal communication plays a major role at several crucial phases in a person's decision to adopt an innovation. The data generally suggest that *personal sources are most effective in inducing adoption, while mass media and impersonal sources (change agents, disseminators) are more effective in transmitting the initial information and knowledge about the innovation to potential adopters.* Furthermore, late adopters tend to rely on personal sources for both information and influence.

Several generalizations have also developed from studies of opinion leaders or opinion leadership. Opinion leaders usually represent those who have obtained high scores on opinion-giving indices by self-scoring, other-nominating, or judge-rating. Opinion leadership is a scale by which the extent of a person's opinion leadership is measured. These studies show that:

1. Opinion leaders (or high scorers on an opinion leadership scale) are more likely to be social norm supporters than are others (Marsh and Coleman, 1956; Rogers and Burdge, 1962; van den Ban, 1964).

2. Opinion leaders in modern, progressive communities tend to have specialized spheres of influence, or to be monomorphic, whereas those in traditional, less developed communities tend to have a general sphere of influence, or to be polymorphic (Emery and Oeser, 1958; Rahim, 1961).

3. Opinion leaders tend to use more mass media and impersonal information sources than do followers (Lionberger, 1953; Rahim, 1961; Rogers and Burdge, 1962).

4. Opinion leaders are more externally oriented than others (Rahudkar, 1960; van den Ban, 1964; Rogers and Meynen, 1965).

5. Opinion leaders are more gregarious than others (Lionberger, 1953; Rahim, 1961; van den Ban, 1964).

6. Opinion leaders are distributed throughout all social levels. However,

people tend to seek advice from those who are slightly above them in social status (Lionberger and Coughenour, 1957). In general, opinion leaders have slightly higher social status than their followers.

7. Opinion leaders tend to be more innovative than others. Furthermore, persons tend to be influenced by slightly earlier adopters or by persons who adopt at about the same time.

Emergent Generalizations Concerning Communication Effects on Behavioral Change

A casual glance at the summarized findings from the mass communication research and the diffusion research may reveal more than a few generalizations about the effect of human communication on behavioral change. This is striking, for the two traditions developed independently, and it was only about a decade ago that researchers in the two traditions began to discover their overlapping interests and theoretical convergence (E. Katz, 1960).

I will now attempt to summarize the various theoretical generalizations about the effects of human communication on behavioral change, drawing evidence mainly from the two research traditions.

DIFFICULTIES OF BEHAVIORAL CHANGE

Behavioral change, in general, is a slow and difficult process. There are three fundamental reasons why this is so: (1) man's basic need for psychological or cognitive closure, (2) the tight ring of his social reinforcement, and (3) his self-fulfilling communication behavior. I will now elaborate.

Man's basic psychological composite resists change. As the cognitive theorists repeatedly point out, men strive for consistency, balance, and congruity. This is not to say that men are closed-minded and unreceptive to new ideas and practices. In fact, men are quite open-minded and receptive to new ideas and practices—insofar as the new ideas and practices are not in direct conflict with their basic beliefs and values. Behavioral change, by definition, implies an overt contradiction of an individual's past behavior; thus it would induce dissonance, imbalance, and incongruity. Such a psychological state is in most cases intolerable and should be avoided.

The psychological closure of an individual is further reinforced by the immediate social environment in which he claims and is claimed to have membership. There are important interdependent dynamics between a person's psychological makeup and his social environment. He strives to make the two dynamic forces compatible and consonant. He survives and thrives in the social environment because it supports and reinforces his beliefs and values, and he is psychologically comfortable and happy when he can participate in the social environment in ways compatible with his beliefs and values. His family, his friends, and his fellow workers, through constant intimate contacts with him, constitute the fundamental relationship between himself and the external world of which his behavioral patterns must take account. Such intimate contacts are interactive in nature, providing immediate feedback and responses to feedback and rewards that are personal and intimate.

Thus constituted psychologically and socially, the individual attempts to construct and organize his communication behavior so that messages of conflicting composition can be carefully avoided. He exposes himself only to the sources and channels that are least likely to carry such antagonistic messages. If and when such antagonistic messages are encountered, he elects to erase or block them from his memory. Furthermore, he is selective in his perception and interpretation of messages, even if distortion or misinterpretation has to be employed. The selective exposure, selective retention, and selective perception or interpretation form a three-layer fence which protects him from potential intrusions of messages that are incompatible with his psychological and social makeup.

For these three reasons, as diagramed roughly in Figure 6−5, inducement of behavioral change is difficult and slow. This is documented by

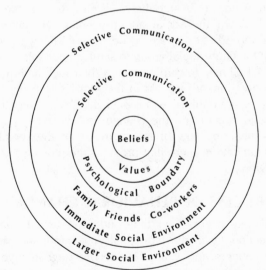

Figure 6−5. The Social and Psychological System of an Individual and His Selective Communications

the findings that once a voter has made up his mind whom he will vote for, the likelihood of his changing his vote intention is less than one in ten, and that it took more than 14 years for hybrid seed corn to be completely adopted in Iowa.

HUMAN COMMUNICATION: THE MOVING FORCE OF BEHAVIORAL CHANGE

Men do change the ways they behave however, even though such changes are infrequent and slow. How, then, does change come about? It seems that behavior change can occur only if one or more of the reinforcement rings have somehow changed their composition relative to the individual or loosened their grip on the individual. Cumulative experiences may crystalize the incompatibility of various beliefs and values. The immediate social environment, for a variety of reasons, may not be perceived as supportive or reinforcing any longer. Antagonistic messages may somehow, even a little at a time, get through. Of the three possible composition changes, a change in psychological makeup is the most difficult and least likely to occur, since it may induce an identity crisis. A change in the support provided by the social environment may occur only when the social climate becomes receptive to change or when physical mobility brings the individual into a different social environment. *Filtering of antagonistic messages,* on the other hand, *occurs almost regularly.* With the growth of mass media and transportation facilities, a person may find it difficult not to be exposed to some antagonistic messages in any given day.

In addition, exposure to such messages may serve as the catalyst necessary to break down the social and psychological compositions which constitute the more basic barriers to behavioral change. Enough exposure on the part of the entire social group to similar antagonistic messages could mold the social climate toward change. When such a climate has formed, change not only gains a foothold in the social system, but will gradually accelerate its impact until the winds of change have swept thoroughly over the entire social system and the change itself becomes part of the social and psychological makeup of the members of the social system. It is human communication, then, that provides the moving force in changing human behavior.

THE PROCESS OF BEHAVIORAL CHANGE

Behavioral change occurs over time and over several *stages.* The *initial stage* is the *encounter* of the individual with information concerning the change, be it voting or innovating. The *second stage* involves his *exchange* with other sources of information and opinion so that the intrinsic composition of the change as well as the social climate toward the change can be determined. His *actual change of behavior,* his commitment, constitutes the *third stage* of behavioral change. Finally, there is a *fourth stage* of behavioral change—*postcommitment reinforcement,* which is the process whereby the individual integrates the change into his psychological and social closure.

In the information encounter stage, both the mass media and personal sources provide important channels for information transmission. Mass media tend to be more effective in transmitting such information in the more modern, industrialized, urban communities, whereas personal sources are the primary information carriers in the more traditional, agricultural, and rural communities. A third type of source, the disseminators who have been specifically charged with responsibility for spreading news of the change, is effective in transmitting information among the more specialized social systems, such as the medical, organizational, educational, and agricultural groups, and in the more traditional, agricultural, and rural communities. These disseminators are most effective when the change is planned on the community or societal level.

After the individual has been exposed to the information about the change, he may go through a stage of exchange with other sources in order to confirm facts about and values (as he perceived) of the change and to evaluate the social climate toward the change before he makes a commitment. The extent of such exchange is determined by a number of factors: (1) the more he is interested in the topic, the more extensive his exchange; (2) the more cross-pressures he experiences or the more ambiguous he feels about the change, the more extensive his exchange; (3) the less social support he perceives for the change, the more extensive his exchange; (4) the less credible the information source, the more extensive his exchange; (5) the more extensive his participation in the social environment, the more extensive his exchange; (6) the less expertise he has in the topic, the more extensive his exchange; (7) the more financial investment involved in the change, the more extensive his exchange.

Mass media, impersonal sources, and personal sources are all likely to be consulted during the exchange, depending on the availability of the sources to the individual and the extent to which the messages relative to the change are carried by these sources. As a whole, because of the relative ease with which they trade information and opinions, personal sources constitute the basic exchange channels.

Finally, the individual commits himself, either to adopting the change or to rejecting it. The *commitment is overwhelmingly more influenced by personal sources than by mass media or impersonal sources.* For the mass media, messages of an informative nature seem more effective in inducing change than messages based on an emotional appeal. *Disseminators are almost as effective as other personal sources in inducing change in the more traditional, rural, or agricultural communities.* "Wrong" sources tend to induce rejection or to delay the commitment (Copp, Sill, and Brown, 1958).

In general, changes are accepted more readily by younger persons, by persons of higher social status, by persons in better financial positions, by persons who have some expertise in the topic, by persons who have access to more information sources, by persons closer to the original sources or disseminators, and by persons who are less bound by the existing social norms.

After the individual has accepted the change, he attempts to bring the change into his social and psychological closure. Again, selective exposure, selective retention, and selective perception and interpretation are utilized to assemble messages which are congruous with the change. Discontinuance of change tends to occur among persons who commit themselves relatively late to the change or among persons who are so oriented toward change in general that they have committed themselves to other changes superseding the previously adopted change.

INTERPERSONAL INFLUENCE ON BEHAVIORAL CHANGE

Probably the most important finding about behavioral change is the role personal sources play. Research attention has consequently focused on the structure of interpersonal communication. Two areas of research have proved interesting and fruitful. One research area focuses on the relative time it takes different individuals to commit themselves to the change; out of this effort has come knowledge about the early adopters and opinion leaders. The other area focuses on the interplay of mass media and personal sources in the process of behavioral change.

The persons who commit themselves to the change *earliest* tend to be *deviants* as far as the prevailing social norms are concerned. Their commitment does not have much impact on other persons in the social system. However, the *opinion leaders* keep a close eye on the effect of the innovators' early commitment and evaluate the results of the change. These opinion leaders can be distinguished from others in the social system by their substantial interest and expertise in the area of the change, their strategic social position, which facilitates their contact with sources and media disseminating the change and knowledge about the change, their gregariousness, their extensive exposure to mass media, and their support for the social norms. *Opinion leaders can be found on all social levels and they tend to be influential with those on the same social level or on the level slightly below.* In the more modern, industrial, and urban communities, opinion leaders tend to be *monomorphic;* in short, different sets of opinion leaders appear in different topic areas. In the more traditional, agricultural, and rural communities, opinion leaders tend to be *polymorphic;* in other words, they give advice on a wide range of topics. Different types of opinion leaders can also be identified. Some opinion leaders specialize primarily in local affairs, while others specialize in cosmopolitan issues. *Formal opinion leaders* do not have direct contact with their followers, but exert influence on younger and moderately well-educated people; *informal leaders,* on the other hand, have frequent personal contact with their followers and tend to exert influence on older and less-educated people. When traditional opinion leaders fail to relate their groups to the larger social system, younger and more cosmopolitan opinion leaders emerge.

While the local, traditional opinion leaders tend to be *stabilizers,* functioning mainly to maintain the group and the social norms, the cosmopolitan and progressive opinion leaders tend to be *movers,* functioning as the link between the group and the larger, fast-moving social system.

It is only when a sufficient number of opinion leaders have committed themselves to the change that a significant number of other members of the social system will follow suit. This momentum—accelerating at a rate which depends on the extent of interpersonal communication, the characteristics of the change, the observable advantages of the change, and the extent of dissemination effort—will then carry the change until it is completely accepted by members of the social system.

The crucial question, then, is whether and to what extent the opinion leaders will commit themselves to the change. One determining factor is the *social climate.* In the more modern, industrial, and urban communities, the social climate is in general favorable to change; thus, the leaders tend to commit themselves to useful changes. In the more traditional, agricultural, and rural communities, the social climate is in general less favorable to change. In these communities, *external authoritative intervention in mobilizing the opinion leaders becomes crucial.*

Since opinion leaders hold key positions in the interpersonal communication networks of the social system, their sharing of opinions and information about the change with others constitutes the most crucial element in the dynamic process of behavioral change.

7

Control and Adaptation:
THE ORGANIZATION
OF HUMAN COMMUNICATION

The previous chapters on encounter, exchange, and influence—the three phases of human communication—may give the reader a false impression that human communication is mostly a one-way process, with a source generating information or message and a receiver who encounters or is influenced by that information or message. At best, the previous discussion gives the impression that while exchange does occur, it is a free-flow interaction situation. Thus, the whole process of human communication seems to be illuminated by the simple input-process-output model where a piece of information or a message is assimilated by an organ which in turn processes the information or message and formulates its response. However, there is another important phase in human communication; *not only is the process two-way*—that is, the receiver also generates information and message for the source—*but the continuation and thriving of human communication depends on such interaction.* This important aspect of human communication will now be discussed under the topic of control and adaptation. *Control indicates the effort put forth by the source to organize communication; adaptation, the effort of the receiver to organize communication.*

When information theory was first introduced in the late 1940s by Shannon and Weaver, another information theorist, Norbert Weiner (1948), proposed a study of the control of communication. He perceived that communication can be maintained only when there is feedback from the receiver to the source. He called the control aspect of communication "cybernetics," a word derived from Latin meaning "governing." The impetus behind cybernetics was an important law in thermodynamics. According to the second law of thermodynamics, a physical system that does not interact with the external environment decays and approaches randomness over time. In information terms, the law states that the tendency toward entropy (maximum disorganization, true equilibrium) is a universal law of nature. In other words, *if a system is closed—if it has no interaction with its environment—it will eventually cease to function.* When this physical law is applied to biological and social systems, it implies that a system, to continue functioning with its presently defined characteristics and goals, will have to interact with its environment. Such an interactive system is called an open system. The most important feature of an open system is its ability to construct and employ a feedback mechanism that permits information about its output to be received and processed by the input unit, which in turn can assess the changes that are necessary relative to the system's structure or process, so that the output can get closer to the expected or desired level of direction. In short, *a social system must either change or perish.*

Functions of Control and Adaptation

Communication is, therefore, the basic ingredient of a surviving social system. In the encounter phase, the intention is to transmit information successfully; that is, we hope to reduce the uncertainty of the information. In the exchange phase, we hope that the meaning intended is the meaning received and interpreted. In the influence phase, we hope that the attitude and behavior will not only change but that they will change in a certain direction and magnitude. How do we know, either as sources or as receivers, that the effect of human communication has approached the intended direction and magnitude? If a source does not evaluate what happens to the information and message as they are received by the receiver, and if the receiver has no way of detecting the response of the source as to what he perceives, understands, and how he is affected by the message, the likelihood of a communication breakdown or communication gap is great. Many world, national, and interpersonal frictions attest to the seriousness of such a gap.

In May 1970, when the United States government decided to send troops into Cambodia, American youth and President Nixon used similar terms in discussing the issue but meant different things. For example, the President emphasized that he and the students both wanted "peace." By "peace," students meant an immediate end to U.S. military involvement in Southeast Asia, whereas the President meant a "just peace" and "self-determination for South Vietnam" (*Time*, August 3, 1970, quoting Heard and Cheek's memorandum to the President regarding college unrest). As a result, the "V" symbol was used by people of all political persuasions to mean whatever they wanted it to mean. The result was that the same symbol had completely different meanings and effects for different people. Such a gap exists in many other forms and societies. To close such a gap, *both the source and the receiver would have to attach identical symbols and meanings* to the information and messages they transmitted. This is the first function served by the adaptation and control of human communication.

Adaptation and control of human communication also serve *to detect the effect of the communication and to adjust it to what the source and the receiver expect.* In other words, in addition to the shared understanding of the information and message, the influence of the communication, if such effect is intended, will be in the direction of and of the magnitude intended by the source of the communication. It may be pointed out that when the information and message transmitted are understood as they were intended to be by the source, the receiver should be affected in the expected direction and magnitude. However, as mentioned in Chapter 4, many variables constrain the consistency between the understanding and attitudinal acceptance of the information or message and the actual behavioral change to take place. Whether the behavior will be in the direction of and of the magnitude advocated by the source depends on many social, psychological, and economic considerations. In addition, the realistic environment restricts the ways in which the receiver can act. Thus, he may have to adjust his actual behavior, in the hope that such adjustment will not alter the expected effect in any way. Unfortunately, such adjustments occur with high frequency; furthermore, they do alter the intended effects. To detect the deviation of the actual behavior from the intended effect requires reliance on control and adaptation analysis—adaptation by the receiver, taking into account the various environmental constraints, and control by the source, to measure and counteract any deviations from the expected effect.

While communication is itself an open system capable of steering its internal structure away from inefficiency (in terms of information and message) and ineffectiveness (in terms of influence), it is also an important mechanism on which all human organizations depend to arrest the tendency toward entropy and therefore to survive. A human organization is defined here as an interrelated aggregate group of people which engages in specific and persistent activities over time and which has certain goals as the ultimate purpose of its existence. An organization can either choose to remain closed and thus risk disorganization or it can choose to change and grow. *As a human organization grows, three things tend to occur within the organization. First, the amount of transaction increases.* The growth of an organization is symbolized by its growth in number of levels, branches, and offices. The transaction of information and messages among the various subsystems also increases as the number of such subsystems increases. *Second, multiple-channel traffic increases.* That is, transactions tend more and more to go through a multiple number of channels rather than to be direct transactions. *Finally, the channels are more and more occupied by undesirable systems of traffic.* As the traffic increases in the channels, provisions have to be made to facilitate specific transactions. However, cumulation of such provisions eventually proves to be ineffective to other transactions and, in fact, becomes a barrier to other transactions. Because of these three factors, *each form of organization has an upper limit of size beyond which it will not function* (Weiner, 1948). Unless the form of the organization itself changes, one effective means to combat these obstacles is to establish a *feedback* mechanism in the organization. The mechanism directs traffic, reduces the number of channels involved in each transaction, and eliminates undesirable cumulative systems of traffic.

Lest the above discussion give the impression that the control and adaptation of human communication are purely mechanical problems, I hasten to point out that human beings have an inherent need to receive information indicating to what extent their behavior and performance and even beliefs are acceptable to others. The control and adaptation of human communication meet this need by transmitting such information to the concerned participants.

In summary, then, control and adaptation of human communication are essential if the communication system itself is to become efficient and effective, if deviations of intended effects are to be detected and adjusted, and if the resulting difficulties of growing organizations are to be reduced or eliminated.

Mechanisms of Control and Adaptation

The control and adaptation of human communication consist of two major components. The first component concerns the *feedback* mechanism, which transmits and processes information and messages from the receivers to the source of communication. The second component focuses on the *dissemination process,* which the source utilizes to adjust its transmission mechanism to achieve more efficient or effective communication.

THE FEEDBACK MECHANISM

Feedback is essentially the mechanism by which the source is informed of the observable effect (intended or unintended) on the receivers of the information and message he has transmitted. Feedback can be either positive or negative. Positive feedback confirms that the intended efficiency and effect has been achieved; *negative feedback* indicates the deviation of the actual efficiency and effect of the communication from the intended one. Of the two types of feedback, negative feedback is by far the more important, for *it is the negative feedback which provides the necessary information on the basis of which control and adaptation of communication can be made.*

Leavitt and Mueller (1951) found that when negative feedback was allowed in experimental communication situations, errors in the accuracy of information transmission were decreased and the participants' confidence in carrying out the assigned task was improved. Tustin (1952) and many others have specifically pointed out that feedback is intended to arrest error. From here on, I will use the word feedback to mean exclusively negative feedback.

The feedback mechanism consists of three major components (Tustin, 1952): *a measuring device, a regulator, and an upper bound of time span.*

The measuring device detects the output direction and magnitude in a given time unit. It is a means whereby the actual outcome of either a communication situation or the achieved output of an organization can be objectively measured. It involves both an accounting system, which keeps track of the quantity of such outcome and output, and an evaluating unit, which assesses the quality of such outcome and output.

The information obtained by the measuring device is then transmitted to the regulating unit. The regulating unit is responsible for comparing the information received from the measuring unit with the intended outcome and output. When discrepancy is detected, as it usually is, the information is fed to the units which compose the production and communication system. These units, based on such information, adjust themselves accordingly and, hopefully, cause the outcome and output to approach the expected goal.

The measuring and regulating activities operate under an important constraint—time. For when these activities take too long, the resulting adjustments and adaptations may not be sufficient to counteract the damage that has already been done to the system or to salvage it. Thus, the third crucial component of the feedback mechanism is a time limit. With the requirement of time span, the measuring and regulating activities will be effective in feeding the necessary information to the system to arrest errors before such errors have deviated so much from the intended goal that the system can no longer survive.

A dynamic view of the systemic adjustment and adaptation resulting from an efficient feedback mechanism is depicted in Figure 7–1.

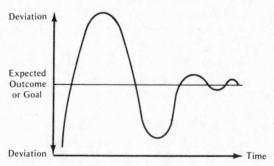

Figure 7–1. Effect of Feedback

While feedback is an important mechanism by which the tendency to entropy in a communication system or an organization is arrested, it may also, by its existence, create other problems.

One possible problem connected with the feedback mechanism is the *hostility* of the elements and the role-occupants toward the *disruption* caused by the feedback and the resulting adjustment. Leavitt and Mueller (1951) found that in a task experiment, the participants were generally hostile to the feedback because it disrupted their routine. A social system of any kind tends to settle down to a routinized procedure in conducting its activities. The role-occupants and units are trained to master such procedures so that activities can be carried out most efficiently. When such training and routinization have formed, it becomes disruptive to the role-occupants and units if changes and adjustments are forced upon them. The hostility and resentment may be a direct function of the amount of change and adjustment required.

Another problem of feedback concerns *oscillation* (Tustin, 1952). As the regulator transmits the feedback information back into the system in order to change the operations back to the expected level, overcorrection may easily result. What tends to happen is that correction of a deviation in one direction will lead to deviation in the opposite direction. When such changes occur regularly, an oscillation results, and when the oscillation reaches a point at which every change or adjustment requires drastic disruption of routines, the system will rapidly approach a breakdown.

A third problem that can result from feedback is that it may cause *imbalance* among the units within the system (Tustin, 1952). The feedback may require change and adjustments in certain specific units of the system. However, because the units in the system are all interrelated, changes in some units affect other units as well. While some units have changed or adjusted their activities, other units may still maintain their routinized activities. As a result, the interdependence among the units breaks down.

The process of feedback itself requires *time*. Time is needed to measure the outcome and output, to assess this information, and to adjust the system. Whether the amount of time invested in such activities can be compensated for by the resulting adjustment and outcome is another important factor in the assessment of the feedback mechanism.

Finally, the feedback mechanism tends to *grow* as the system grows or as greater precision of the outcome and the output is required. Haire (1959) noted that in the biological organism, the pressure for information in the interest of integration is answered partly by the growth of the nervous system into a more complex network and partly by a simple increase in the speed of the transmission of the signal. In social systems, the speed of message transmission can be improved, but not substantially due to mechanical limitations. Thus, it is more efficient and probable that as the system grows, expansion of the feedback mechanism into a more complex network will take place. The growth of the feedback mechanism itself accentuates the before-mentioned problems. In addition, the feedback itself becomes an enormous operational organization which faces breakdown and entropy. Thus, the feedback will approach the entropy itself as it grows bigger and bigger. What this means is that no organization can grow indefinitely. There is an upper limit of size beyond which an organization will not function for the simple reason that an effective feedback mechanism ceases to be feasible (Weiner, 1948). Deutsch (1952) also points out that a system can grow only if it continues to: (1) increase in openness, (2) increase in internal coherence, (3) increase in power, and (4) increase in learning capacity. As a system increases in size, these activities become harder to perform and maintain.

THE DISSEMINATION MECHANISM

Strictly speaking, the dissemination mechanism is a part of the feedback mechanism; when the information is transmitted from the measuring device to the regulating unit, the resultant necessary adjustments and changes will have to be delivered to and enforced by units within the system. The deliberate transmission of such information to the units in the system is the dissemination process. However, there are situations where dissemination occurs without feedback. This may occur either when no previous outcome or output exist or when such outcome and output are not available for assessment. Propaganda directed to an audience in enemy territory is one example; many initiations of technical, industrial, agricultural, health, and educational innovations (especially in less developed or developing countries) are another. Thus, I single out the dissemination mechanism for discussion.

The dissemination mechanism is utilized extensively by governments, social reformists, agencies of planned change, and marketing specialists. It consists of three major defining characteristics: (1) It occurs in a *well-defined target system;* (2) it requires *deliberate transmission* on the part of the source; and (3) the source or initiator of the dissemination has relatively rigid *control over the transmission process.*

Dissemination can occur only when the target system is defined beforehand. This does not imply that the target system must be thoroughly analyzed or understood. In fact, many target systems are not completely analyzed or understood by the disseminator. However, a definite conception of the "enemy territory" or "enemy" is necessary before propaganda can be disseminated. When an insurance firm attempts to sell a particular policy, the target system is that specific segment of the population which qualifies to buy it. Without such definition, dissemination cannot take place or have an effect.

Dissemination involves deliberate transmission. In other words, the source intention is clearly demonstrated, even though such intention may be concealed from the target system. Thus, the transmission is enforced by the source at all times and the intended purpose of the source is to see to it that the transmission is delivered to the audience in the target system.

The third element of dissemination is the transmission control. The disseminators have control over the selection of channels and the messages to be transmitted in the primary transmission. The primary transmission is the transmission which connects the source of the dissemination with the channel, while the secondary transmission consists mainly of the communication activities that take place between a secondary source and other units or members in the delivery and/or target system. Thus, dissemination involves a relative description of and control over the primary channels and messages to be utilized in the transmission by the source and the disseminators.[1]

Dynamic Contribution of Disorganization

While this discussion has focused on the means by which the tendency toward entropy may be arrested, it must be pointed out that disorganization is also an important element in human communication and human organization. For human communication, the *total elimination of uncertainty or entropy would mean that no information was being received by the receiver.* In other words, the transmission would be wasted, since the receiver would already possess the information. While the efficiency of the transmission depends, during the transmission, on the degree of uncertainty reduction, complete lack of uncertainty is also undesirable. Similarly, human organization cannot stay at a point where all activities are completely routinized. That a natural balance between uncertainty and redundancy is sought in such diversified phenomena as language, animal survival, and even news delivery shows that *there is an optimal level of balance between organization and disorganization.* While feedback arrests the tendency toward total uncertainty (entropy), neither communication nor other social systems should strive for a totally efficient feedback system. Such a system would prove to be too costly, time-consuming, and entropy-inducing. The system should, instead, leave room for growth, change, and therefore disorganization. *A certain degree of disorganization performs a number of important functions for a social system:*

1. *It increases and maintains the openness of the system.* All social systems are open systems, interacting with the external environment and therefore receiving and producing activities and energies across the boundary. Such exchange is bound to present the social system with situations it has not experienced before. If the social system does not allow any disorganization, such encounter will either decrease the efficiency of the system or damage the system severely enough to threaten its survival. If a certain amount of disorganization is tolerated, eventually the feedback

---

1. These characteristics essentially differentiate the dissemination process from the diffusion process. In the diffusion process, some or all of these characteristics will be lacking.

mechanism will absorb the effect of such disorganization and adjust the system so that the elements of the disorganization can be integrated into the routines of the system's activities.

2. Related to the openness of the system, disorganization also *provides the system with opportunities to learn.* Learning is the process by which a stimulus coming from the environment is processed so that subsequently a systematic response deemed appropriate by and beneficial to the system can be generated. Disorganization permits such stimuli to filter into the system so that new response patterns can be established in the best interests of the system.

3. Another important function of disorganization is to *generate renewal of the system.* An accumulation of learning by the system because of disorganization actually improves its chances of survival, assuming that it continues to adjust itself to stimuli coming from the environment. As mentioned earlier, the system has a natural tendency toward entropy and therefore death; disorganization can disrupt the deteriorating pattern and thereby renew the system so that the activities and goals of the system are refreshed and oriented in a new direction.

Disorganization can benefit the social system only under two conditions. One condition is that *the amount of disorganization is tolerable* to the system. When disorganization damages the routines substantially, the foundations of the system will be shaken and the ability of the system to survive may be damaged. Thus, the amount of disorganization has an upper limit—which is the amount of organization in the system. I speculate that *this upper limit is somewhere below the 50 percent mark in terms of the total uncertainty,* since many natural efficient systems possess an optimal distribution of 50 percent and 50 percent between uncertainty and redundancy.

Another condition is that *the system can and will respond to the disorganization.* In other words, the system has a built-in learning capacity. For a system without such ability, disorganization will simply accumulate over time and eventually overwhelm the organization of the system. Thus, it is essential for the system to respond to disorganization—not to suppress it but to absorb its implications and adjust the system itself so that the disorganization can be integrated and routinized.

Summary

In this brief chapter, I have attempted to point out that communication is not only a two-way process but that the survival of the social system involved may depend on it. Such a two-way process makes possible the adaptation and control of the organization of communication. Such adaptation and control are essential if the communication system is to become efficient and effective, if deviations from intended effects are to be detected and adjusted, and if the resulting difficulties of organizational growth are to be reduced or eliminated.

The adaptation and control of communication consists of two components—feedback (negative) and dissemination. Negative feedback, defined as the mechanism by which the source is informed of the observable effect on the receivers of the information and messages that it has transmitted, consists of a measuring device, a regulator, and a specific time limit. Dissemination is a communication process in which the target system is well-defined, the transmission is the deliberate effort of the source, and the source has control over the transmission process.

While feedback and dissemination promote control and organization of human communication, a certain degree of disorganization is not only permissible but also necessary. As long as the disorganization does not totally destroy the social system in question and as long as the system can and will respond, such disorganization increases and maintains the system's openness, promotes its learning capabilities and opportunities, and generates renewal of the system. Thus, disorganization may actually contribute to the adaptation of the system as it communicates with its external environment.

8

Toward Theorization of Human Communication Research

In this book, I have attempted to sketch our knowledge, based on both conceptual discussions and empirical evidence, of human communication. The development of theoretical statements, however, remains limited, uneven, and fragmentary. In one research area, the psychological influence of communication, important propositions have been advanced and empirically tested, while in another, the behavioral influence of communication, investigations have advanced only a few propositions, only some of which have gained substantial empirical support. In other areas, such as encounter, exchange, and control, our theorizing task is only at the preliminary stage, though powerful measurements have been available to us since the late forties.

In this concluding chapter, I propose to examine the theoretical issues in human communication research from two separate angles. First, I will discuss the concept of theory and the process of scientific investigation. Such discussion will equip us (1) to examine critically the current strata of various so-called theories and (2) to suggest potential avenues for constructing theories about human communication. Second, I will critically examine one particular theoretical proposition as a potential theory and suggest an alternate theoretical framework and propositions to be derived from it. Thus, I will provide an example of how the discussions of theory constructions in the first part can fruitfully guide our theorization of human communication in the future.

The Concept of Theory and the Process of Scientific Investigation

The ultimate goal of science is to explain, by means of a set of theories, events that are observed. One theory can be compared with another in terms of (1) its generality (how many observable facts can it explain?), (2) its pervasiveness of extension (how many other theoretical statements can be deduced from it?), and (3) its simplicity (how parsimonious is it?). A theory consists of three main parts: concepts, propositions, and contingency (Homans, 1964).

ELEMENTS OF A THEORY

A theory has a set of concepts or a conceptual scheme. These concepts are either primitive (they are not defined) or operative (they can be found empirically). For example, when we say that sentiment varies with interaction, both sentiment and interaction are considered primitive concepts that are left undefined. When we say that sentiment varies with the frequency of telephone calls, the frequency of telephone calls is a concept that has its empirical meaning equivalence—that is, we can actually observe and count the number of telephone calls taking place between two persons.

In addition to concepts, a theory also contains a number of propositions. Let us consider the following set of propositions:

1. Sentiment varies with interaction.

2. Interaction varies with the frequency of telephone calls between two persons.

3. Therefore, sentiment should vary with the frequency of telephone calls between two persons.

4. The frequency of telephone calls between John and Judy is greater than between Joe and Jane.

5. So, it should be the case that the sentiment between John and Judy is greater than the sentiment between Joe and Jane.

This set of propositions constitutes the deductive system of a theory. The first proposition is the most abstract and general. Proposition 2 begins to specify a linkage between a primitive term, interaction, and an operative term, the frequency of telephone calls. Proposition 3 is directly deduced from Propositions 1 and 2. Proposition 4 becomes even more specific; it concerns a given situation with all terms operative in nature. Proposition 5 is the consequent proposition; again, it is deduced from Propositions 3 and 4.

Thus, a theory contains a set of concepts and a deductive set of propositions—deductive in terms of the flow from abstract to concrete, from general to specific, from a higher-order proposition to a number of lower-order propositions. As a result of the deductive set of propositions, a theory can be verified empirically because lower-order propositions such as 4 and 5 are directly accessible to observation and measurement (the psychological concept, sentiment, is assumed to be operationalizable in that some measurement instrument can be devised to tap it empirically). In this sense, a theory is contingent—on its direct access to empirical verification. Strictly speaking, a theory can be said to exist only if such a verification process has been completed, only if its empirical verification has been substantiated.

In the social sciences, of which human communication is one area of concern, we have many so-called theories, but only a few of them are true theories in the sense that they fulfill all three of the requirements of a theory. When we have a set of statements consisting of a number of concepts and some propositions, which are not contingent—not empirically verified—then we have a hypothesis. A hypothesis is a potential theory, but it is not an actual one until the last condition, contingency, has been fulfilled. We also have many statements which contain a set of concepts and an incomplete set of propositions (usually only the higher-order propositions phrased in abstract terms), but which do not have lower-order propositions; contingency is not fulfilled in the case of these statements either. These statements are speculations, not theories. They may help point out the potential approaches to a theory, but they themselves can only be regarded as pre-theory statements.

THE POWER OF A THEORY

The chief function of a theory is to summarize a variety of observable events and situations by means of a limited set of propositions (the higher-order propositions). Thus, the *power of a theory is evaluated in terms of the number of empirical (lower-order) propositions which can be deduced from the higher-order propositions.* In this sense, the power of a theory depends on more than how "true" it is. Some "true" theories can be relatively powerless. For example, we may state, "The sun is observable every morning, when there are no clouds." It is a theory that can be and has been verified. However, because almost no other propositions can be deduced from this proposition, we say that this theory is relatively powerless.

A theory is not airtight, or all-inclusive. If it is airtight, then we call it a law. However, because a theory is always contingent upon observations, it is inevitably probabilistic in nature. A theory can be falsified. In fact, *an essential characteristic of a theory is its falsifiability.* When the propositions in a theory become discrepant with those in another theory, or with those observed, we say that a theoretical crisis is present. A theoretical crisis is a healthy event in the process of scientific development, because it provides the opportunity for alternative theories to arise. When an alternative theory can resolve the crisis, either we have additional propositions in the existing theory or we have a new theory. This process of crisis-generating and crisis-resolving is the fundamental contribution of theorization to the growth of science (Kuhn, 1962).

DEDUCTION AND INDUCTION

Although a theory contains a deductive set of propositions, the *construction of a theory can take either of two routes—the deductive approach or the inductive approach.* In the deductive approach, we start with a set of higher-order propositions and deduce lower-order propositions from them. Empirical tests can be made to test these lower-order propositions. In the inductive approach, we begin with a set of lower-order propositions which are empirically observed. From these propositions, we induce general principles which become the tentative higher-order propositions. Again, just as with the deductive approach, we must deduce other lower-order propositions from these tentative higher-order propositions and make them available for empirical verification. It must be pointed out that a great number of significant theories are inductively constructed. Homans (1964), in fact, warns us that in the social sciences, empirical observations are most important and that the use of the inductive approach cannot be overemphasized.

CONSTRUCTION AND EVALUATION OF THEORIES AND POTENTIAL THEORIES

Are there optimal strategies for constructing theories? And are there objective ways to evaluate the various propositions that have been called "theories"? The most powerful means we have to construct and evaluate propositions is through the use of models.

A *model* is defined here as a *representation of some aspect of a theory*. This definition is probably different from most definitions the reader will find in philosophy of science books. The philosophers of science tend to view the model as some representation of a theory. In this context, however, we view models as tools we use while constructing a theory. When we have a theory, we no longer need to worry about models. In reality, models are generally used in this way, especially in the social sciences and especially in the nonmathematical variety. (I consider the mathematical "models" as theories or hypotheses, but more precise conditions and formulas make them easier to be empirically tested.)

Since models are tools for constructing and evaluating a theory, there are several *levels of modeling*—according to the extent to which the model resembles a complete theory.

I. *The dimensional model.* A dimensional model is intended to specify the dimensions of a concept. The dimensions are derived either from theory or from data. However, a valid dimensional model must satisfy or approximate two criteria: (1) *The dimensions specified should be exclusive;* in other words, they should be independent dimensions; and (2) *the dimensions specified should be relatively exhaustive;* they should constitute the major components, if not the only components, of the concept. For example, Osgood and Tannenbaum (1955) derived the three dimensions of meaning as contained in adjectives: evaluation, potency, and activity. Berlo, Lemert, and Mertz (1970) isolated the components of source credibility: competence, dynamism, and safety. These are examples of dimensional models derived from empirical data. Parsons (1951) specified three components of human actions: the personality system, the social system, and the cultural system; and he derived these systems from theoretical considerations. Whether these models are of any value in our attempt to construct a theory with them depends on empirical verification of their exclusiveness and exhaustiveness. Another important aspect of the dimensional model is that there are concepts which are not specified or cannot be specified in concrete dimensions or components. Many psychological concepts such as attitude and belief are intrinsically continuous. So are many sociological variables such as education, opinion leadership, earliness of information exposure, or earliness of adoption. In these cases, when we are dealing with a *continuous concept,* care must be taken so that the constructed scale represents (1) *the full range of values* and (2) *the proper distribution form.* The requirement for the full-range coverage is to insure that exhaustiveness is approximated. The proper distribution form means that when the observed values tend to fall in a limited range, there must be sufficient scale points to differentiate such values. Let us look at the following example. If we were to gather data on the extent of awareness in a given population of President Kennedy's assassination four hours after the event in terms of (1) those who were aware and (2) those who were not aware, we might find the following distributions for the sample respondents:

(1) Aware: 95%
(2) Not aware: 5%

It is evident that the great majority of the observed responses fall into the first scale category and this makes the scale useless. What we need, then, is a scale that is sensitive to the particular range where the majority of the responses is likely to fall. For example, we might need to specify the exact time of earliest awareness for each respondent; thus, instead of using a dichotomous two-category response scale, we need a continuous time scale of initial awareness.

The dimensional model is the most basic of the models we use in attempting to construct a theory. It specifies the components or values in the concepts that are the building blocks in our potential theory.

II. *The typological model.* A typological model specifies the cross-distributions of two or more concepts. If we have constructed dimensional models for two concepts and both concepts are involved in the potential theory, we may then construct a typology based on the cross-classifications of the dimensions of the two concepts. The various influence typologies suggested by D. Katz (1960), Kelman (1961), Parsons (1963), and Lin (1967), as discussed in Chapter 4, are attempts at typological models. Several criteria help us to assess the soundness of a typological model. One basic criterion is *whether the dimensions specified for each concept approach exclusiveness and exhaustiveness*—in other words, whether a dimensional model for each concept is included. Another criterion focuses on the *extent of the analytic contribution such a model can provide.* The extent of analytic contribution is defined as the degree to which the analysis can explain or predict a certain phenomenon of interest to the scientist. In many cases, the analytic contribution of a typological model is not known until the theory itself is tested. But sound and thorough conceptual analysis of a typological model can quite often aid in the eventual assessment of the theory.

III. *The associative model.* An associative model specifies the tendency or relationships among the concepts specified. The *first two models are pre-theory models, but the associative model is a first approximation of a theory.* Here, not only have the concepts been cross-classified over their specified dimensions, but, in addition, a pattern or ordering among the types is imposed. For example, in the study of the psychological influence of communication, the component approach usually manipulates one or two communication variables (such as source credibility or fear-appealing message) and evaluates their effect on the change of a subject's attitude toward a certain issue. The hypothesis is usually in the form of "the more credible the source, the more the change of attitude." This is basically an associative model being constructed. Most of the hypothesis-testing approaches utilized in human communication research are of the associative model variety.

While the associative model would be most solidly built upon existing dimensional and typological models—that is, when all the requirements for a dimensional model and a typological model have been met—there are occasions when, for analytic purposes, only a selected and limited number of dimensions of the concepts (and, therefore, a limited number of types) is being tested in an associative model. For example, in nonverbal communication research, the specification of all dimensions of many nonverbal modalities is difficult to exhaust because such a number may be very large. Nevertheless, many associative models have been constructed on the basis of either known dimensions or dimensions thought by the researchers to contribute most analytically. Such a strategy is useful and necessary, but the generalizability of the model must be constrained and limited within the dimensions incorporated.

IV. *The functional model.* A functional model specifies a one-to-one relationship between two or more concepts. As defined in mathematics, a function is the relationship where the specification of a value of one variable has one and only one corresponding value of another variable. The variable with the given or specified value is usually called the independent, or predictor, variable, and the variable with the unique value, the dependent, or predicted, variable. The terms "independent" and "dependent" here do not have the usual meaning of unrelatedness or relatedness. Thus, when we say that variable A is a function of B, we mean that given a value of B, there is one and only one corresponding value of A.

In other words, given the values of B, we can predict with complete accuracy the values of A.

The statement, "A is a function of B," does not necessarily imply the statement, "B is a function of A." In many instances, one variable is a function of another variable, but the second variable is not a function of the first variable. Take the example of Y and X in the following relationship:

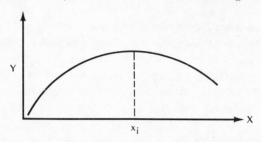

Here we say that Y is a function of X; given a value of X, one and only one value is specified for Y. However, X is not a function of Y; given a value of Y, there can be more than one corresponding value of X.

When A is a function of B and B is also a function of A, we say that the inverse function of A exists. For the example given above, one way to have the inverse function would be to specify the value ranges for the variables. We may say, for example, that the inverse function exists for Y when X is less than x_i and that a different inverse function exists for Y when X is greater than x_i.

A functional model, then, should at least be able to state a functional relationship between a set of variables. Furthermore, it should be able to specify the conditions under which the inverse function exists. A functional model is only a step away from a complete theory; it has completely specified the relationship between some subset of concepts in the potential theory. We have few such models in human communication research. In the study of encounter, many potential functional models exist because of the rigor of the information measurement. But only a few have actually been attempted on an empirical basis. DeFleur and Larsen's model (1958) is an outstanding example. In the study of the behavioral influence of communication, Coleman (Coleman, Katz, and Menzel, 1966) has constructed a functional model for the relationship between the extent of a physician's social integration and his earliness in adopting a new drug.

V. *The generalized model.* The final model is one in which all the relations among the concepts in a theory are functionally specified, exhaustively. The generalized model is a representation of a theory. This model indicates the *final phase of theory building.* In fact, as soon as a generalized model is realized, the "mission" of models is accomplished and the model can be discarded, insofar as the particular theory is concerned.

Of the five models discussed, the first two—dimensional and typological

—are pre-theory models, and we have many of them in the study of human communication. The third model—associative—is approximating a theory, and there are also many of them in the study of human communication. But the last two models—truly theoretical models—are rare. As the reader goes back to earlier chapters, he may now attempt to assess for each research effort the specific model and therefore the level of theorization it attempted.

ANALYTIC STRATEGIES IN RESEARCH

When a researcher becomes interested in a theoretical concept, he can employ one or both of two strategies: (1) the causal factors of the concept of crucial interest, or (2) the consequent factors of the concept. The strategy he follows in his study has important analytic implications. The first strategy leads to a causal analysis; the second leads to an effectual analysis.

I. *Causal analysis.* When a researcher is interested in determining the causes, or predecessor factors, of a concept or variable, he is investigating a potential causal relationship. He attempts analytically to use a *number of variables which theoretically and/or temporally precede the variable of interest.* The analytic strategy is to explain the variation of the variable in terms of the causal, or predecessor, variables. I call this strategy the *convergence* approach, and it can be represented in Figure 8–1.

II. *Effectual analysis.* When a researcher is interested in determining the consequences or impacts on a number of variables of a given variable, he is investigating a potential effectual relationship. What is to be analyzed is the extent to which the *variation of the variable of interest theoretically and/or temporally leads to different consequences.* I call this strategy the *divergence* approach, and it can be represented in the graph in Figure 8–2.

III. *The complete analysis.* When a researcher is interested in analyzing both the causes and the consequences of a variable or a concept, he is attempting the complete analysis. Such an analysis can be diagramed (for Concept Y) as in Figure 8–3.[1]

All three strategies are valuable to theory building and should be utilized fully. However, in the social sciences and in the study of human communication, *we have utilized the convergence approach much more frequently than we have the other approaches.* The main reason for this is that the popular analytic methods we use fit more conveniently into the convergence approach (analysis of variance, regression analysis, etc.). With recent methodological innovations (such as discriminant analysis and path analysis) in the social sciences, we should pay more attention to the theoretical problems of the divergent nature. Again, the reader is advised to keep these strategies in mind as he reviews the book. He should try to formulate

1. Y, in fact, can be a set of concepts instead of a single concept.

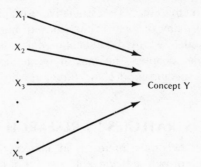

Figure 8-1. Causal Analysis of Concept Y

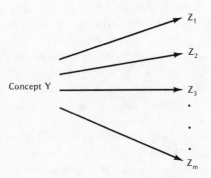

Figure 8-2. Effectual Analysis of Concept Y

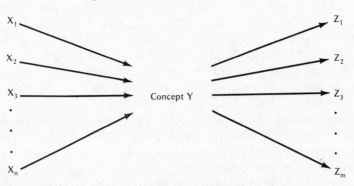

Figure 8-3. Complete Analysis of Concept Y

what kind of strategy has been used and what kind of strategy should be used
to help build a better theory.

IMPORTANCE OF CONTINGENT HYPOTHESES

The most common process of theory building consists of the following steps: (1) specification of concepts and relationships (this may be a result of empirical information), (2) deduction of lower-level propositions, (3) postulation of hypotheses, (4) testing of the hypotheses with empirical data, and (5) confirmation of or failure to confirm the hypotheses. The hypothesis represents the linkage between a theoretical proposition and empirical observations. In actual research practice, when a hypothesis is not confirmed, the usual excuses include: bad sample ("college sophomores are probably too unique"), bad setting ("the lights in the laboratory might have been too dim," "the passing train interfered with the quietness"), bad instrument ("the scale did not provide good response point distribution"). These are "excuses" because the scientist could have foreseen these problems and planned accordingly. Such excuses are also invoked in another contingency—when the scientist does not have anything theoretical to fall back on. *Most analytic methods allow only a statement of the extent of confirmation, not rejection.* A hypothesis is either confirmed or not confirmed; it cannot be rejected.

One way to tackle this problem theoretically is to construct *contingent hypotheses* before testing the main hypothesis. The scientist should ask himself, "What theoretical alternatives are there if the hypothesis fails to be confirmed?" He should think of contingent hypotheses, for potentially alternative theoretical propositions. To test these contingent hypotheses, he may incorporate additional concepts or variables to be measured and tested in the empirical test. If and when the original hypothesis fails to be confirmed, he should then proceed to test the contingent hypotheses. If these are confirmed, he can report the results, suggest modifications of the theoretical propositions, and deduce further propositions from the modified theoretical statements to be tested empirically. This procedure is especially valuable in the social sciences, since they are at a relatively primitive stage of development and since current theoretical statements must be regarded as preliminary and subjected to revisions.

A Critical Assessment and Reformulation of the Process of Communication's Influence on Behavior

In this section, I will utilize our knowledge about the nature of theory and the process of scientific investigation to critically examine one aspect of human communication and to suggest an alternative theoretical framework for future research.

The aspect selected for examination is the influence of human communication on behavior. The theoretical discussion will take as its point of departure the two-step flow hypothesis, since the hypothesis has had a pervasive impact on the area for the last two decades and since no alternative theoretical framework has been proposed.

THE DEVELOPMENT OF THE TWO-STEP FLOW HYPOTHESIS

Let us begin at that point in the research history when the hypothesis was initially proposed. The hypothesis, as stated by Lazarsfeld and his associates (Lazarsfeld, Berelson, and Gaudet, 1948), suggested that "ideas often flow from radio and print to the opinion leaders and from them to the less active sections of the population" (Lazarsfeld, Berelson, and Gaudet, 1948, p. 151). The earliest evidence of such a process came from a panel study conducted during the 1940 presidential election in Erie County, Ohio. The researchers found that the self-designated opinion leaders "read and listened to campaign material much more than the nonopinion leaders." Furthermore, among those few who changed their voting intentions during the last six months of the campaign, a substantial proportion cited other persons as the primary sources of influence (p. xiii).

The hypothesis subsequently gained further attention in another study, conducted by Katz, Lazarsfeld, and their associates (Katz and Lazarsfeld, 1955) in Decatur, Illinois during 1945. The study focused mainly on women's opinions and behavior relative to public affairs, fashion buying, movie selections, and food marketing. Other studies conducted by the Columbia University group (Berelson, Lazarsfeld, and McPhee, 1954; Coleman, Katz, and Menzel, 1966) also bore on the hypothesis.

Further empirical studies which directly or indirectly tested the hypothesis were conducted by Troldahl (1963, 1966) in Boston and Detroit, by van den Ban (1964) in Holland, and by Arndt (1968) in Harvard University married students' housing facilities.

The cumulative evidence concerning the hypothesis has been, at best, inconclusive. Yet the hypothesis has dominated our conceptualization of mass communication for the past two decades. That it may continue to do so is attested by the fact that hardly any reasonable research report on mass communication fails to mention some variation of the hypothesis as its theoretical framework.

THEORETICAL AND EMPIRICAL EVALUATIONS

We may now begin to evaluate the two-step flow hypothesis as a potential theory, utilizing the definition of a theory or a potential theory discussed earlier.

The Concepts in the Hypothesis

There are three identifiable and important concepts in the hypothesis: ideas, opinion leaders versus nonopinion leaders, and the mass media. The third concept, mass media, originally designated radio and print only. However, this term, as used in later formulations and studies bearing on the hypothesis, also includes specialized media such as professional periodicals and farm journals as well as TV.

The first concept, "ideas," was left undefined in the original proposal (Lazarsfeld, Berelson, and Gaudet, 1948). However, the data that were provided implied both information (reading, listening, and exposure in general) and influence (voting intention changes). This dual nature of the concept was further emphasized in a later statement: "A personal contact or a radio advertisement will indiscriminately be called a factor, an influence, an exposure, or a source. We will not make too stuffy a distinction between impact, effectiveness, and influence" (Katz and Lazarsfeld, 1955, p. 174). Later studies (Berelson, Lazarsfeld, and McPhee, 1954; van den Ban, 1964; Coleman, Katz, and Menzel, 1966; Troldahl, 1966; Arndt, 1968) all accepted this definition of the concept, usually stressing the information aspect in the first step of the flow (from mass media to some persons) and the influence aspect in the second step (from persons to others).

The definition of the opinion leader versus nonopinion leader dichotomy is also unclear and the problem is further confounded by varying operationalizing methods. In the Erie County study, as well as in the Elmira studies, a set of self-designated questions on general information and influence-relaying activities was asked of each respondent. On the other hand, the later studies (van den Ban, 1964; Coleman, Katz, and Menzel, 1966; Troldahl, 1966; Arndt, 1968) all used a nominating method: each respondent was asked to name some others from whom he sought information (discussion) and advice (influence). The Decatur study used both self-designated and nominating methods on general activities. Thus, the definition of opinion leadership has been derived either from the self-designation method or from the nomination method. Furthermore, these questions address themselves either to the specific activity at hand or to the general activities in the area.

The effect of self-designation versus nomination methods created some ambiguity. While the Decatur study showed that more than two-thirds of the respondents confirmed the roles attributed to them, it has been shown that the two methods of defining opinion leadership yield significant (better than zero relationship) but low correlations, stably ranging from .23 to .40 (Rogers and Cartano, 1962). The effect of general versus specific content has yet to be researched.

Mass media, although seemingly easy to define, have been operationalized in various empirical forms. In addition to the generally accepted forms of printed (newspapers, magazines) and electronic (radio and television) media, specialized media (farm journals, medical journals, special bulletins) have also been used in studies (van den Ban, 1964; Coleman, Katz, and Menzel, 1966; Troldahl, 1966; Arndt, 1968). It would seem that the differential definition is a necessary one, due to the types of topics under study. (Topics may be relevant either to the general public, in which case they are available in the popular mass media—radio, television, newspapers, and magazines—or they may be relevant to the specialized audience and thus available only in specialized media.) However, advertising media such as are distributed door to door become difficult to classify. Furthermore, nothing is known about how the differential definitions applied to mass media affect their relationship to various flow patterns.

In sum, then, both its original proposers and other authors attempting to verify (or falsify) it, have failed to make clear, either conceptually or empirically, the concepts employed in the two-step flow hypothesis.

The Propositions in the Hypothesis

The hypothesis can be formalized in the diagram in Figure 8–4. The arrows point to the flow of "ideas" (information, or influence, or both).

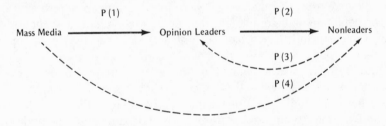

Figure 8–4. The Two-Step Flow Hypothesis

Each paired relationship can be called a patterned activity, indicated by P. Thus, the abstract proposition of the hypothesis can be stated: *Pattern one, P(1), and Pattern two, P(2), should follow one another over time and in a one-to-one (isomorphic) relationship.* Operationally, the flow of an idea should be initiated from a mass medium to an opinion leader, and then from *this* opinion leader to a nonleader. To test such a proposition *directly*, we need to trace the linkage between the mass media and the potential receivers, and the linkage among the potential receivers, for a given idea over time.

We can also construct lower-level propositions. Instead of mapping out completely and precisely the mass and interpersonal networks over time, we can *indirectly* test the proposition by verifying the relative strengths of the two following propositions:

1. P(1) > P(4)
2. P(2) > P(3)

In other words, aggregate data collected relative to the flow of the idea should show both of the following trends significantly: (1) The flow from the mass media to the opinion leaders should be significantly greater than the flow from the mass media to the nonleaders; and (2) the flow from the opinion leaders to the nonleaders should be significantly greater than that from the followers to the opinion leaders. Two points need clarification. First, note that *both these low-level propositions must be true in order to confirm the hypothesis indirectly.* Also, because aggregate data (marginal frequencies) are used, the low-level propositions only provide an indirect test of the hypothesis.

While confirmation of the low-level propositions in a given study may or may not verify the high-level proposition—the acceptance of the high-level proposition needs an accumulation of such indirect confirmations —*the lack of confirmation of the low-level propositions can certainly be taken as evidence that the high-level proposition is false,* since it assures the improbability of confirmation of the direct test.

Contingency (or Falsification) of the Hypothesis

Now we may review the various studies and evaluate the extent to which the empirical data have verified or falsified the high-level and low-level propositions derived from the two-step flow hypothesis.

The high-level proposition. *No empirical study* has been designed to verify the hypothesis through a *direct test* of the high-level proposition. Methodologically, it would be a quite complex operation, because it would involve the tracing of the flow of the idea (either information, or influence, or both) for all potential receivers. Such a task would be extremely difficult when the social system to be studied was of a medium to large size (usually more than 200 respondents), as is usually the case in mass communication research.

The low-level propositions. All the empirical studies have focused on the indirect verification of the hypothesis through testing of the two low-level propositions. For the first proposition, $P(1) > P(4)$, and focusing on information flow, confirmation data came from the Erie County study (Lazarsfeld, Berelson, and Gaudet, 1948, pp. 49–51), the Elmira study (Berelson, Lazarsfeld, and McPhee, 1954, pp. 109–115), the Decatur study (Katz and Lazarsfeld, 1955, pp. 310–312), and the Harvard study (Arndt, 1968). Two studies (van den Ban, 1964; Troldahl, 1966) failed to confirm the proposition. *For the second proposition,* $P(2) > P(3)$, *and focusing on influence (advice) flow, no single study confirmed it,* though five studies tested it (Berelson, Lazarsfeld, and McPhee, 1954; van den Ban, 1964; Coleman, Katz, and Menzel, 1966, p. 124; Troldahl, 1966; and Arndt, 1968). In the Decatur study, the relationship was significant at the .05 level only for one of the four topics (fashion) and only for the low-education group.[2]

---

2 Based on a statistical test (X^2) of data presented in Katz and Lazarsfeld (1955, p. 318).

In sum, there has been *no direct confirmation* of the hypothesis. The overwhelming evidence relative to the indirect tests is that the first-step flow may be true and the second-step flow cannot be confirmed. Because one of the two low-level propositions tested was not confirmed, we may safely conclude that there has been *no indirect confirmation* of the hypothesis either.

Reconceptualization of Communication's Influence on Behavior

Since the two-step flow hypothesis does not hold, what can we say theoretically about the behavioral influence process of communication? Clearly some reorientation in our thinking about the process is necessary if we are to move ahead in our theorization. While criticisms of the two-step flow hypothesis have been voiced time and again (for example, Lazarsfeld and Menzel, 1963; van den Ban, 1964; Bostian, 1970), no other systematic theoretical position or framework has been proposed. In the following pages, I will present a conceptual framework which builds on the cumulative evidence of research, mainly on that conducted during the past ten years. In the proposed framework, instead of replacing the two-step flow hypothesis, I will attempt to take into account the various research contributions generated by the development and testing of this hypothesis. Thus in a sense, the framework represents a further theoretical development of the two-step flow hypothesis.

RECONCEPTUALIZATION OF THE CONCEPTS

It should be clear by now that one major source of confusion in connection with the two-step flow hypothesis is the unclarity of its concepts. I will now attempt to reexamine the concepts employed.

It seems, first of all, that the concept "ideas" is too vague and too encompassing for theoretical development. Various operational definitions employed in the studies suggest that at least two kinds of "ideas" should be considered, namely, information and influence (Lin, 1971). Information can be defined as the extent of reception and comprehension of the codes transmitted, while influence can be defined as the extent of response (either psychological or behavioral) to the meanings contained in the message. The definition of information is derived directly from the information theory (Garner, 1962; Edwards, 1964) and that of influence from the research on meaning (Osgood, Suci, and Tannenbaum, 1957), attitude change (Cohen, 1964; Kiesler, Collins, and Miller, 1969), and behavioral change (Lewin, 1943; Rogers, 1962). In fact, the call for distinguishing between information flow and influence flow was sounded as early as a decade and a half ago (Katz and Lazarsfeld, 1955, p. 309, footnote 1). However, no theoretical distinction had been employed in any study until recently (Lin, 1971).

As research in news diffusion (Miller, 1945; Larsen and Hill, 1954; Deutschmann and Danielson, 1960; and Greenberg, 1964a) testifies, the process involved in the flow of information (news events) is drastically different from that involved in the flow of influence (Hovland, Janis, and Kelley, 1953; Klapper, 1960; Rogers, 1962).

A CONCEPTUAL SCHEME

We may now attempt to construct a conceptual scheme for the primary concepts just mentioned. A conceptual scheme is simply a way of tying central concepts together. For our purpose here, we may construct a scheme for the concepts along a time dimension:

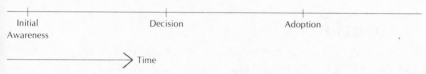

Here, we specify the three concepts in their most salient (distinguishable and measurable) forms: the initial awareness represents the first point in time of the information flow; the decision point (the psychological commitment) represents the major psychological consequence of influence; and the adoption point represents the major behavioral indicator of influence. The distances between the three points in the scheme can now be given significance as we derive other concepts from this conceptual scheme.

DERIVED CONCEPTS

From the conceptual scheme presented, we may now derive some other concepts:

1. *The decision period.* This concept is defined as the time distance between a person's initial awareness and his decision (either positive or negative).

2. *Communication participation* (exchange). This concept is defined as the extent to which the person has engaged in information and advice (influence) seeking, receiving, and relaying activities.

3. *Commitment actualization.* This concept is defined as the time distance between a person's decision (positive) and his behavioral adoption.

4. *Sustained adoption* (practice). This concept is defined as the extent to which a person, after his initial adoptive behavior, continues to commit himself to the action (be it an idea or practice) over the span of time when such action is accessible.

Now, we may expand the initial conceptual framework, incorporating the derived concepts as follows:

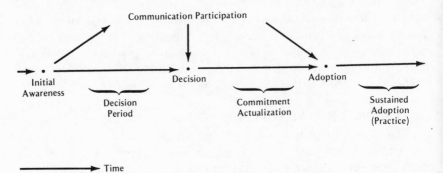

Figure 8–5. A Conceptual Framework of Behavioral Change

PROPOSITIONS

Our next task will be to propose a number of statements relative to the suggested concepts. Most of the propositions to be discussed are empirically and/or theoretically supported by past research.

For Initial Awareness

Proposition 1. Information flow is transmitted significantly more from the mass media (the popular forms) to people than it is from interpersonal sources. The effectiveness of the mass media is constrained by (1) the information's saliency to the people as a whole, (2) the degree of accessibility of the mass media, (3) the specific time of the information's availability relative to the physical locale of the potential receivers, and (4) the time of a potential receiver's awareness relative to the time of the information's initial availability.

The data on mass communication research, including news diffusion and innovation diffusion, overwhelmingly support the thesis that the mass media are more effective than personal sources in transmitting information (see Chapters 2 and 6). However, several exceptions do exist and these concern: (1) the nature of the information—interpersonal flow is stronger when the information is of medium saliency to the population (Greenberg, 1964a); (2) the accessibility of the mass media—interpersonal flow is stronger when mass media are not accessible to the potential receivers, as in primitive villages in underdeveloped countries (Greenberg, 1964b; Rogers and Shoemaker, 1971); (3) the time when information first reaches the locale—odd hours, such as midnight and early morning, and weekends induce stronger interpersonal flow (Miller, 1945); and (4) the relative time of awareness—late knowers tend to learn the information through interpersonal sources (Ryan and Gross, 1943; Rogers, 1962).

For the Decision Period

The *decision periods* can be categorized by a first approximation into (1) the *undefined* case (when information flow is the sole concern, such as in studies of news diffusion), (2) the *instantaneous* period (when the initial information exposure and the psychological commitment occur simultaneously), (3) the *protracted* period (when initial information exposure and commitment are linked over a period of time between instantaneity and infinity), and (4) the *infinite* period (when initial information exposure and commitment are linked over an infinite period of time) (Lin, 1971). For the first category, the concept of decision-making is trivial.

Proposition 2. Instantaneous decision-makers as compared with protracted decision-makers tend to have more traditional (as opposed to modern) personalities, to be more socially integrated, to be more interested and ego-involved in the issue at hand, and to experience less cross-pressure.

In other words, the differentiation between instantaneous and protracted decision-making is mainly derived from personality structure, degree of integration in the social structure, extent of interest and ego-involvement in the issue, and amount of cross-pressure or competing events. In one study conducted in a developing country (Lin, 1971), the instantaneous decision-makers were found more often to be better educated and male. In addition, they tended to be locally born and to attend church more often. Thus, the preliminary evidence suggests both modernity and social integration hypotheses. Further verification is needed to assess the relative magnitude of the contributions of the two factors in explaining the two types of decision-makers. In the 1940 Erie County study, Lazarsfeld and his associates (1948) found that the earlier decision-makers tended to show more interest in the election and to feel less pressure from the party and the candidate for which they did not intend to vote. Deutschmann and Fals Borda (1962), in a study in a Colombian village, also found a substantial proportion of instantaneous decision-makers—for all 12 agricultural innovations studied, over half the respondents reported one or more instantaneous decisions—within the traditional village. Future research should systematically investigate the typology of decision-makers. Also important will be a determination of the polymorphism/monomorphism distinction between decision-makers, or the extent to which people consistently use one type of decision-making process in most of their patterned activities requiring decisions or the extent to which each type of decision-making process is used only in a given set of activities involving decisions.

The phenomenon of the infinite decision-making process has been researched very little. Further data must be gathered before propositions can be made about it and its relationship to other decision-making processes.

For Communication Participation

There is strong evidence that information and influence seeking, receiving, and relaying take place during the decision-making period and subsequent to the decision (Wright and Cantor, 1967; Troldahl, 1966; Arndt, 1968; Hingson and Lin, 1971). Furthermore, such activities induce decisions and adoptions. The data all suggest that instead of dichotomizing opinion leaders versus nonleaders, perhaps a more fruitful strategy would be to study the active and passive communication participants. In a recent study in El Salvador, we found that there was a strong correlation between a housewife's socioeconomic and educational background and the extent to which she participated in information and influence seeking and relaying during a mass immunization campaign. Furthermore, active participation in such communication activities correlated with a higher family- and self-receptivity to inoculation.

Additional evidence suggests that a person's interpersonal communication activities are related to his strategic position in the spatial and social networks and that such activities are also related to his exposure to mass and specialized media (such as radio, TV, newspapers, magazines, specialized and professional journals and bulletins, and salesmen) (Carlson, 1965; Coleman, Katz, and Menzel, 1966).

Thus, it is clear that active communication participation serves as an important contributing factor in moving a person toward behavioral commitment (adoption).

Proposition 3a. Higher socioeconomic status, a more critical location in the spatial and social networks, and a higher educational level contribute to a person's participation in communication activities relative to a specific issue;

Proposition 3b. Active communication participation promotes a person's eventual behavioral commitment.

For Adoption

Proposition 4a. Influence flow is more likely to be transmitted through the interpersonal network than through the mass media;

Proposition 4b. Interpersonal influence is facilitated by status contiguity and perceptual identification between the source and the receiver;

Proposition 4c. The amount of antagonistic information assimilated will decrease over time toward the adoption point.

The first proposition is derived from discussions and research evidence (see Chapter 6). The second proposition is supported by evidence that influence is greater if the source and the receiver are contiguous, but not necessarily homophilous, in their social status, or if the source and the receiver can empathize with each other (Merton, 1949; Lerner, 1958; Rogers and Bhomik, 1970). The third proposition is a direct derivation from the dissonance theory, which states that as a person commits himself to a specific behavior, he tends to reduce his psychologically unfavorable attitude and to avoid antagonistic information (see Chapter 5).

For Commitment Actualization

The probable discrepancy between psychological commitment and behavioral commitment has recently inspired considerable discussion (see Chapter 5). Preliminary indications support:

Proposition 5. Commitment actualization is facilitated by less social distance, less social constraint, and greater consistency of role-perceptions.

DeFleur and his associates (DeFleur and Westie, 1958; Warner and DeFleur, 1969) found that when they took social distance and social constraint into account, the predictability of behavioral commitment from psychological commitment (attitude) was much improved. Another little-researched but useful concept is the differential role-perception at the time of psychological commitment and at the time of potential behavioral commitment. As a person perceives himself in a differing role relative to the given situation, the commitment actualization will show strong variation (for example, he may declare his support for X party's candidate at a rally given by the X party since he is a member of that party but then vote for Y party's candidate who advocates reduction of unemployment if he is out of a job at the time of election).

For Sustained Adoption

The initial behavioral commitment does not necessarily imply a long-term commitment. In fact, for many actions and people, the initial commitment is not sustained unless a number of factors persist.

Proposition 6. Sustained adoption is contingent upon effective feedback, effective dissemination, and continuous accessibility of the action.

As discussed in Chapter 7, through the feedback mechanism, the source of the action is provided with important information for evaluating the effects, both intended and unintended, of the action on the system. Such information permits the source to reinforce or modify the target adopters' behavior in line to the intended goal. Reinforcement and modifications are brought about through dissemination. Dissemination is further enhanced by social and local pressure on the target adopters and by the reinforcement surrounding the target adopters. Social influence, as discussed by Kelman (1961) can be exerted by way of compliance (ends-means control), identification (attractiveness), or internalization (value recognition), each of which has differential antecedent and consequent characteristics.

Another important ingredient is the continuous accessibility of the action. Recently, family planning programs in some developing countries have taken a turn for the worse. For example, the use of IUD's in some areas has decreased (Fawcett, 1970; Rogers, 1970). This is partly because a continuous supply of IUD's to the local communities has not been maintained. A few such instances of nonsupply may be sufficient to discourage the adopters (users) and to cause them to abandon their continuous commitment; commitment in this case has simply become impractical.

CONTINGENCY OF THE PROPOSITIONS

The concepts and propositions discussed here must be subjected to rigorous falsification tests. In the discussion, I have drawn empirical support from various research traditions, among them mass communication, diffusion of innovations, news diffusion, and experimental social psychology. Most of the data are consistent with the proposed conceptual scheme and propositions. From now on, the conceptual scheme and the propositions can and should be submitted to further verifications and modifications.

Concluding Remarks

In this chapter, I have briefly described the nature of theory and the scientific process and utilized such knowledge to critically examine one particular theoretical proposition in human communication research. Finally, I advanced a reconceptualization of the potential theory, suggesting a conceptual framework and a number of propositions. While it was not my intention to utilize such a conceptual framework to map out the entire communication process (in fact, many issues are left out of the scheme, for instance, the nature of information and message and modes of exchange), the reader should have realized by now that human communication is becoming an integrated scientific discipline and that the growth of this discipline will be further facilitated by our continuous concern with theorization.

References

Ackoff, R. L.
    1958.   Toward a behavioral theory of communication. *Management Science* 4:218–234.

Adams, J. B., and Muller, J. J.
    1968.   Diffusion of the news of a foreign event: a nationwide study. Paper presented at the Association for Education in Journalism convention, Lawrence, Kansas.

Adams, J. S.
    1961.   Reduction of cognitive dissonance by seeking consonant information. *Journal of Abnormal and Social Psychology* 62:74–78.

Allen, I. L., and Colfax, J. D.
    1968.   The diffusion of news of LBJ's March 31 decision. *Journalism Quarterly* 45:321–324.

Allen, T. J., and Cohen, S.
    1969.   Information flow in research and development laboratories. *Administrative Science Quarterly* 14:12–19.

Allport, G. W.
    1935.   Attitudes. In *Handbook of Social Psychology,* ed. C. Murchison, pp. 798–884. Worcester, Mass.: Clark University Press.

Altman, I., and Haythorn, W.
    1967.   The ecology of isolated groups. *Behavioral Science* 12:169–182.

Argyle, M., and Dean, J.
    1965.   Eye contact, distance, and affiliation. *Sociometry* 28:289–304.

Argyle, M., Lalljee, M., and Cook, M.
    1968.   The effects of visibility on interaction in a dyad. *Human Relations* 21:3–17.

Arndt, J.
    1968.   A test of the two-step flow in diffusion of a new product. *Journalism Quarterly* 45:457–465.

Aronson, E.
    1961.   The effect of effort on the attractiveness of rewarded and unrewarded stimuli. *Journal of Abnormal and Social Psychology* 63:375–380.

Aronson, E., and Carlsmith, J. W.
    1963.   Effect of the severity of threat on the devaluation of forbidden behavior. *Journal of Abnormal and Social Psychology* 66:584–588.

Aronson, E., and Golden, B. W.
    1962.   The effect of relevant and irrelevant aspects of communication credibility on opinion change. *Journal of Personality* 30:135–146.

Aronson, E., and Mills, J.
    1959.   The effect of severity of initiation on liking for a group. *Journal of Abnormal and Social Psychology* 59:177–181.

Asch, S. E.
    1951.   Effects of group pressure upon the modification and distortion of judgments. In *Groups, Leadership and Men,* ed. Harold Guetzkow, pp. 177–190. Pittsburgh: Carnegie Press.
    1956.   Studies of independence and conformity: a minority of one against a unanimous majority. *Psychological Monographs* 70–9 (Whole No. 416).

Ashby, W. R.
    1956.   *An Introduction to Cybernetics.* New York: John Wiley and Sons.

Barnlund, D.
    1962.   Toward a meaning-centered philosophy of communication. *Journal of Communication* 11:198–202.

Barnlund, D., and Harland, C.
    1963.   Propinquity and prestige as determinants of communication networks. *Sociometry* 26:467–479.

Baron, R. M.
    1963.   A cognitive model of attitude change. Unpublished Ph.D. dissertation, New York University.

Bateson, G.
    1951.   Information, codification, and metacommunication. In *Communication: The Social Matrix of Psychiatry,* J. Ruesch and G. Bateson, eds., pp. 168–186 and 212–214. New York: Norton and Company.

Bavelas, A.
    1950.   Communication patterns in task-oriented groups. *Journal of the Acoustical Society of America* 22:725–730.

Beal, G. M., and Rogers, E. M.
    1960.   *The Adoption of Two Farm Practices in a Central Iowa Community.* Ames, Iowa: Iowa Agricultural and Home Economics Experiment Station Special Report.

Becker, M. H.
    1970.   Sociometric location and innovativeness: reformulation and extension of the diffusion model. *American Sociological Review* 35:267–282.

Bem, D. J.
    1965.   An experimental analysis of self-persuasion. *Journal of Experimental Social Psychology* 1:199–218.
    1967.   Self-perception: an alternative interpretation of cognitive dissonance phenomena. *Psychological Review* 74:183–200.

Bennis, W. G., Benne, K. D., and Chin, R., eds.
    1961.   *The Planning of Change.* New York: Holt, Rinehart and Winston.

Ben-Zeev, S., and White, I. S.
    1962.   Effects and implications. In *The Great Debates,* ed. S. Kraus, pp. 331–337. Bloomington, Indiana: Indiana University Press.

Berelson, B.
    1959.   The state of communication research. *Public Opinion Quarterly* 23:1–15.

Berelson, B., Lazarsfeld, P. F., and McPhee, W. N.
1954.   *Voting: A Study of Opinion Formation in a Presidential Campaign.* Chicago: University of Chicago Press.

Berkowitz, L., and Goranson, R. E.
1964.   Motivational and judgmental determinants of social perception. *Journal of Abnormal and Social Psychology* 69:296–302.

Berlo, D. K.
1960.   *The Process of Communication.* New York: Holt, Rinehart and Winston.

Berlo, D. K., Lemert, J. B., and Mertz, R. J.
1970.   Dimensions for evaluating the acceptability of message sources. *Public Opinion Quarterly* 33:563–576.

Berne, E.
1964.   *Games People Play.* New York: Grove Press.

Bettinghaus, E. P.
1966.   *Message Preparation: The Nature of Proof.* Indianapolis: Bobbs-Merrill.

Bingham, W. E., Jr.
1943.   A study of the relations which the galvanic skin response and sensory reference bear judgments of the meaningfulness, significance, and importance of 72 words. *Journal of Psychology* 16:21–34.

Birdwhistell, R. L.
1952.   *Introduction to Kinesics.* Louisville: University of Louisville Press.
1970.   *Kinesics and Context.* Philadelphia: University of Pennsylvania Press.

Blau, P.M.
1964.   *Exchange and Power in Social Life.* New York: John Wiley and Sons.

Bloch, B., and Trager, G. L.
1942.   *Outline of Linguistic Analysis.* Baltimore: Linguistic Society of America.

Bloomfield, L.
1933.   *Language.* New York: Holt, Rinehart and Winston.

Boas, F.
1938.   *The Mind of Primitive Man.* New York: Macmillan.

Boomer, D. S.
1963.   Speech disturbance and body movement in interviews. *Journal of Nervous and Mental Disease* 136:263–266.

Boomer, D. S., and Dittmann, A. T.
1964.   Speech rate, filled pause, and body movement in interviews. *Journal of Nervous and Mental Disease* 139:324–327.

Bostian, L. R.
1970.   The two-step flow theory: cross-cultural implications. *Journalism Quarterly* 47:109–117.

Brazier, M. A. B., ed.
1960.   *The Central Nervous System and Behavior.* New York: Josiah Macy, Jr., Foundation.

Brehm, J. W.
1956.   Post-decision changes in the desirability of alternatives. *Journal of Abnormal and Social Psychology* 52:384–389.

1960. Attitudinal consequences of commitment to unpleasant behavior. *Journal of Abnormal and Social Psychology* 60:379–383.

1962a. Motivational effects of cognitive dissonance. In *Nebraska Symposium on Motivation,* ed. M. R. Jones. Lincoln, Nebraska: University of Nebraska Press.

1962b. An experiment on coercion and attitude change. In *Explorations in Cognitive Dissonance,* J. W. Brehm and A. R. Cohen, eds., pp. 84–88. New York: John Wiley and Sons.

1962c. An experiment on thirst. In *Explorations in Cognitive Dissonance,* J. W. Brehm and A. R. Cohen, eds., pp. 137–143. New York: John Wiley and Sons.

Brehm, J. W., and Cohen, A. R.

1959a. Re-evaluation of choice alternatives as a function of their number and qualitative similarity. *Journal of Abnormal and Social Psychology* 58:373–387.

1959b. Choice and chance relative deprivation as determinants of cognitive dissonance. *Journal of Abnormal and Social Psychology* 58:383–387.

1962. *Explorations in Cognitive Dissonance.* New York: John Wiley and Sons.

Brehm, J. W., and Crocker, J. C.

1962. An experiment on hunger. In *Explorations in Cognitive Dissonance,* J. W. Brehm and A. R. Cohen, eds., pp. 133–136. New York: John Wiley and Sons.

Bremel, D. A.

1962. A dissonance theory approach to defensive projection. *Journal of Abnormal and Social Psychology* 64:121–129.

1963. Selection of a target for defensive projection. *Journal of Abnormal and Social Psychology* 66:318–324.

Brock, T. C.

1962. Cognitive restructuring and attitude change. *Journal of Abnormal and Social Psychology* 64:264–271.

1963. Effects of prior dishonesty on post-decision dissonance. *Journal of Abnormal and Social Psychology* 66:325–331.

Brock, T. C., and Buss, A. H.

1962. Dissonance, aggression, and evaluation of pain. *Journal of Abnormal and Social Psychology* 65:197–202.

Burke, K.

1945. *A Grammar of Motives.* Englewood Cliffs, New Jersey: Prentice-Hall.

Calhoun, J. B.

1950a. A behavioral sink. In *Roots of Behavior,* ed. E. L. Bliss, chap. 22. New York: Harper.

1950b. The study of wild animals under controlled conditions. *Annals of the New York Academy of Sciences* 51:113–122.

1962. Population density and social pathology. *Scientific American* 206:139–146.

Campbell, D. T.
    1963.   Social attitudes and other acquired behavioral dispositions. In *Psychology: A Study of a Science,* ed. S. Koch, pp. 94–172. New York: McGraw-Hill.

Canon, J. K.
    1964.   Self-confidence and selective exposure to information. In *Conflict, Decision, and Dissonance,* ed. L. Festinger, pp. 83–95. Stanford, California: Stanford University Press.

Caplow, T., and Forman, R.
    1950.   Neighborhood interaction in a homogeneous community. *American Sociological Review* 15:351–366.

Carlsmith, J. M., Collins, B. E., and Helmreich, R. L.
    1966.   Studies on forced compliance: I. The effect of pressure for compliance on attitude change produced by face-to-face role-playing and anonymous essay writing. *Journal of Personality and Social Psychology* 4:1–13.

Carlson R. O.
    1965.   *Adoption of Educational Innovations.* Eugene, Oregon: The Center for the Advanced Study of Educational Administration, University of Oregon.

Carter, C. F., and Williams, B. R.
    1957.   *Industry and Technical Progress: Factors Governing the Speed of Application of Science.* London: Oxford University Press.

Carter, R. F.
    1962.   Some effects of the debates. In *The Great Debates,* ed. S. Kraus, pp. 253–270. Bloomington, Indiana: Indiana University Press.

Cartwright, D., and Harary, F.
    1956.   Structural balance: a generalization of Heider's theory. *Psychological Review* 63:277–293.
    1970.   Ambivalence and indifference in generalizations of structural balance. *Behavioral Science* 15:497–513.

Cathcart, R.
    1966.   *Post Communication: Criticism and Evaluation.* Indianapolis: Bobbs-Merrill.

Cerha, J.
    1967.   *Selective Mass Communication.* Stockholm, Sweden: Kungl. Boktryckeriet.

Chapin, F. S.
    1928.   *Cultural Change.* New York: Century.

Chase, S.
    1954.   *Power of Words.* New York: Harcourt, Brace & World.

Cherry, C.
    1957.   *On Human Communication.* Cambridge and New York: The M.I.T. Press and Wiley.

Chomsky, N.
    1956.   Three models for the description of language. *I. R. E. Transactions on Information Theory* IT–2:113–124.

Cohen, A. R.
  1957.   Need for cognition and order of communication as determinants of opinion change. In *The Order of Presentation in Persuasion,* ed. C. I. Hovland, pp. 79–97. New Haven, Conn.: Yale University Press.
  1959.   Some implications of self-esteem for social influence. In *Personality and Persuasibility,* C. I. Hovland and I. L. Janis, eds., pp. 102–120. New Haven, Conn.: Yale University Press.
  1962.   'Forced-compliance' experiment on repeated dissonance. In *Explorations in Cognitive Dissonance,* J. W. Brehm and A. R. Cohen, eds., pp. 97–104. New York: John Wiley and Sons.
  1964.   *Attitude Change and Social Influence.* New York: Basic Books.
Cohen, A. R., Brehm, J. W., and Latané, B.
  1959.   Choice of strategy and voluntary exposure to information under public and private conditions. *Journal of Personality* 27:63–73.
Cohen, A. R., and Latané, B.
  1962.   An experiment on choice in commitment to counter-attitudinal behavior. In *Explorations in Cognitive Dissonance,* J. W. Brehm and A. R. Cohen, eds., pp. 88–91. New York: John Wiley and Sons.
Cohen, A. R., and Zimbardo, P. G.
  1962.   An experiment on avoidance motivation. In *Explorations in Cognitive Dissonance,* J. W. Brehm and A. R. Cohen, eds., pp. 143–151. New York: John Wiley and Sons.
Colby, B. N.
  1958.   Behavioral redundancy. *Behavioral Science* 3:317–322.
Coleman, J. S., Katz, E., and Menzel, H.
  1957.   The diffusion of an innovation. *Sociometry* 20:253–270.
  1966.   *Medical Innovation.* Indianapolis: Bobbs-Merrill.
Coleman, J. S., Menzel, H., and Katz, E.
  1959.   Social processes in physicians' adoption of a new drug. *Journal of Chronic Diseases* 9:1–19.
Condon, W. S., and Ogston, W. D.
  1967a.   A method of studying animal behavior. *Journal of Auditory Research* 7:359–365.
  1967b.   A segmentation of behavior. *Journal of Psychiatric Research* 5:221–235.
Copp, J. H., Sill, M. L., and Brown, E. J.
  1958.   The function of information sources in the farm practice adoption process. *Rural Sociology* 23:146–157.
Crane, D.
  1969.   Social structure in a group of scientists: a test of the "invisible college" hypothesis. *American Sociological Review* 34:335–352.
  In Press. *Invisible Colleges: Diffusion of Knowledge in Scientific Communities.* Chicago: University of Chicago Press.
Creelman, M. B.
  1966.   *The Experimental Investigation of Meaning.* New York: Springer.
Cronkhite, G.
  1969.   *Persuasion: Speech and Behavioral Change.* Indianapolis: Bobbs-Merrill.

Crystal, D., and Quirk, R.
    1964. *Systems of Prosodic and Paralinguistic Features in English.* The Hague: Mouton.

Davis, K. E., and Jones, E. E.
    1960. Changes in interpersonal perceptions as a means of reducing cognitive dissonance. *Journal of Abnormal and Social Psychology* 61:402–410.

DeFleur, M. L.
    1966. *Theories of Mass Communication.* New York: David McKay.

DeFleur, M. L., and DeFleur, L. B.
    1967. The relative contribution of television as a learning source for children's occupational knowledge. *American Sociological Review* 32:777–789.

DeFleur, M. L., and Larsen, O. N.
    1958. *The Flow of Information.* New York: Harper.

DeFleur, M. L., and Westie, F. R.
    1958. Verbal attitudes and overt acts: an experiment on the salience of attitudes. *American Sociological Review* 23:667–673.

Deutsch, K. W.
    1952. On communication models in the social sciences. *Public Opinion Quarterly* 16:356–380.
    1963. *The Nerves of Government: Models of Political Communication and Control.* New York: Free Press.

Deutsch, K. W., Platt, J., and Senghaas, D.
    1971. Conditions favoring major advances in social science. *Science* 171:450–459.

Deutsch, M., and Gerard, H. B.
    1955. A study of normative and informational social influences upon individual judgment. *Journal of Abnormal and Social Psychology* 51:629–636.

Deutsch, M., Krauss, R. M., and Rosenau, N.
    1962. Dissonance or defensiveness? *Journal of Personality* 30:16–28.

Deutschmann, P. J.
    1962. Viewing, conversation, and voting intention. In *The Great Debates,* ed. S. Kraus, pp. 232–252. Bloomington, Indiana: Indiana University Press.

Deutschmann, P. J., and Danielson, W.
    1960. Diffusion of knowledge of the major news story. *Journalism Quarterly* 37:345–355.

Deutschmann, P. J., and Fals Borda, O.
    1962. *Communication and Adoption Patterns in an Andean Village.* San Jose, Costa Rica: Programa Interamericano de Información Popular and Facultad de Sociologia, Universidad Nacional de Colombia.

Dichter, E.
    1966. How word-of-mouth advertising works. *Harvard Business Review* 44:147–166.

Dimit, R. M.
   1954. Diffusion and adoption of approved farm practices in 11 counties in southwest Virginia. Unpublished Ph.D. dissertation, Iowa State University.

Dittmann, A. T.
   1962. The relationship between body movements and moods in interviews. *Journal of Consulting Psychology* 26:480.

Dittmann, A. T., Parloff, M. B., and Boomer, D. S.
   1965. Facial and bodily expression: a study of receptivity of emotional cues. *Psychiatry* 28:239–244.

DiVesta, F. J., and Stover, D. O.
   1962. The semantic mediation of evaluative meaning. *Journal of Experimental Psychology* 64:467–475.

Duncan, S. D., Jr.
   1965. Paralinguistic behaviors in client-therapist communication in psychotherapy. Ph.D. dissertation, University of Chicago.
   1969. Nonverbal communication. *Psychological Bulletin* 72:118–137.

Easton, D.
   1965. *A Framework for Political Analysis.* Englewood Cliffs, New Jersey: Prentice-Hall.

Edwards, E.
   1964. *Information Transmission.* London: Chapman and Hall.

Efran, J. S., and Broughton, A.
   1966. Effect of expectancies for social approval on visual behavior. *Journal of Personality and Social Psychology* 4:103–107.

Efron, D.
   1941. *Gesture and Environment.* New York: King's Crown.

Ehrlich, D., Guttman, I., Schönbach, P., and Mills, J.
   1957. Post-decision exposure to relevant information. *Journal of Abnormal and Social Psychology* 54:98–102.

Eisenson, J., Auer, J. J., and Irwin, J. V.
   1963. *The Psychology of Communication.* New York: Appleton-Century-Crofts.

Eisenstadt, S. N.
   1952. Communication processes among immigrants in Israel. *Public Opinion Quarterly* 16:42–58.
   1955. *The Absorption of Immigrants.* Glencoe, Ill.: Free Press.

Ekman, P., and Friesen, W. V.
   1969a. Nonverbal leakage and clues to deception. *Psychiatry* 32:88–106.
   1969b. The repertoire of nonverbal behavior: categories, origins, usage, and coding. *Semiotica* 1:49–98.

Ekman, P., Sorenson, E. R., and Friesen, W. V.
   1969. Pan-cultural elements in facial displays of emotion. *Science* 164:86–88.

Elms, A. C.
   1967. Role playing, incentive, and dissonance. *Psychological Bulletin* 68:132–148.

Elms, A. C., and Janis, I. L.
    1965. Counter-norm attitudes induced by consonant versus dissonant conditions of role playing. *Journal of Experimental Research in Personality* 1:50–60.

Emery, F. E., and Oeser, O. A.
    1958. *Information, Decision and Action: A Study of the Psychological Determinants of Changes in Farming Techniques.* New York: Cambridge University Press.

Exline, R. V.
    1963. Explorations in the process of person perception: visual interaction in relation to competition, sex, and need for affiliation. *Journal of Personality* 31:1–20.

Exline, R. V., Gray, D., and Schuette, D.
    1965. Visual behavior in a dyad as affected by interview content and sex of respondent. *Journal of Personality and Social Psychology* 1:201–209.

Exline, R. V., Thibaut, J., Brannon, C., and Gumpert, P.
    1966. *Visual Interaction in Relation to Machiavellianism and an Unethical Act.* Technical Report No. 16, University of Delaware, Contract Nonr-2285(02), Office of Naval Research.

Exline, R. V., and Winters, L. C.
    1965. Affective relations and mutual glances in dyads. In *Affect, Cognition, and Personality,* S. S. Tompkins and C. E. Izard, eds. New York: Springer.

Fawcett, J. T.
    1970. *Psychology and Population.* New York: Population Council.

Fearing, F.
    1953. Toward a psychological theory of human communication. *Journal of Personality* 22:71–78.

Felipe, N. J., and Sommer, R.
    1966. Invasions of personal space. *Social Problems* 14:206–214.

Feshbach, S., and Singer, R. D.
    1970. *Television and Aggression.* San Francisco: Jossey-Bass.

Festinger, L. A.
    1950. Informal social communication. *Psychological Review* 57:271–281.
    1957. *A Theory of Cognitive Dissonance.* Evanston, Ill.: Row, Peterson.
    1964a. *Conflict, Decision and Dissonance.* Stanford, California: Stanford University Press.
    1964b. Behavioral support for opinion change. *Public Opinion Quarterly* 28:404–417.

Festinger, L. A., and Carlsmith, J. M.
    1959. Cognitive consequences of forced compliance. *Journal of Abnormal and Social Psychology* 58:203–210.

Festinger, L. A., Schachter, S., and Back, K.
    1950. *Social Pressures in Informal Groups.* Stanford, California: Stanford University Press.

Fishbein, M.
  1965.   The relationships between beliefs, attitudes and behavior. Paper presented at the Prospects and Problems in the Psychology of Knowledge conference, Philadelphia, Pennsylvania.
Fishbein, M., and Hunter, R.
  1964.   Summation versus balance in attitude organization and change. *Journal of Abnormal and Social Psychology* 69:505–510.
Fliegel, F. C., and Kivlin, J. E.
  1966a.   Farmers' perceptions of farm practice attributes. *Rural Sociology* 31:197–206.
  1966b.   Attributes of innovations as factors in diffusion. *American Journal of Sociology* 72:235–248.
Fliegel, F. C., Kivlin, J. E., and Sekhon, G. S.
  1968.   A cross-national comparison of farmers' perceptions of innovations as related to adoption behavior. *Rural Sociology* 33:437–449.
Frank, R. L.
  1957.   Tactile Communication. *Genetic Psychology Monographs* 56: 209–255.
Freedman, J. L.
  1965.   Long-term behavioral effects of cognitive dissonance. *Journal of Experimental Social Psychology* 1:145–155.
Freedman, J. L., and Sears, D.
  1966.   Selective exposure. In *Advances in Experimental Social Psychology*, ed. L. Berkowitz. New York: Academic Press.
Galluhorn, J.
  1952.   Distance and friendship as factors in the gross interaction matrix. *Sociometry* 15:123–134.
Garfinkel, H.
  1964.   Studies of the routine grounds of everyday activities. *Social Problems* 11:225–250.
Garner, W. R.
  1962.   *Uncertainty and Structure as Psychological Concepts.* New York: John Wiley and Sons.
Garvey, W. D., Lin, N., and Nelson, C. E.
  1970a.   Some comparisons of communication activities in the physical and social sciences. In *Communication Among Scientists and Engineers*, C. E. Nelson and D. K. Pollock, eds., pp. 61–84. Lexington, Mass.: D. C. Heath.
  1970b.   Communication in the physical and social sciences. *Science* 170: 1166–1173.
Gerard, H. B.
  1961.   Disagreement with others, their credibility, and experienced stress. *Journal of Abnormal and Social Psychology* 62:559–564.
Gerard, H. B., and Mathewson, G. C.
  1966.   The effect of severity of initiation on liking for a group: a replication. *Journal of Experimental Social Psychology* 2:278–287.

Gerbner, G.
1956.   Toward a general model of communication. *Audio-Visual Communication Review* 4:3–11.

Gibb, J. R.
1961.   Defensive communication. *Journal of Communication* 11:141–148.

Goffman, E.
1957.   Alienation from interaction. *Human Relations* 10:47–59.
1959.   *The Presentation of Self in Everyday Life.* Garden City, New York: Doubleday.
1961.   *Encounters.* Indianapolis: Bobbs-Merrill.
1963.   *Behavior in Public Places.* Glencoe, Ill.: Free Press.
1967.   *Interaction Ritual.* Garden City, New York: Doubleday.
1969.   *Strategic Interaction.* Philadelphia: University of Pennsylvania Press.

Graham, S.
1956.   Class and conservatism in the adoption of innovations. *Human Relations* 9:91–100.

Grant, E. C.
1969.   Human facial expression. *Man* 4:525–536.

Greenberg, B. S.
1964a.   Diffusion of news of the Kennedy assassination. *Public Opinion Quarterly* 28:225–232.
1964b.   Person-to-person communication in the diffusion of news events. *Journalism Quarterly* 41:489–494.

Greenberg, J. H.
1954.   The linguistic approach. In *Psycholinguistics: Survey of Theory Research Problems,* C. E. Osgood and T. A. Sebeok, eds. Indiana University Publications in Anthropology and Linguistics, International Journal of American Linguistics, Memoir 10.

Greenberg, J. H., Osgood, C. E., and Saporta, S.
1954.   Language change. In *Psycholinguistics: Survey of Theory Research Problems,* C. E. Osgood and T. A. Sebeok, eds. Indiana University Publications in Anthropology and Linguistics, International Journal of American Linguistics, Memoir 10.

Griffin, K., and Heider, M.
1967.   The relationship between speech anxiety and the suppression of communication in childhood. In *The Psychiatric Quarterly Supplement,* Part 2. Utica, New York: State Hospital Press.

Griffin, Kim, and Patton, B. R. eds.
1971.   *Basic Readings in Interpersonal Communication.* New York: Harper & Row.

Guetzkow, H., and Simon, H. A.
1955.   The impact of certain communication nets upon organization and performance in task-oriented groups. *Management Science* 1:233–250.

Hägerstrand, T.
1952.   *The Propagation of Innovation Waves.* Lund Studies in Geography, Lund, Sweden: Royal University of Lund.

1965. Quantitative techniques for analysis of the spread of information and technology. In *Education and Development,* C. A. Anderson and M. J. Bowman, eds. Chicago: Aldine.

Haire, M., ed.
1959. *Modern Organization Theory.* New York: John Wiley and Sons.

Hall, E. T.
1959. *The Silent Language.* Garden City, New York: Doubleday.
1963. A system for the notation of proxemic behavior. *American Anthropologist* 65:1003–1026.
1966. *The Hidden Dimension.* Garden City, New York: Doubleday.

Hall, S.
1964. The importance of choice and attitudinal discrepancy in the study of extreme attitudes. M.S. thesis, Ohio State University.

Haney, W. V.
1967. *Communication and Organizational Behavior Text and Cases.* Homewood, Illinois: Richard D. Irwin.

Harris, Z. S.
1951. *Methods in Structural Linguistics.* Chicago: University of Chicago Press.

Harrison, R.
In Press. *Nonverbal Communication.* Englewood Cliffs, New Jersey: Prentice-Hall.

Hayakawa, S. I.
1941. *Language in Thought and Action.* New York: Harcourt, Brace & World.

Heider, F.
1946. Attitudes and cognitive organization. *Journal of Psychology* 21:107–112.

Hildum, D. C., and Brown, R. W.
1956. Verbal reinforcement and interviewer bias. *Journal of Abnormal and Social Psychology* 53:108–111.

Himmelweit, H., Oppenheim, A. N., and Vince, P.
1958. *Television and the Child.* London: Oxford University Press.

Hingson, R., and Lin, N.
1971. Communication participation and individual receptivity to a public health program. Mimeo report. Baltimore: Department of Social Relations, Johns Hopkins University.

Homans, G. C.
1950. *The Human Group.* New York: Harcourt, Brace & World.
1964. Contemporary theory in sociology. In *Handbook of Modern Sociology,* ed. R. E. L. Fans, pp. 951–977. Chicago: Rand McNally.

Horowitz, M. W., Lyons, J., and Perlmutter, H. V.
1951. Induction of forces in discussion groups. *Human Relations* 4:57–76.

Hovland, C. I.
1959. Reconciling conflicting results derived from experimental and survey studies of attitude change. *American Psychologist* 14:8–17.

Hovland, C. I., et al.
1957. *The Order of Presentation in Persuasion.* New Haven, Conn.: Yale University Press.

Hovland, C. I., Harvey, O. J., and Sherif, M.
1957. Assimilation and contrast effects in reactions to communication and attitude change. *Journal of Abnormal and Social Psychology* 55:244–252.

Hovland, C. I., and Janis, I. L., eds.
1959. *Personality and Persuasibility*. New Haven, Conn.: Yale University Press.

Hovland, C. I., Janis, I. L., and Kelley, H. H.
1953. *Communication and Persuasion*. New Haven, Conn.: Yale University Press.

Hovland, C. I., Lumsdaine, A. A., and Sheffield, F. D.
1949. *Experiments on Mass Communication*. Princeton, New Jersey: Princeton University Press.

Hovland, C. I., and Mandell, W.
1952. An experimental comparison of conclusion-drawing by the communicator and by the audience. *Journal of Abnormal and Social Psychology* 47:581–588.

Hovland, C. I., and Weiss, W.
1951. The influence of source credibility on communication effectiveness. *Public Opinion Quarterly* 15:635–650.

Hutchinson, J.
1970. Using TV to recruit family planning patients. *Family Planning Perspectives* 2:8–11.

Hutt, C., and Vaizey, M. J.
1966. Differential effects of group density on social behavior. *Nature* 209:1371–1372.

Inkeles, A.
1958. *Public Opinion in Soviet Russia*. Cambridge, Mass.: Harvard University Press.

Izard, C. E.
1968. The emotions and emotion constructs in personality and culture research. In *Handbook of Modern Personality Theory*, ed. R. B. Cattell. Chicago: Aldine.

Janis, I. L.
1959. Motivational factors in the resolution of decisional conflict. *Nebraska Symposium on Motivation*, ed. M. R. Jones. Lincoln: University of Nebraska Press.

Janis, I. L., and Feshbach, S.
1953. Effects of fear-arousing communications. *Journal of Abnormal and Social Psychology* 48:78–92.

Janis, I. L., and Gilmore, J. B.
1965. The influence of incentive conditions on the success of role-playing in modifying attitudes. *Journal of Personality and Social Psychology* 1:17–27.

Janis, I. L., Hovland, C. I., et al.
1959. *Personality and Persuasibility*. New Haven, Conn.: Yale University Press.

Janis, I. L., Lumsdaine, A. A., and Gladstone, A. I.
   1951.   Effects of preparatory communications on reactions to a subsequent news event. *Public Opinion Quarterly* 15:487–518.
Janis, I. L., and Terwilliger, R. F.
   1962.   An experimental study of psychological resistances to fear-arousing communications. *Journal of Abnormal and Social Psychology* 65:403–410.
Jenkins, J. J.
   1963.   Medical associations: paradigms and situations. In *Verbal Behavior and Learning: Problems and Processes,* C. N. Cofer and B. S. Musgrave, eds. New York: McGraw-Hill.
Johnson, D. E., and van den Ban, A. W.
   1959.   The dynamics of farm practice change. Paper presented at the Midwest Sociological Society meeting, Lincoln, Nebraska.
Jones, R. A.
   1966.   Forced compliance dissonance predictions: obvious, non-obvious, or non-sense? Paper presented at the American Psychological Association meeting, September, New York.
Jones, R. A., and Brehm, J. W.
   1970.   Persuasiveness of one- and two-sided communications as a function of awareness there are two sides. *Journal of Experimental Social Psychology* 6:47–56.
Jones, R. A., Linder, D. E., Kiesler, C. A., Zanna, M., and Brehm, J. W.
   1968.   Internal states or external stimuli—observers' attitude judgments and the dissonance theory-self persuasion controversy. *Journal of Experimental Social Psychology* 4:247–269.
Joos, M.
   1950.   Description of language design. *Journal of the Acoustical Society of America* 22:701–708.
Jourard, S. M.
   1966.   An exploratory study of body-accessibility. *British Journal of Social and Clinical Psychology* 5:221–231.
Jung, C. G.
   1918.   *Studies in Word Association.* London: William Heinemann.
Kaplan, A.
   1964.   *The Conduct of Inquiry.* San Francisco: Chandler Publishing Co.
Katz, D.
   1960.   The functional approach to the study of attitudes. *Public Opinion Quarterly* 24:163–204.
Katz, E.
   1960.   Communication research and the image of society: convergence of two traditions. *American Journal of Sociology* 65:435–440.
   1961.   The social itinerary of technical change: two studies on the diffusion of innovation. *Human Organization* 20:70–82.
   1963.   The diffusion of new ideas and practices. In *The Science of Human Communication,* ed. W. Schramm, pp. 77–93. New York: Basic Books.

Katz, E., and Feldman, J. J.
1962. The debates in the light of research: a survey of surveys. In *The Great Debates*, ed. S. Kraus, pp. 173–223. Bloomington, Indiana: Indiana University Press.

Katz, E., and Lazarsfeld, P. F.
1955. *Personal Influence*. New York: Free Press.

Katz, E., Levin, M. L., and Hamilton, H.
1963. Traditions of research on the diffusion of innovation. *American Sociological Review* 28:237–252.

Kelley, H. H.
1951. Communication in experimentally created hierarchies. *Human Relations* 4:39–56.

Kelley, H. H., and Volkhart, E. H.
1952. The resistance to change of group-anchored attitudes. *American Sociological Review* 17:453–465.

Kelley, H. H., and Woodruff, C. L.
1956. Members' reactions to apparent group approval of a counter norm communication. *Journal of Abnormal and Social Psychology* 52:67–74.

Kelman, H. C.
1961. Processes of opinion change. *Public Opinion Quarterly* 25:57–78.

Kelman, H. C., and Cohler, J.
1959. Reactions to persuasive communications as a function of cognitive needs and styles. Paper presented at the 30th Annual Meeting of the Eastern Psychological Association, Atlantic City, New Jersey.

Kelman, H. C., and Hovland, C. I.
1953. Reinstatement of the communicator in delayed measurement of opinion change. *Journal of Abnormal and Social Psychology* 48:327–335.

Kendon, A.
1967. Some functions of gaze-direction in social interaction. *Acta Psychologica* 26:22–63.

Kiesler, C. A.
1963. Attraction to the group and conformity to group norms. *Journal of Personality* 31:559–569.

Kiesler, C. A., Collins, B. E., and Miller, N.
1969. *Attitude Change*. New York: John Wiley and Sons.

Kiesler, C. A., and Corbin, L. H.
1965. Commitment, attraction, and conformity. *Journal of Personality and Social Psychology* 2:890–895.

Kiesler, C. A., and DeSalvo, J.
1967. The group as an influencing agent in a forced compliance paradigm. *Journal of Experimental Social Psychology* 3:160–171.

Kiesler, C. A., and Singer, R. D.
1963. The effects of similarity and guilt on the projection of hostility. *Journal of Clinical Psychology* 19:157–162.

Kiesler, C. A., Zanna, M., and DeSalvo, J.
  1966.   Deviation and conformity: opinion change as a function of commit-
                ment, attraction, and presence of a deviate. *Journal of Personality
                and Social Psychology* 3:458–467.

King, M., Jr.
  1961.   Sociometric status and sociometric choice. *Social Forces* 39:
                199–206.

King, R. G.
  1969.   *Forms of Public Address.* Indianapolis: Bobbs-Merrill.

Kirk, J. R., and Talbott, G. D.
  1959.   The distortion of information. *Etc.* 17:5–27.

Kivlin, J. E., and Fliegel, F. C.
  1967.   Differential perceptions of innovations and rate of adoption. *Rural
                Sociology* 32:78–91.

Klapper, J. T.
  1957–58. What we know about the effects of mass communication: the brink
                of hope. *Public Opinion Quarterly* 21:453–474.
  1960.   *The Effects of Mass Communication.* Glencoe, Ill.: Free Press.

Knapp, M. L.
  In Press. *Nonverbal Communication.* New York: Holt, Rinehart and Winston.

Kraus, S., ed.
  1962.   *The Great Debates.* Bloomington, Indiana: Indiana University Press.

Kraus, S., and Smith, R. G.
  1962.   Issues and images. In *The Great Debates,* ed. S. Kraus, pp. 289-312.
                Bloomington, Indiana: Indiana University Press.

Kuhn, T. S.
  1962.   *The Structure of Scientific Revolutions.* Chicago: University of
                Chicago Press.

Kutner, B., Wilkins, C., and Yarrow, P. R.
  1952.   Verbal attitudes and overt behavior involving racial prejudice.
                Journal of Abnormal and Social Psychology 27:649–652.

Laing, R. D., Phillipson, H., and Lee, A. R.
  1966.   *Interpersonal Perception: A Theory and a Method of Research.*
                New York: Springer.

Lambert, W. W., and Lambert, W. E.
  1964.   *Social Psychology.* Englewood Cliffs, New Jersey: Prentice-Hall.

Lang, K., and Lang, G. E.
  1962.   Reactions of viewers. In *The Great Debates,* ed. S. Kraus, pp. 313–
                330. Bloomington, Indiana: Indiana University Press.

La Piere, R. T.
  1934.   Attitudes vs. actions. *Social Forces* 13:230–237.

Larsen, O. N., and Hill, R. J.
  1954.   Mass media and interpersonal communication in the diffusion of
                a news event. *American Sociological Review* 19:426–453.
  1958.   Social structure and interpersonal communication. *American Journal
                of Sociology* 63:497–505.

Lasswell, H. D.

    1948. The structure and function of communication in society. In *The Communication of Ideas,* ed. L. Bryson, pp. 37–51. New York: Institute for Religious and Social Studies.

Lazarsfeld, P. F., Berelson, B., and Gaudet, H.

    1948. *The People's Choice.* New York: Columbia University Press.

Lazarsfeld, P. F., and Menzel, H.

    1963. Mass media and personal influence. In *The Science of Human Communication,* ed. W. Schramm, pp. 94–115. New York: Basic Books.

Lazarsfeld, P. F., and Merton, R. K.

    1954. Friendship as a social process: a substantive and methodological analysis. In *Freedom and Control in Modern Society,* ed. M. Berger et al. New York: Van Nostrand.

Lazer, W., and Bell, W. E.

    1966. The communication process and innovation. *Journal of Advertising Research* 6:2–7.

Leavitt, H. J.

    1951. Some effects of certain communication patterns on group performance. *Journal of Abnormal and Social Psychology* 46:38–50.

Leavitt, H. J., and Mueller, R. A. H.

    1951. Some effects of feedback on communication. *Human Relations* 4:401–410.

Leiderman, P. H., and Shapiro, D., eds.

    1964. *Psychobiological Approaches to Social Behavior.* Stanford, California: Stanford University Press.

Lemert, J. B.

    1969. Status conferral and topic scope. *Journal of Communication* 19: 4–13.

Lerner, D.

    1958. *The Passing of Traditional Society.* Glencoe, Ill.: Free Press.

Leventhal, H., and Perloe, S. I.

    1962. A relationship between self-esteem and persuasibility. *Journal of Abnormal and Social Psychology* 64:385–388.

Levitt, E. A.

    1964. The relationship between abilities to express emotional meanings vocally and facially. In *The Communication of Emotional Meaning,* ed. J. R. Davitz, pp. 87–100. New York: McGraw-Hill.

Lewin, K.

    1943. Forces behind food habits and methods of change. *Bulletin of the National Research Council* 108:35–65.

Lin, N.

    1967. Note on a typological analysis of the decision-making processes of innovation assimilation. Mimeo report. Baltimore: Department of Social Relations, Johns Hopkins University.

    1971. Information flow, influence flow, and the decision-making process. *Journalism Quarterly* 48:33–40.

Lin, N., Garvey, W. D., and Nelson, C. E.
    1970. A study of the communication structure of science. In *Communication Among Scientists and Engineers,* C. E. Nelson and D. K. Pollock, eds., pp. 23–60. Lexington, Mass.: D. C. Heath.

Lin, N., and Hingson, R.
    1969. The communication process in a mass immunization campaign in four Honduran communities. Mimeo report. Department of Social Relations, Johns Hopkins University, Baltimore.

Lin, N., Hingson, R., and Allwood-Paredes, J.
    1971. *Mass immunization campaign in El Salvador, 1969.* HSMHS Health Reports 860:1112–1121.

Linder, D. E., Cooper, J., and Jones, E. E.
    1967. Decision freedom as a determinant of the role of incentive magnitude in attitude change. *Journal of Personality and Social Psychology* 6:245-254.

Lionberger, H. F.
    1953. Some characteristics of farm operators sought as sources of farm information in a Missouri community. *Rural Sociology* 18:327–338.
    1960. *Adoption of New Ideas and Practices.* Ames, Iowa: Iowa State University Press.

Lionberger, H. F., and Coughenour, C. M.
    1957. *Social Structure and Diffusion of Farm Information.* Columbia, Missouri: Missouri Agricultural Experiment Station Research Bulletin.

Little, K. B.
    1968. Cultural variations in social schemata. *Journal of Personality and Social Psychology* 10:1–7.

Liu, A. P. L.
    1971. *Communications and National Integration in Communist China.* Berkeley: University of California Press.

Livant, W. P.
    1963. Antagonistic functions of verbal pauses: filled and unfilled pauses in the solution of additions. *Language and Speech* 6:1–4.

Lowe, F. E., and McCormick, T. C.
    1956. A study of the influence of formal and informal leaders in an election campaign. *Public Opinion Quarterly* 20:651–662.

Loy, J. W., Jr.
    1969. Social psychological characteristics of innovators. *American Sociological Review* 34:73–82.

Lumsdaine, A. A., and Janis, I. L.
    1953. Resistance to 'counter propaganda' produced by one-sided and two-sided 'propaganda' presentation. *Public Opinion Quarterly* 17:311–318.

Lund, F. H.
    1925. The psychology of belief. IV. The law of primacy in persuasion. *Journal of Abnormal and Social Psychology* 20:183–191.

Maccoby, E. E.
1963. The effects of television on children. In *The Science of Human Communication,* ed. W. Schramm, pp. 116–127. New York: Basic Books.

McGuire, W. J.
1961a. Resistance to persuasion conferred by active and passive prior refutation of the same and alternative counter-arguments. *Journal of Abnormal and Social Psychology* 63:326–332.
1961b. The effectiveness of supportive and refutational defenses in immunizing and restoring beliefs against persuasion. *Sociometry* 24:184–197.
1962. Persistence of the resistance to persuasion induced by various types of prior belief defenses. *Journal of Abnormal and Social Psychology* 64:241–248.
1968. The nature of attitudes and attitude change. In *Handbook of Social Psychology,* vol. 4, G. Lindzey and E. Aronson, eds., pp. 136–314. Reading, Mass.: Addison-Wesley.

McGuire, W. J., and Papageorgis, D.
1961. The relative efficacy of various types of prior belief-defense in producing immunity against persuasion. *Journal of Abnormal and Social Psychology* 62:327–337.
1962. Effectiveness of forewarning in developing resistance to persuasion. *Public Opinion Quarterly* 26:24–34.

McLuhan, M.
1964. *Understanding Media.* New York: McGraw-Hill.

Maloney, J. C.
1964. Advertising research and an emerging science of mass persuasion. *Journalism Quarterly* 41:517–525.

Manis, M.
1960. The interpretation of opinion statements as a function of recipient attitude. *Journal of Abnormal and Social Psychology* 60:360–364.

Marsh, C. P., and Coleman, L.
1956. Group influences and agricultural innovations: some tentative findings and hypotheses. *American Journal of Sociology* 61:588–594.

Marshall, G. R., and Cofer, C. N.
1963. Associative indices as measures of word-relatedness–a summary and comparison of ten methods. *Verbal Behavior* 1:408–421.

Mead, G. H.
1934. *Mind, Self, and Society.* Chicago: University of Chicago Press.

Meeker, B. F.
1971. Decisions and exchange. *American Sociological Review* 36:485–495.

Mehrabian, A.
1968. Relationship of attitude to seated posture, orientation, and distance. *Journal of Personality and Social Psychology* 10:26–30.
1969. Significance of posture and position in the communication of attitude and status relationship. *Psychological Bulletin* 71:359–372.

1970.   A semantic space for nonverbal behavior. *Journal of Counseling and Clinical Psychology* 35:248–257.

In Press. *Secret Messages.* Belmont, California: Wadsworth.

Mehrabian, A., and Ferris, S. R.

1967.   Inference of attitudes from nonverbal communication in two channels. *Journal of Counseling Psychology* 31:248–252.

Mehrabian, A., and Wiener, M.

1967.   Decoding of inconsistent communications. *Journal of Personality and Social Psychology* 6:109–114.

Merton, R. K.

1949.   Patterns of influence: a study of interpersonal influence and communication behavior in a local community. In *Communication Research 1948–1949*, P. F. Lazarsfeld and F. Stanton, eds., pp. 180–219. New York: Harper and Brothers.

1957.   Priorities in scientific discovery: a chapter in the sociology of science. *American Sociological Review* 22:655–659.

Milgram, S.

1967.   The small world problem. *Psychology Today* 1:61–67.

Miller, D. C.

1945.   A research note on mass communication. *American Sociological Review* 10:691–694.

Miller, G. R.

1966.   *Speech Communication: A Behavioral Approach.* Indianapolis: Bobbs-Merrill.

Mills, J. E.

1966.   Interest in supporting and discrepant information. In *Cognitive Consistency*, ed. S. Feldman. New York: Academic Press.

Mills, J., Aronson, E., and Robinson, H.

1959.   Selectivity in exposure to information. *Journal of Abnormal and Social Psychology* 59:250–253.

Mitnick, L. L., and McGinnies, E.

1958.   Influencing ethnocentrism in small discussion groups through a film communication. *Journal of Abnormal and Social Psychology* 50:82-90.

Morris, C. W.

1946.   *Signs, Language, and Behavior.* Englewood Cliffs, New Jersey: Prentice-Hall.

Mulder, M.

1960.   The power variable in communication experiments. *Human Relations* 13:241–257.

Mulford, C. L.

1959.   Relation between community variables and local industrial development corporations. Unpublished M.S. thesis, Iowa State University.

Myren, D. T.

1962.   The rural communications media as a determinant of the diffusion of information about improved farming practices in Mexico. Paper presented at the Rural Sociological Society meeting, August, Washington, D.C.

Newcomb, T. M.
1953. An approach to the study of communicative acts. *Psychological Review* 60:393–404.
1956. The prediction of interpersonal attraction. *American Psychologist* 11:575–586.
Newman, E. B., and Gerstman, L. S.
1952. A new method for analyzing printed English. *Journal of Experimental Psychology* 44:114–125.
Newman, J. B.
1960. A rationale for a definition of communication. *Journal of Communication* 10:115–124.
Nilsen, T. R.
1966. *Ethics of Speech Communication.* Indianapolis: Bobbs-Merrill.
North Central Rural Sociology Subcommittee for the Study of Diffusion of Farm Practices
1955. Bibliography of research on social factors in the adoption of farm practices. Mimeo bulletin. Ames, Iowa: Iowa Agricultural Extension Service.
Ogden, C. K., and Richards, I. A.
1923. *The Meaning of Meaning.* New York: Harcourt, Brace & World.
Osgood, C. E.
1952. The nature and measurement of meaning. *Psychological Bulletin* 49:197–237.
1960. Cognitive dynamics in the conduct of human affairs. *Public Opinion Quarterly* 24:341–365.
1963. An exploration into semantic space. In *The Science of Human Communication,* ed. W. Schramm, pp. 28–40. New York: Basic Books.
1966. Dimensionality of the semantic space for communication via facial expressions. *Scandinavian Journal of Psychology* 7:1–30.
Osgood, C. E., Suci, G. J., and Tannenbaum, P. H.
1957. *The Measurement of Meaning.* Urbana, Ill.: University of Illinois Press.
Osgood, C. E., and Tannenbaum, P. H.
1955. The principle of congruity in the prediction of attitude change. *Psychological Review* 62:42–55.
Panek, D. M., and Martin, B.
1959. The relationship between GSR and speech disturbance in psychotherapy. *Journal of Abnormal and Social Psychology* 58:402–405.
Parsons, T.
1951. *The Social System.* New York: Free Press.
1963. On the concept of influence. *Public Opinion Quarterly* 27:37–62.
Pavlov, I. P.
1927. *Conditioned Reflexes.* London: Oxford University Press.
Pemberton, H. E.
1936. The curve of culture diffusion rate. *American Sociological Review* 1:547–556.
1937. The effect of a social crisis on the curve of diffusion. *American Sociological Review* 2:55–61.

Pennington, D. F., Jr., Haravey, F., and Bass, B. M.
    1958.   Some effects of decision and discussion on coalescence, change, and effectiveness. *Journal of Applied Psychology* 42:404–408.

Phillips, G. M.
    1966.   *Communication and the Small Group*. Indianapolis: Bobbs-Merrill.

Popper, K. R.
    1959.   *The Logic of Scientific Discovery*. New York: Harper.

Powell, F. A.
    1965.   Source credibility and behavioral compliance as determinants of attitude change. *Journal of Personality and Social Psychology* 2: 669–676.

Price, D. J. de Solla
    1963.   *Little Science, Big Science*. New York: Columbia University Press.

Pye, L. W., ed.
    1963.   *Communications and Political Development*. Princeton, New Jersey: Princeton University Press.

Rahim, S. A.
    1961.   *The Diffusion and Adoption of Agricultural Practices: A Study in a Village in East Pakistan*. Comilla, Pakistan: Pakistan Academy for Village Development.

Rahudkar, W. B.
    1960.   Local leaders and the adoption of farm practices. *Nagpur Agriculture College Magazine* 34:1-13.

Rapoport, A.
    1953a.   *Operational Philosophy*. New York: Harper.
    1953b.   What is information. *Etc.* 10:247–260.

Razran, G. H.
    1939.   A quantitative study of meaning by a conditioned salivary technique. *Science* 90:89–90.

Rhine, R. J.
    1958.   A concept-formation approach to attitude acquisition. *Psychological Review* 65:362–370.

Richardson, L., ed.
    1969.   *Dimensions of Communication*. New York: Appleton-Century-Crofts.

Riley, J. W., Jr., and Riley, M. W.
    1959.   Mass communication and the social system. In *Sociology Today: Problems and Prospects*, R. K. Merton, L. Broom, and L. S. Cottrell, Jr., eds., pp. 537–578. New York: Basic Books.

Roethlisberger, F. J.
    1952.   Barriers to communication between man. *Etc.* 9:89–93.

Rogers, E. M.
    1957.   Personality correlates of the adoption of technological practices. *Rural Sociology* 22:267–268.
    1958.   Categorizing the adopters of agricultural practices. *Rural Sociology* 23:345–354.
    1961.   The adoption period. *Rural Sociology* 26:77–82.
    1962.   *Diffusion of Innovations*. New York: Free Press.

1965. Mass media exposure and modernization among Colombian peasants. *Public Opinion Quarterly* 29:614–625.

1970. Communication research and family planning. Mimeo report.

In Press. Communication channels in the diffusion of technology: combining mass media and interpersonal channels. In *Handbook of Communication,* ed. W. Schramm et al. Chicago: Rand McNally.

Rogers, E. M., Ascroft, J. R., and Röling, N. G.

1970. Diffusion of innovations in Brazil, Nigeria, and India. Mimeo report 24. East Lansing, Mich.: Department of Communication, Michigan State University.

Rogers, E. M., and Bhowmik, D. K.

1970. Homophily-heterophily: relational concepts for communication research. *Public Opinion Quarterly* 34:523–538.

Rogers, E. M., and Burdge, R. J.

1962. *Community Norms, Opinion Leadership, and Innovativeness Among Truck Growers.* Wooster, Ohio: Ohio Agricultural Experiment Station Research Bulletin.

Rogers, E. M., and Cartano, D. G.

1962. Methods of measuring opinion leadership. *Public Opinion Quarterly* 26:435–441.

Rogers, E. M., and Meynen, W. L.

1965. Communication sources for 2, 4-D weed spray among Colombian peasants. *Rural Sociology* 30:213–219.

Rogers, E. M., and Shoemaker, F.

1971. *Communication of Innovations.* New York: Free Press.

Rokeach, M.

1966a. Attitude change and behavioral change. *Public Opinion Quarterly* 30:529–550.

1966b. The nature of attitudes. In *International Encyclopedia of Social Sciences.* New York: Macmillan.

Rokeach, M., and Rothman, G.

1965. The principle of belief congruence and the congruity principle as models of cognitive interaction. *Psychological Review* 72:128–142.

Rosen, S.

1961. Post-decision affinity for incompatible information. *Journal of Abnormal and Social Psychology* 63:188–190.

Rosenberg, M.J., et al., eds.

1960. An analysis of affective-cognitive consistency. In *Attitude Organization and Change,* M. J. Rosenberg, C. I. Hovland, W. J. McGuire, R. P. Abelson, and J. W. Brehm, eds., pp. 15–64. New Haven, Conn.: Yale University Press.

1965. When dissonance fails: on eliminating evaluation apprehension from attitude measurement. *Journal of Personality and Social Psychology* 1:28–42.

Rosenberg, M. J., and Abelson, R. P.

1960. An analysis of cognitive balancing. In *Attitude Organization and Change,* M. J. Rosenberg, C. I. Hovland, W. J. McGuire, R. P. Abelson, and J. W. Brehm, eds., pp. 112–163. New Haven, Conn.: Yale University Press.

Rosenberg, M. J.
1960. *Attitude Organization and Change: An Analysis of Consistency among Attitude Components.* New Haven, Conn.: Yale University Press.

Rosnow, R. L., and Robinson, E. J., eds.
1967. *Experiments in Persuasion.* New York: Academic Press.

Ross, D. H.
1958. *Administration for Adaptability.* New York: Metropolitan School Study Council.

Ruesch, J., and Bateson, G.
1968. *Communication: The Social Matrix of Psychiatry.* New York: Norton and Company.

Ruesch, J., and Kees, W.
1956. *Nonverbal Communication.* Berkeley: University of California Press.

Ryan, B., and Gross, N. C.
1943. The diffusion of hybrid seed corn in two Iowa communities. *Rural Sociology* 8:15–24.

Sainesbury, P.
1955. Gestural movement during psychiatric interview. *Psychosomatic Medicine* 17:458–469.

Satir, V.
1967. *Conjoint Family Therapy.* Palo Alto, California: Science and Behavior Books.

Schatz, L., and Strauss, A.
1955. Social class and modes of communication. *American Journal of Sociology* 60:329–338.

Scheflen, A. E.
1966. Natural history method in psychotherapy: communicational research. In *Methods of Research in Psychotherapy,* L. A. Gottschalk and A. H. Auerbach, eds. New York: Appleton-Century-Crofts.

Schramm, W.
1955. Information theory and mass communication. *Journalism Quarterly* 32:131–146.
1960. *Mass Communication.* Urbana, Ill.: University of Illinois Press.
1963. Communication research in the United States. In *The Science of Human Communication,* ed. W. Schramm, pp. 1–16. New York: Basic Books.

Schramm, W., Lyle, J., and Parker, E. B.
1961. *Television in the Lives of Our Children.* Stanford, California: Stanford University Press.

Schramm, W., and Roberts, D. F., eds.
1971. *The Process of Effects of Mass Communication.* Revised Edition. Urbana, Ill.: University of Illinois Press.

Scott, W. A.
1957. Attitude change through reward of verbal behavior. *Journal of Abnormal and Social Psychology* 55:72–75.
1959a. Cognitive consistency, response reinforcement and attitude change. *Sociometry* 22:219–229.

1959b.   Attitude change by response reinforcement: replication and exten-
          sion. *Sociometry* 22:328–335.
Selltiz, C., Edrich, H., and Cook, S. W.
1965.   Ratings of favorableness of statements about a social group as an
          indicator of attitude toward the group. *Journal of Personality and
          Social Psychology* 2:408–415.
Shannon, C. E.
1951.   Prediction and entropy of printed English. *Bell System Technical
          Journal* 30:50–64.
Shannon, C. E., and Weaver, W.
1949.   *The Mathematical Theory of Communication.* Urbana, Ill.: Univer-
          sity of Illinois Press.
Shaw, M. E., Rothschild, G. H., and Stickland, J. F.
1957.   Decision processes in communication nets. *Journal of Abnormal
          and Social Psychology* 54:323–330.
Sherif, C. W., Sherif, M., and Nebergall, R. E.
1965.   *Attitude and Attitude Change: The Social Judgment-Involvement
          Approach.* Philadelphia, Pa.: W. B. Sanders Company.
Sherif, M., and Cantril, H.
1947.   *The Psychology of Ego-Involvement.* New York: John Wiley and
          Sons.
Sherif, M., and Hovland, C. I.
1961.   *Social Judgment: Assimilation and Contrast Effects in Communica-
          tion and Attitude Change.* New Haven, Conn.: Yale University Press.
Singer, R. D.
1961.   Verbal conditioning and generalization of prodemocratic responses.
          Journal of Abnormal and Social Psychology 63:43–46.
Smith, B. L., Lasswell, H. D., and Casey, R. D.
1946.   *Propaganda, Communication, and Public Opinion.* Princeton, New
          Jersey: Princeton University Press.
Smith, E. E.
1961.   The power of dissonance techniques to change attitudes. *Public
          Opinion Quarterly* 25:626–639.
Stephenson, W.
1967.   *The Play Theory of Mass Communication.* Chicago: University of
          Chicago Press.
Stevens, S.
1950.   A definition of communication. *Journal of the Acoustical Society of
          America* 22:689–690.
Sutherland, A.
1959.   The diffusion of an innovation in cotton spinning. *Journal of Indus-
          trial Economics* 7:118–135.
Tannenbaum, P. H.
1953.   Attitude toward source and concept as factors in attitude change
          through communications. Unpublished Ph.D. dissertation, Univer-
          sity of Illinois.
Tannenbaum, P. H., Greenberg, B. S., and Silverman, F. S.
1962.   Candidate images. In *The Great Debates,* ed. S. Kraus, pp. 271–288,
          Bloomington, Indiana: Indiana University Press.

Thaibaut, J.
1950. An experimental study of the cohesiveness of underprivileged groups. *Human Relations* 3:251–278.

Thistlewaite, D. L., de Haan, H., and Kamenetsky, J.
1955. The effect of 'directive' and 'nondirective' communication procedures on attitudes. *Journal of Abnormal and Social Psychology* 51:107–113.

Tomkins, S. S.
1962. *Affect, Imagery, Consciousness,* vol. 1. *The Positive Affects.* New York: Springer.
1963. *Affect, Imagery, Consciousness,* vol. 2. *The Negative Affects.* New York: Springer.

Trager, G. L.
1958. Paralanguage: a first approximation. *Studies in Linguistics* 13:1–12.
1960. Taos III: paralanguage. *Anthropological Linguistics* 2:24–30.
1961. The typology of paralanguage. *Anthropological Linguistics* 3:17–21.

Travers, J., and Milgram, S.
1969. An experimental study of the small world problem. *Sociometry* 32:425–443.

Triandis, H. C., and Fishbein, M.
1965. Cognitive interaction in person perception. *Journal of Abnormal and Social Psychology* 67:446–453.

Troldahl, V. C.
1963. *The Communication of Horticultural Information and Influence in a Suburban Community.* Boston University Communications Research Center Report No. 11.
1966. A field test of a modified 'two-step flow of communication' model. *Public Opinion Quarterly* 30:609–623.

Troldahl, V. C., and Van Dam, R.
1965. Face-to-face communication about major topics in the news. *Public Opinion Quarterly* 29:626–634.

Tustin, A.
1952. Feedback, *Scientific American* 187:48–54.

United States Bureau of the Census.
1970. *Statistical Abstract of the United States: 1970.* Washington, D.C.: Department of Commerce.

van den Ban, A. W.
1957. Some characteristics of progressive farmers in the Netherlands. *Rural Sociology* 22:205–212.
1961. Research in the field of advisory work. *Netherlands Journal of Agricultural Science* 9:122–133.
1964. A revision of the two-step flow of communication hypothesis. *Gazette* 10:237–250.

Wade, S., and Schramm, W.
1969. The mass media as sources of public affairs, science, and health knowledge. *Public Opinion Quarterly* 33:197–209.

Walster, E.
  1964. The temporal sequence of post-decision processes. In *Conflict, Decision, and Dissonance,* ed. L. Festinger, pp. 112–128. Stanford, California: Stanford University Press.

Ward, C. D.
  1965. Ego-involvement and absolute judgment of attitude statements. *Journal of Personality and Social Psychology* 2:202–208.

Warner, L. G., and DeFleur, M. L.
  1969. Attitude as an interactional concept: social constraint and social distance as intervening variables between attitudes and action. *American Sociological Review* 34:153–182.

Watson, O. M., and Graves, T. D.
  1966. Quantitative research in proxemic behavior. *American Anthropologist* 68:971–985.

Weaver, W.
  1949. The mathematics of communication. *Scientific American* 181:11–15.

Weick, K. E.
  1964. Reduction of cognitive dissonance through task enhancement and effort expenditure. *Journal of Abnormal and Social Psychology* 68:533–539.

Weiner, N.
  1948. *Cybernetics.* Cambridge, Mass.: The M.I.T. Press.

Weiss, R. F.
  1962. Persuasion and acquisition of attitudes: models from conditioning and selective learning. *Psychological Reports* 11:709–732.

Westley, B. H., and MacLean, M. S., Jr.
  1957. A conceptual model for communication research. *Journalism Quarterly* 34:31–38.

Whorf, B. L.
  1956. *Language, Thought, and Reality.* New York: The Technology Press and John Wiley and Sons.

Wicker, A. W.
  1969. Attitudes versus actions: the relationship of verbal and overt behavioral responses to attitude objects. *Journal of Social Issues* 25:41–78.

Wilkening, E. A.
  1953. Adoption of improved farm practices as related to family factors. Mimeo report. Madison, Wis.: Wisconsin Experiment Station.

Wilkening, E. A., et al., eds.
  1962. Communication and acceptance of recommended farm practices among dairy farmers of Northern Victoria. *Rural Sociology* 27:116–197.

William, F., and Sundene, B.
  1965. Dimensions of recognition: visual vs. vocal expression of emotion. *Audio-Visual Communications Review* 13:44–52.

Willis, F. N.
  1966. Initial speaking distance as a function of the speakers' relationship. *Psychonomic Science* 5:221–222.

Wright, C. R.
   1959.   *Mass Communication*. New York: Random House.
Wright, C. R., and Cantor, M.
   1967.   The opinion seeker and avoider: steps beyond the opinion leader concept. *Pacific Sociological Review* 10:33–43.
Wright, D.
   1970.   What is friendship? *New Society* 16:632–634.
Yeracaris, C. A.
   1961.   Social factors associated with the acceptance of medical innovations. Paper presented at the American Sociological Association meeting, August, St. Louis.
Yu, F. T. C.
   1964.   *Mass Persuasion in Communist China*. New York: Frederick A. Praeger.
Zavalloni, M., and Cook, S. W.
   1965.   Influence of judges' attitudes on ratings of favorableness of statements about a social group. *Journal of Personality and Social Psychology* 1:43–54.
Zax, M., and Klein, A.
   1960.   Measurement of personality and behavior changes following psychotherapy. *Psychological Bulletin* 57:435–448.
Zimbardo, P. G.
   1965.   The effect of effort and improvisation on self-persuasion produced by role-playing. *Journal of Experimental Social Psychology* 1:103–120.
Zimbardo, P. G., Weisenberg, M., Firstone, I., and Levy, B.
   1965.   Communication effectiveness in producing public conformity and private attitude change. *Journal of Personality* 33:233–255.
Zipf, G. K.
   1945.   The repetition of words, time perspective and semantic balance. *Journal of General Psychology* 32:127–148.

Index

ABCX model, 7
Abelson, R. P., 125
Ackoff, R. L., 8
Adams, J. B., 50, 136
Adaptation. *See* Control
Adoption, 147, 161-162, 162-176, 210
 discontinuance of, 174-175
 stages of, 166
Adopters, 162, 164, 166, 170-171, 174, 180
 categories of, 162, 171
 characteristics of, 162, 166, 170, 174
Allen, I. L., 50
Allen, T. J., 47
Allwood-Paredes, J., 169-170
Altman, I., 73
Amount of change advocated, 109-110
Analytic strategies, 199-200
Argyle, M., 72
Arndt, J., 155, 202-205, 210
Aronson, E., 110, 133, 136
Asch, S. E., 21, 116
Ascroft, J. R., 169
Assign, 59-61
Assimilation, 119, 120
Attitude, 17-18, 95-96, 97, 98-100, 102, 103-104
 relationship with behavior, 18
Attitude change, 90-92, 96-97, 102-144
 cognitive approach, 122-140
 comparisons of approaches, 140-144
 component approach, 106-118
 measurements of, 102-105, 143
 social judgment approach, 118-122
Awareness. *See* Information

Balance, 5-6, 123-125, 138-140
 balance configurations, 5-6
 imbalanced configurations, 5-6
Barnlund, D., 47
Baron, R. M., 114
Bass, B. M., 116
Bateson, G., 71, 86
Bavelas, A., 20
Beal, G. M., 11, 171
Becker, M. H., 169
Behavior, 17-19, 97, 98-100, 145
 relationship with attitude, 18, 95-100, 145
Behavioral change, 97-98, 145-181, 201-212
 assessment and reformulation, 201-212
 difficulties of, 176-178
 indicators, 146-147

interpersonal influence on, 180-181
 moving forces of, 178
 process of, 178-180
Bem, D. J., 135
Bennis, W. G., 21
Ben-Zeev, S., 157
Berelson, B., 7n, 9, 11, 19, 150-152, 154, 202-205
Berkowitz, L., 122
Berlo, D. K., 4, 66, 109, 195
Bhowmik, D. K., 46, 210
Bingham, W. E., Jr., 62
Birdwhistell, R. L., 68, 69, 71
Blau, P. M., 76
Bloch, B., 58
Bloomfield, L., 58
Boas, F., 74
Body motion, 69, 76
Boomer, D. S., 72
Bostian, L. R., 206
Brannon, C., 72
Brazier, M. A. B., 62
Brehm, J. W., 11, 111, 130-132, 133, 135, 136
Bremel, D. A., 133
Brock, T. C., 132, 133
Broughton, A., 72
Brown, E. J., 179
Brown, R. W., 115
Burdge, R. J., 175
Burke, K., 4
Buss, A. H., 133

Calhoun, J. B., 45, 46
Campbell, D. T., 103, 141
Canon, J. K., 136
Cantor, M., 210
Cantril, H., 18
Caplow, T., 44
Carlsmith, J. M., 10, 132-133, 134
Carlson, R. O., 160, 166-167, 210
Cartano, D. G., 203
Carter, C. F., 160
Carter, R. F., 157
Cartwright, D., 20, 124, 139
Casey, R. D., 12
Change agents. *See* Impersonal channels
Channel, 41-44
 capacity, 41-44
 of the English language, 42-43
 of humans, 42
Chapin, F. S., 162

Cherry, Colin, 12, 16
Chomsky, N., 58
Classical conditioning, 61-62
Classification of human communication,
    13-15
Closed system. See Open system
Cofer, C. N., 63
Cognition, 122
Cognitive consistency, 122-123
Cognitive dissonance, 122-123, 128-137, 138
    controversies over, 133-136
    criticisms of, 136-137
    hypotheses of, 129-130
    limitations of, 134
Cognitive models, 137-140, 141
    assumptions, 137
    comparisons, 138-140
Cohen, A. R., 11, 98, 106, 112, 113, 114,
    117, 118, 132, 133, 136, 206
Cohen, S., 47
Cohler, J., 114
Colby, B. N., 81
Coleman, J. S., 11, 167-169, 171, 172, 198,
    202-205, 210
Coleman, L., 159, 175
Colfax, J. D., 50
Collins, B. E., 102, 106, 119, 121n, 122, 125,
    129, 130, 134, 136, 206
Commitment actualization, 207, 210-211
Communication participation. See Exchange
Compliance, 88-90
Component approach, 106-118, 140-144
Components of communication, 106-118
Condon, W. S., 71
Congruity principle, 125-128, 138-140
Contingent hypotheses, 201
Contrast, 119, 120
Control, 19-21, 182-191
    functions of, 183-185
    mechanisms of, 185-189
Convergent analysis, 142-143, 199-200
Cook, M., 72
Cook, S. W., 122
Cooper, J., 134
Co-orientation, 6, 125, 138-140
Copp, J. H., 179
Corbin, L. H., 125
Coughenour, C. M., 176
Counterargument, 117-118
Crane, D., 80
Creelman, M. B., 67
Crocker, J. C., 133
Crowding, 45-46
Crystal, D., 68
Cybernetics. See Control; Feedback

Danielson, W., 49, 77, 207
Davis, K. E., 133
Dean, J., 72

Decatur study, 153-154, 202, 203, 205
Deception, 71, 73, 82
Decision-making, 151, 158, 164, 166, 170,
    173, 207, 209
Decoding, 36-41
Deduction, 194-195
Deese, J., 12
Definitions, of communication, 3-9
    dimensional approach, 4-5
    functional approach, 7-8
    implicit, 8
    problems of, 8-9
    process approach, 5-7
DeFleur, L. B., 50
DeFleur, M. L., 18, 48, 50, 52-54, 56, 99,
    148, 149, 198, 211
de Haan, H., 111
Delivery, 15-16, 22-23, 44-52
    analysis of, 44-52
    system, 15-16, 22-23
    See also Network
De Salvo, J., 125, 133
Deutsch, K., 12, 160, 188
Deutsch, M., 116-117, 132
Deutschmann, P., 12, 49, 77, 157, 160, 165,
    171, 172-173, 207, 209
Diffusion, 48-54, 77, 147, 148-149, 160-176
    comparison with mass communication,
        148-149, 161
    elements of, 160
    levels of, 161-162
    of news, 16, 48-54, 77, 160
    prinicples of, 170-176
    rates of, 161-162, 163, 169-170, 170-173
Dimit, R. M., 171
Disorganization, 189-190, 191
Dissemination, 19-20, 185, 188-189, 191
    characteristics of, 188-189
Disseminators. See impersonal channels
Dissonance reduction, 129, 136, 137, 139
Distortion, 82-83
Dittmann, A. T., 72
Divergent analysis, 142-143, 199-200
DiVesta, F. J., 62
Duncan, S. D., Jr., 68, 72

Easton, D., 9
Edrich, H., 122
Edwards, E., 16, 39, 42, 206
Efran, J. S., 72
Efron, D., 70
Ego involvement, 99-100, 119-122
Ehrlich, D., 132
Eisenstadt, S. N., 160
Ekman, P., 68, 69, 70, 73, 76, 82
Elmira study, 154, 203, 205
Elms, A. C., 134
Emery, F. E., 165, 175
Empathy, 174

Encoding, 34-36
Encounter, 22-56, 57, 178 *See also* Delivery;
    Information; Network; Uncertainty
Entropy. *See* Open system; Uncertainty
Erie County study, 150-152, 153, 154, 202,
    203, 205, 209
Exchange, 57-85, 178-179, 207, 209-210
  barriers to, 80-84
  functions of, 76-80
  generality and specificity of, 74-76
Exline, R. V., 72

Facial expression, 69, 71, 76
Fals Borda, O., 160, 165, 171, 172-173, 209
Fawcett, J. T., 211
Fearing, F., 8
Feedback, 19-20, 158, 182-183, 184,
    185-188, 189, 191
  components of, 186
  negative, 19, 185
  positive, 19, 185
Feldman, J. J., 157
Felipe, N. J., 76
Ferris, S. R., 71
Feshbach, S., 112-113, 156
Festinger, L. A., 10, 11, 20, 44, 98, 128-130,
    132-133, 135, 138-140
Field, P. B., 113
Firstone, I., 133
Fishbein, M., 128
Fliegel, F. C., 173
Forman, R., 44
Frank, R. L., 73
Freedman, J. L., 133, 136
Free word-association, 62-63
Friendship, 78-79
Friesen, W. V., 68, 69, 70, 73, 76, 82

Galluhorn, J., 44
Gallup, G., 12
Garfinkel, H., 76
Garner, W. R., 12, 16, 39, 42, 206
Garvey, W. D., 13, 47
Gaudet, H., 7n, 11, 19, 150-152, 202-205
Gerard, H. B., 116-117, 133
Gerbner, G., 4
Gestalt psychology, 122
Gestural relativity, 76
Gilmore, J. B., 134
Gladstone, A. I., 117
Goffman, E., 17, 77-78, 82
Golden, B. W., 110
Goranson, R. E., 122
Graham, S., 173
Grant, E. C., 69
Graves, T. D., 173
Gray, D., 72
Greenberg, B. S., 7, 16, 49-50, 51, 157, 207,
    208

Greenberg, J. H., 34, 58
Griffith, B., 13
Gross, N. C., 11, 160, 164-165, 171, 172, 208
Group identification and differentiation,
    79-80
Guetzkow, H., 79
Gumpert, P., 72
Guttman, I., 132

Hägerstrand, T., 45
Haire, M., 187
Hall, E. T., 8, 45, 68, 73, 75
Hall, S., 133
Hamilton, H., 161
Harary, F., 20, 124, 139
Haravey, F., 116
Harland, C., 47
Harris, Z. S., 58
Harrison, R., 74
Harvey, O. J., 119-121
Haythorn, W., 73
Heider, F., 5, 21, 123, 138-140
Helmreich, R. L., 134
Hesitation, 72
Hildum, D. C., 115
Hill, R. J., 46, 48-49, 207
Himmelweit, H., 156
Hingson, R., 169-170, 171, 173, 210
Homans, G. C., 78, 193, 195
Horowitz, M. W., 6
Hovland, C. I., 9, 10, 97, 106-110, 110-112,
    113, 118-121, 134, 207
Hull, C. L., 142
Hunter, R., 128
Hutchinson, J., 158
Hutt, C., 73

Identification, 88-90
Immunization effect. *See* Inoculation analysis
Impersonal channels, 164-165, 167, 169-170,
    175, 179
Impression management. *See* Interaction ritual
Incentive effects, 134
Induction. *See* Deduction
Influence, 80, 86-101, 151-156, 164-181,
    201-212
  definition of, 86
  functions of, 90-92
  paradigms of, 87-95
  processes of, 88-90
  source of, 151-156, 164-165, 167-169
  types of, 87-88
Information, 23-44, 48-56, 77, 157-158, 162,
    166-167, 170, 175, 179, 203, 206, 208
  application of, 34-44
  characteristics of, 29-32
  comparison with correlational and variance
    analyses, 39
  measurement, 24-29

source of, 48-52, 54-56, 157-158, 164, 166, 167, 170, 175, 179
system, 15-16, 22
Inkeles, A., 150
Innovation, 160, 162, 165, 173
characteristics of, 162, 173
See also Diffusion; Innovative behavior
Innovative behavior, 146-147, 162, 166, 174-175
Innovators. *See* Innovative behavior
Inoculation analysis, 117-118
Interaction ritual, 77-78
Internalization, 88-90
Interpersonal channels, 46-47, 48-52, 53-54, 55-56, 151, 153, 155, 158-160, 164-165, 166, 167-169, 170, 175-176, 179, 180-181, 209-210
Invisible colleges, 80
Izard, C. E., 76

Janis, I. L., 10, 106, 111, 112-113, 117, 134, 207
Jenkins, J. J., 12, 63
Johnson, D. E., 174
Jones, E. E., 133, 134
Jones, R. A., 111, 135
Joos, M., 58
Jourard, S. M., 73
Jung, C. G., 62
Justification of choice, 130-132
Justification of forced compliances, 132-133

Kamenetsky, J., 111
Kaplan, A., 8n
Katz, D., 86, 90-92, 94, 95, 196
Katz, E., 7n, 9, 11, 21, 48, 147, 148, 153-154, 157, 159, 160, 161, 167-169, 171, 176, 198, 202-205, 207, 210
Kelley, H. H., 10, 46, 106, 111, 113, 115, 134, 207
Kelman, H. C., 86, 88-90, 94, 95, 109, 114, 196, 211
Kendon, A., 72, 73
Kerrick, J. S., 128
Kiesler, C. A., 102, 106, 119, 120, 121n, 122, 125, 129, 130, 133, 134, 135, 136, 206
Kinesics. *See* Body motion
King, M., Jr., 47
Kirk, J. R., 82-84
Kivlin, J. E., 173
Klapper, J. T., 11, 21, 47, 48, 157, 158, 207
Klein, A., 99
Knapp, M. L., 74
Kraus, S., 157
Krauss, R. M., 132
Kuhn, T. S., 194
Kutner, B., 99

Lalljee, M., 72
Lambert, W. E., 72
Lambert, W. W., 72
Lang, G. E., 157
Lang, K., 157
Language, 58, 66-67, 74-75, 87
La Piere, R. T., 98-99
Larsen, O. N., 46, 48-49, 52-54, 56, 198, 207
Lasswell, H. D., 4, 11-12, 21
Latané, B., 133, 136
Lazarsfeld, P. F., 7n, 11, 19, 21, 46, 48, 149, 150-152, 153-154, 158, 159, 168, 202-205, 206, 207, 209
Leavitt, H. J., 79, 185, 187
Legitimation, 92-94
Leiderman, P. H., 102
Lemert, J. B., 66, 86, 109, 195
Lerner, D., 12, 210
Leventhal, H., 113
Levin, M. L., 161
Levitt, E. A., 71
Levy, B., 133
Lewin, K., 10, 21, 115-116, 122, 206
Lin, N., 13, 47, 86, 92-94, 169-170, 171, 173, 196, 206-207, 209, 210
Linder, D. E., 134, 135
Linguistic relativity, 74
Lionberger, H. F., 11, 173, 175, 176
Little, K. B., 75
Liu, A. P. L., 150
Livant, W. P., 72
Lowe, F. E., 159
Loy, J. W., Jr., 162
Lumsdaine, A. A., 10, 106, 109n, 110-111, 117
Lund, F. H., 112
Lyle, J., 156
Lyons, J., 6

Maccoby, E. E., 156
McCormick, T. C., 159
McGinnies, E., 116
McGuire, W. J., 103, 106, 117-118, 142-143
MacLean, M. S., Jr., 7, 12, 21, 56
McLuhan, M., 12, 44
McPhee, W. N., 11, 154, 202-205
Mandell, W., 111, 112
Manis, M., 122
Markov chain, 55-56
Marsh, C. P., 159, 175
Marshall, G. R., 63
Martin, B., 72
Mass communication, 147, 148-160
comparisons with diffusion, 148-149
effects of, 149-160
principles of, 158-160
See also Mass media
Mass media, 47-48, 48-52, 53-54, 55-56,

148-160, 164, 166, 169, 170, 175, 178, 179, 180, 203-205
  growth of newspaper, 50, 149-150
  growth of radio, 47, 50, 149
  growth of television, 47, 50, 149
  See also Mass communication
Mass network. *See* Mass media
Mathewson, G. C., 133
Mead, G. H., 13-14
Meaning, 17, 57-85
  classical conditioning model of, 61-62
  connotative and denotative, 81-82
  definition of, 58-61
  free word-association model of, 62-63
  measurement of nonverbal, 67-76
  measurement of verbal, 61-67
  mediated word-association model of, 63-67
  representational model of, 59-60
  surface and latent, 82
Mediated word-association, 63-67
Mehrabian, A., 68, 71, 73, 74
Menzel, H., 11, 13, 149, 158, 167-169, 171, 198, 202-205, 206, 210
Merton, R. K., 11, 46, 80, 152-153, 210
Mertz, R. J., 66, 109, 195
Message analysis, 110-113
  appeals, 112-113
  one-sided versus two-sided, 110-111
  order of presentation, 111-112
  stating a conclusion, 11
Meynen, W. L., 175
Milgram, S., 47
Miller, D. C., 48, 207, 208
Miller, G. A., 12, 16
Miller, N., 102, 106, 119, 121n, 122, 125, 129, 130, 134, 136, 206
Mills, J., 132, 133, 136
Mitnick, L. L., 116
Model, 195-199
Model of communication, 4-7
Morris, C. W., 59
Mueller, R. A. H., 185, 187
Mulder, M., 79
Mulford, C. L., 173
Muller, J. J., 50
Multi-step flow of communication, 154
Myren, D. T., 165

Nebergall, R. E., 121, 137
Neighborhood effect, the, 45
Nelson, C. E., 47
Network, 44-55, 77
  mass, 47-48, 48-54, 55
  social 46-47, 48-54, 55, 77
  spatial, 44-46, 48-54, 55
Newcomb, T. M., 6, 21, 79, 124-125, 138-140
New Jersey study, 152-153
Newman, J. B., 8
Noise, 37-39

Nonverbal meaning, 67-74
  measurement of, 67-68
Nonverbal modalities, 68-72
  categories of, 68, 69-70

Oeser, O. A., 165, 175
Ogden, C. K., 59
Ogston, W. D., 71
Open system, 182-183, 184
Opinion leaders, 151-156, 159-160, 167, 169, 175, 180-181, 203-205
  formal versus informal, 159, 180-181
  local versus cosmopolitan, 152-153, 159, 180
  polymorphic versus monomorphic, 159, 175, 180
  and social norms, 159, 160, 175, 180
  socioeconomic status of, 152, 154, 155, 159, 175, 180
Oppenheim, A. N., 156
Organization, 80-81, 184
Oscillation, 187
Osgood, C. E., 12, 34, 58, 59, 60, 63-66, 73, 125-128, 138-140, 195, 206

Paisley, W., 13
Panek, D. M., 72
Papageorgis, D., 117
Paralanguage, 68
Parker, E. B., 156
Parloff, M. B., 72
Parsons, T., 86, 87-88, 94, 95, 195, 196
Patterns of habits, 146, 147
Pavlov, I. P., 61
Pemberton, H. E., 162-164, 171
Pennington, D. F., Jr., 116
Periodical commitment, 146, 147
Perlmutter, H. V., 6
Perloe, S. I., 113
Phases of human communication, 15-21
  adaptation and control, 19-20
  encounter, 15-16
  exchange, 16-17
  importance, 20-21
  influence, 17-19
Platt, J., 160
Play, 79
Pool, I. de S., 12
Popper, K. R., 8n
Postcommitment reinforcement, 178-179
Powell, F. A., 113-114
Practice, 207, 211
Price, D. J. de Solla, 80
Primacy effect, 111-112
Proxemics, 69, 73, 75-76
Psychological influence, 90-92, 95-97, 102-144
Pye, L. W., 12, 21

Quirk, R., 68

Rahim, S. A., 165, 173, 175
Rahudkar, W. B., 175
Rapoport, A., 8n, 34
Razran, G. H., 61-62
Receiver analysis, 113-115
    authoritarianism, 113-114
    cognitive variations, 114
    self-estimate, 113
Recency effect, 111-112
Recognition, 80
Redundancy, 31, 33-34, 43-44, 55, 80-81
Reference group analysis, 115-117
Region of acceptance, 119-121
Region of noncommitment, 119-121
Region of rejection, 119-121
Representational model of meaning, 59-60
Rhine, R. J., 115
Richards, I. A., 59
Riley, J. W., Jr., 4
Riley, M. W., 4
Robinson, E. J., 106
Robinson, H., 136
Rogers, E. M., 9, 11, 21, 46, 160, 166,
        169, 171, 174, 175, 203-206, 207,
        208, 210, 211
Rokeach, M., 18, 96, 99, 102, 103, 128,
        136
Roling, N. G., 169
Rosen, S., 136
Rosenau, N., 132
Rosenberg, M. J., 10, 106, 125, 134
Rosnow, R. L., 106
Ross, D. H., 160, 166
Rothman, G., 128
Ryan, B., 11, 160, 164-165, 171, 172, 208

S-shaped diffusion curve, 162-164, 165,
        170-173
Sainesbury, P., 72
Saporta, S., 34
Schatz, L., 79
Scheflen, A. E., 71
Schönbach, P., 132
Schramm, W., 9, 12, 34, 43, 47, 50, 82, 156
Schuette, D., 72
Scott, W. A., 115
Sears, D., 136
Sekhon, G. S., 173
Selltiz, C., 122
Semantic differential, 65-66, 126
Semantic generalization, 61-62
Semantic space, 63-67, 74
    dimensions of, 65
    measurement of, 64-65, 66
Senghaas, D., 160
Shannon, C. E., 4, 12, 16, 182

Shapiro, D., 102
Shaw, M. E., 79
Sheffield, F. D., 10, 106, 109n, 110-111
Sherif, C. W., 99-100, 121, 137
Sherif, M., 18, 106, 118-121, 137
Shoemaker, F., 160, 173, 174, 208
Sign, 59-61
Significate, 59-61
Sill, M. L., 179
Silverman, F. S., 157
Simon, H. A., 79
Singer, R. D., 115, 133, 156
Situational intervention, 99
Sleeper effect, 108-109
Smith, B. L., 12
Smith, E. E., 133
Smith, K., 149
Smith, R. G., 157
Social constraint, 99
Social incentive, 99
Social interaction. See Interpersonal channels
Social judgment, 18, 118-122, 140-144
Social network. See Interpersonal channels
Social pressure, 99
Sommer, R., 76
Sorenson, E. R., 76
Source analysis, 106-110
Source credibility, 106-108, 109-110
Spatial network, 44-46, 48-52, 54, 55-56, 158
Spatial relativity, 76
Spencer, H., 142
Stephenson, W., 79
Stevens, S., 8
Stimulus, 61
Stover, D. O., 62
Strain toward symmetry, 124-125
Strauss, A., 79
Suci, G. I., 58, 59, 60, 206
Sundene, B., 74
Sutherland, A., 173
System, 19

Tactile communication, 73
Talbott, G. D., 82-84
Tannenbaum, P. H., 58, 59, 60, 125-128,
        157, 195, 206
Television, 149, 156-158
    effects on children, 156-157
    and voting decision, 157
    See also Mass communication; Mass media
Terwilliger, R. F., 113
Thaibaut, J., 46, 72
Theorization, 141-142, 192-212
Theory, 193-199
    elements of, 193-194
    power of, 194
Thistlewaite, D. L., 111
Tomkins, S. S., 70
Touching. See Tactile communication

Traditions of communication research, 9-13
Trager, G. L., 58, 68
Travers, J., 47
Triandis, H. C., 128
Troldahl, V. C., 155, 202-205, 210
Tustin, A., 185, 186, 187
Two-step flow hypothesis, 19, 152, 153-154,
    154-156, 158, 202-206
  development of, 202
  evaluations of, 202-206

Uncertainty, 22, 23, 34, 38-39, 43-44, 55,
    80-81, 189-191
  characteristics of, 29-32
  functions, 32-33, 38-39
  maximal, 31
  optimal, 33-34, 43-44, 80-81
  relative, 31, 33
  See also Channel capacity; Decoding;
    Encoding

Vaizey, M. J., 73
van den Ban, A. W., 155, 165, 174, 175,
    202-205, 206
Verbal meaning, 61-67, 71
Vince, P., 156
Visual interaction, 72-73
Volkart, E. H., 115

Wade, S., 47
Walster, E., 132
Ward, C. D., 122

Warner, L. G., 18, 99, 211
Watson, J., 59
Watson, O. M., 73
Weaver, W., 4, 7-8, 12, 16, 34, 182
Weich, K. E., 133
Weiner, N., 182, 184, 188
Weisenberg, M., 133
Weiss, W., 106-109, 142
Welles, O., 149
Wells, H. G., 149
Westie, F. R., 18, 211
Westley, B. H., 7, 12, 21, 56
White, I. S., 157
Whorf, B. L., 74
Wicker, A. W., 99
Wiener, M., 71
Wilkening, E. A., 11, 165, 173
William, F., 74
Williams, B. R., 160
Willis, F. N., 73
Winters, L. C., 72
Woodruff, C. L., 115
Wright, C. R., 14, 210
Wright, D., 78, 79

Yeracaris, C. A., 173
Yu, F. T. C., 150

Zanna, M., 125, 135
Zavalloni, M., 122
Zax, M., 99
Zimbardo, P. G., 133, 134

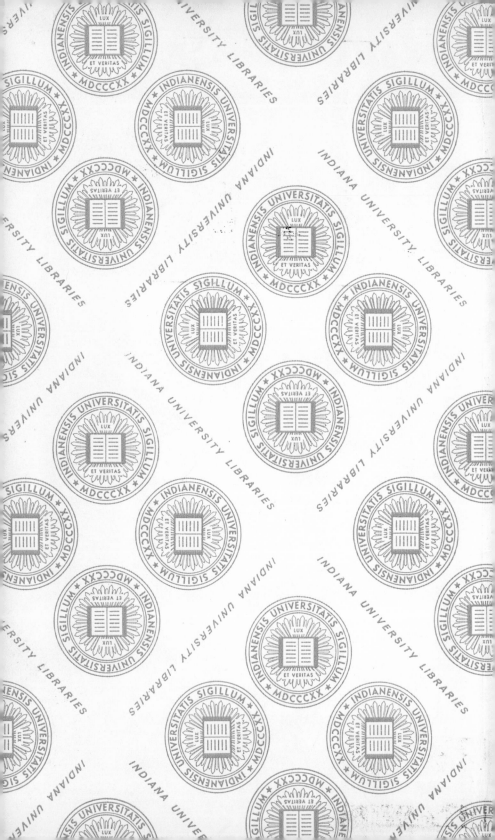